3/31/97

Dearest Hilary,
I love you. Grow
in Him. We love you!
Love
Mom

Published by World Publishers, Inc., Grand Rapids, MI 49418

ISBN

Printed in the United States of America
1 2 3 4 5 6 — 00 99 98 97 96 95

A Devotional for
Early Teens

Carolyn Larsen

INTRODUCTION

Did you ever take a big bite of meatloaf and wonder what in the world is in that all-American mystery meat?

Well, here's a general recipe: Toss some chopped meat (There's the mystery) with a little diced onion. (What in the world does diced mean?) Add tomato sauce and seasoning. (The spicier the better.) Dump in bread crumbs and egg. (Yuck, slimey.) Now stick in your bare hands and mix it up, squeeze it through your fingers, (Gross!) pound it into loaf shape, toss it in a pan, and—voilà—you have meatloaf!

Does that sound anything at all like your life? A little bit of this and a little bit of that all dumped together, then squeezed (bam!), pounded (kablooey!), and shaped (ouch!). Well, if it does, you're not alone.

Life is basically made up of a pound or two of school stuff, a pinch of insecurity, a tablespoon of pride, and a whole bunch of God things. Everything is mixed and squeezed, shaped and pounded. Then it's cooked at a high temperature, sliced up and slapped between the bread slices of parents and friends. Whew! That's why "Life Is A Meatloaf Sandwich!"

This book will take a look at all the stuff that goes into your life. Sometimes it might not be easy to admit what you're really like, deep inside where no one except you and God can see. But, God loves you, and he wants you to love him, yourself, and those around you. And the best news yet—he will help you get rid of the bad stuff and concentrate on the good.

So, dig in. A few minutes a day with this book might be just the right amount of ketchup on your meatloaf sandwich!

CONTENTS

Thursday — Obeying Pays Off • Joshua 2; 6:22-23
Friday — Obeying: Take Two • Jonah
Saturday — To Obey or Not to Obey • Review

Week Six ☞ You're Safe Now

Sunday — This Is Scary! • Genesis 19:4-16
Monday — Please, Help My Brother • Exodus 2:1-10
Tuesday — Safety Rules • Exodus 12:1-30
Wednesday — Take a Stand • Esther
Thursday — You Have No Choice! • Daniel 3
Friday — You Can't Pray Here! • Daniel 6
Saturday — Your Insurance Plan • Review

Week Seven ☞ Guidelines Make Life Easier

Sunday — Follow Your Leader • Exodus 20:3
Monday — Watch Your Mouth • Exodus 20:7
Tuesday — Too Tired Doesn't Count • Exodus 20:8-11
Wednesday — You Gotta Have Respect • Exodus 20:12
Thursday — Treat Others As You Want to Be Treated • Exodus 20:13-16
Friday — If It's Not Yours, Leave It Alone • Exodus 20:17
Saturday — Live By the Rules • Exodus 20:3-20

Week Eight ☞ Look at the Big Picture

Sunday — What about My Dreams? • Genesis 37
Monday — Can Good Come from Bad? • Genesis 42, 45
Tuesday — Hang In There! • Ruth
Wednesday — I Really Care about This! • Nehemiah 2
Thursday — Sing, Girl, Sing • Daniel 2
Friday — Good Job, God! • 1 Samuel 16:1-13
Saturday — Have A Plan • Review

Week Nine ☞ You Mean He Planned Families?

Sunday — Love My Family? • Genesis 4:2
Monday — Live Life Well • Genesis 21:1—7
Tuesday — Am I Gonna Get Married? • Genesis 24
Wednesday — Brothers! • Genesis 25:19-34; 27:42-45
Thursday — Big Sister Blues • Exodus 2:4, 7
Friday — I Want This More Than Anything! • 1 Samuel 1
Saturday — Tell the Truth Now • Psalm 100

Week Ten ☞ The Strongest of the Strong

Sunday — Who's the New Guy? • Joshua 3
Monday — Sick of Being Picked On • Judges 4:6-15
Tuesday — Bigger Doesn't Mean Better • Judges 7:1-22
Wednesday — Friends Forever • Ruth 1
Thursday — Turn the Other Cheek • 1 Samuel 24
Friday — Live By the Golden Rule • 2 Samuel 5:1-5
Saturday — Strength for Today • Psalm 28:7

Week Eleven ☞ You're Never Alone

Sunday — Alone in a Crowd • Genesis 8
Monday — Home Alone! • Genesis 28:10-22
Tuesday — Expect Tough Times • Genesis 39:20-23
Wednesday — Prove It! • Exodus 13:17-22
Thursday —It's HOT! • Exodus 15:22-25
Friday — Your Job, Man • Joshua 1:1-5
Saturday — Don't Be Chicken! • Review

Week Twelve ☞ The Ultimate Love

Sunday — Best Friends • 1 Samuel 20
Monday — Lovin' the Creeps • 2 Samuel 9
Tuesday — Sometimes Life Stinks • 2 Kings 2:1-11
Wednesday — Sweat It Not! • 2 Kings 4:1-7
Thursday — Feelin' Sick • 1 Chronicles 22:6-7; 2 Chronicles 3—4
Friday — Nah! It Can't Be • Ezra 1:1-11
Saturday — Stay Close to the Source • 1 Corinthians 13

Week Thirteen ☞ Wisdom from Above

Sunday — It's Greek to Me • Genesis 41:1-40
Monday — Learning from My Parents? • Deuteronomy 11:19-21; 32:47
Tuesday — Choose Smart! • 1 Samuel 25:1-35
Wednesday — Make a Wish; Any Wish • 1 Kings 3:5-13
Thursday — Use Your Brain • 1 Kings 3:16-28
Friday — Now What Do I Say? • Daniel 5
Saturday — Wise Guys • Review

Week Fourteen ☞ You Gonna Argue with God?

Sunday — Show a Little Patience, Will Ya? • Genesis 17:15-19; 21:1-2
Monday — Promises, Promises • Genesis 9:8-17
Tuesday — Hurry Up, God! • Exodus 16:1-15
Wednesday — Who Ya Gonna Call? • Numbers 21:4-9
Thursday — Leave the Crowd Behind • 1 Samuel 8:6-22
Friday — Show Me • Judges 6:11-23
Saturday — All or Nothing • 2 Timothy 3:16

Week Fifteen ☞ When God Talks People Listen

Sunday — Read Your Mind • Genesis 37:5-10
Monday — Did You Hear Something? • 1 Samuel 3
Tuesday — Open Your Ears • Daniel 2
Wednesday — Bible Messages • Genesis 18:1-15
Thursday — Dream Time • Genesis 28:10-22
Friday — Learn from Experience • Exodus 3:1-10
Saturday — If You Wanna Hear, You Gotta Listen • Review

Week Sixteen ☞ Warm Fuzzies

Sunday —Feelin' Crummy • Genesis 21:14-21
Monday — This Hurts • 2 Kings 4:8-37

Tuesday – Digging Through the Ashes • Job 1
Wednesday – Doesn't God Care? • 2 Kings 5:1-15
Thursday – Ask for Life • 2 Kings 20:1-6
Friday – Don't Give Up • 1 Kings 19:1-18
Saturday – Don't Let Worry Paralyze You • Philippians 4:6-7

Week Seventeen ☞ Fallin' In Line

Sunday – Take a Good Look at Yourself • Romans 3:23
Monday – You Gotta Choose: Death or Life • Romans 6:23
Tuesday – Who Loves Ya, Babe? • John 3:16
Wednesday – You Gotta Believe • John 14:6
Thursday – Confession Is Good for the Soul • 1 John 1:9
Friday – Turn Around • Acts 3:19
Saturday – Your Turn • Review

Week Eighteen ☞ Good Guys Versus Bad Guys

Sunday – You Win or Lose by the Way You Choose • Psalm 1
Monday –Take Control of Your Mind • Psalm 36
Tuesday – Why Do the Bad Guys Win? • Psalm 37
Wednesday – Stay Focused • Psalm 73
Thursday – Good Things Come to Those Who Do Good • Psalm 112
Friday – You Gotta Read the Book • Psalm 119:1-8; 90-96
Saturday – Bottom Line • Review

Week Nineteen ☞ Thanks for Everything

Sunday – Hide Here • Psalm 18
Monday – Sing Praise! • Psalm 33
Tuesday – Safety Insurance • Psalm 66
Wednesday – Spiritual 9-1-1 • Psalm 107
Thursday – Love Never Fails • Psalm 118
Friday – Ya Got No Secrets • Psalm 139
Saturday – Just Say Thanks • Review

Week Twenty ☞ Nuggets of Truth

Sunday – Be an Original • Proverbs 1:8-19
Monday – Make God #1 • Proverbs 3:5-6
Tuesday – Pack a Punch • Proverbs 4:23
Wednesday – Get Movin' • Proverbs 6:6-11
Thursday – This Hurts Me More Than It Does You • Proverbs 13:24; 22:6
Friday – Show Your Smarts • Proverbs 8:12-36
Saturday – Don't Give Up • Colossians 3:23

Week Twenty-One ☞ Usin' the Backboard

Sunday – Watch Your Mouth! • Proverbs 11:12-13
Monday – Inside Out Happiness • Proverbs 15:16; 16:8
Tuesday – Learn from the Best • Proverbs 15:31-33
Wednesday – Make a Good Rep • Proverbs 22:1
Thursday – How to be Popular • Proverbs 25:17-20

Friday — This Is Lots of Work! • Proverbs 31:10-31
Saturday — Fortune Cookies • Review

Week Twenty-Two ☞ The Miracle Begins

Sunday — Anything You Say • Luke 1:26-38
Monday — A Plan Comes Together • Luke 2:1-5
Tuesday — A New Baby! • Luke 2:6-7
Wednesday — All Right! • Luke 2:8-18
Thursday — Star Travel • Matthew 2:1-12
Friday — Rollin' with the Punches • Matthew 2:13-18
Saturday — Real People • Luke 2:1-20

Week Twenty-Three ☞ A Person Like Me

Sunday — Parents Make Me Nuts • Luke 1:31; 2:33, 41-52
Monday — Tripping Over Your Own Feet • Luke 2:7
Tuesday — You Don't Know How Hard It Is! • Luke 4:1-13
Wednesday — Enjoy Your Friends! • John 11:5
Thursday — Sorrow! • John 11:33-38
Friday — Death Is Part of Life! • Luke 23:44-49
Saturday — Just Like Me • Review

Week Twenty-Four ☞ Stay Within the Lines

Sunday — Livin' with Yourself • Matthew 5:4
Monday — Hidden Strength • Matthew 5:5
Tuesday — You Gotta Want It! • Matthew 5:6
Wednesday — Getting Even • Matthew 5:7
Thursday — Input • Matthew 5:8
Friday — Keep the Peace • Matthew 5:9
Saturday — School of Life • Matthew 5:4-9

Week Twenty-Five ☞ A Powerful Sermon

Sunday — Salt Shaker Livin' • Matthew 5:13
Monday — Don't Hide Your Light • Matthew 5:14-16
Tuesday — Cut to the Quick • Matthew 5:21-26
Wednesday — Be Careful Little Mouth • Matthew 5:33-37
Thursday — Love My Who? • Matthew 5:43-48
Friday — Yo! Look At Me! • Matthew 6:1-4
Saturday — Read the Instructions • Review

Week Twenty-Six ☞ Listen and Learn

Sunday — What Are You Worried About? • Matthew 6:25-34
Monday — Take a Good Look at Yourself • Matthew 7:1-6
Tuesday — Just Ask, Will Ya? • Matthew 7:7-12
Wednesday — Stick to the Rules • Matthew 7:13-14
Thursday — Produce the Goods! • Matthew 7:15-23
Friday — You Gotta Live with Your Choices • Matthew 7:24-29
Saturday — No Double Standards • Matthew 7:1-6

Week Twenty-Seven ☞ Did You See That?

Sunday — Oh Yeah? Prove It • John 2:1-11
Monday — How Can You Sleep? • Mark 4:35-41
Tuesday — That's Not Important Enough • Mark 6:35-41
Wednesday — It's a Ghost! • Matthew 14:22-27
Thursday — Try Again • Luke 5:4-11
Friday — The Glory of God • John 11:1-44
Saturday — Seein' Is Believin' • Review

Week Twenty-Eight ☞ Totally Awesome!

Sunday — I Can See! I Can See! • Mark 10:46-52
Monday — Talk, Talk, Talk • Mark 7:31-37
Tuesday — Groupies! • Luke 8:43-48
Wednesday — Thank You, Thank You, Thank You • Luke 17:11-19
Thursday — Do Mothers Cry? • Matthew 9:18-26
Friday — The Bossy Sister • Luke 7:1-10
Saturday — Fix It, God! • Mark 11:22-24

Week Twenty-Nine ☞ Life Stories

Sunday — I'm Not Listening! • Matthew 13:1-23
Monday — Bad Seed • Matthew 13:24-30, 36-43
Tuesday — It's the Real Thing • Mark 4:30-32
Wednesday — I Want THAT One! • luke 15:4-7
Thursday — Drop It, Already! • Matthew 18:21-24
Friday — That's Not Fair! • Matthew 20:1-16
Saturday — Tell Me a Story • Matthew 13:10-17

Week Thirty ☞ Stories with a Point

Sunday — You Can Be Replaced • Matthew 22:2-14
Monday — Be Ready! • Matthew 25:1-13
Tuesday — Use It or Lose It • Matthew 25:14-30
Wednesday — Walk the Talk • Matthew 21:28-32
Thursday — You Can't Take It With You • Luke 12:16-21
Friday — You Count • Luke 15:8-10
Saturday — One Foot in Front of the Other • Review

Week Thirty-One ☞ Hidden Messages

Sunday — Don't Touch Him • Luke 10:25-37
Monday — What Have You Got to Lose? • Luke 15:11-32
Tuesday — Nagging • Luke 11:5-13
Wednesday — Justice Served • Luke 18:2-8
Thursday — Hurrah for Me! • Luke 18:9-14
Friday — Hey Kid, Ya Gotta Have a Ticket • Matthew 13:47-50
Saturday — Computer Games • Review

Week Thirty-Two ☞ Jesus' Friends

Sunday — Leavin' Everything • Matthew 4:18-22
Monday — Leavin' the Trash Behind • Matthew 9:9-13

Tuesday — Being a Sub • Matthew 3:1-17
Wednesday — Acting on Impulse • Matthew 14:22-33
Thursday — Beating the Odds • Mark 14:3-9
Friday — Tryin' Harder • Luke 19:1-10
Saturday — Work as a Team • 1 Corinthians 12:12-28

Week Thirty-Three ☞ Get Along with These Guys?

Sunday — Ya Get Back What Ya Give Out • Ephesians 4:25-32
Monday — Carbon Copy • Ephesians 5:1-5
Tuesday — Light Up My Life • Ephesians 5:8-14
Wednesday — It's Your Choice! • Ephesians 5:15-20
Thursday — I'm Sick of Obeying! • Ephesians 6:1-3
Friday — Wear Your Life Protector • Ephesians 6:10-25
Saturday — Don't Lose Your Temper! • Ephesians 4:26

Week Thirty-Four ☞ The End Is Near

Sunday — A Crystal Ball • Mark 8:31
Monday — A Hero's Welcome • Matthew 21:1-11
Tuesday — Who Can You Trust? • Matthew 26:14-16
Wednesday — Saying Goodbye • Matthew 26:17-30
Thursday — To Be Continued... • Luke 23:2-49
Friday — A Man's Gotta Do What A Man's Gotta Do • Luke 23:50-56
Saturday — Face Reality • Review

Week Thirty-Five ☞ It Ain't Over 'til It's Over

Sunday — V-I-C-T-O-R-Y • Matthew 28:1-8
Monday — I'm Back • John 20:11-28
Tuesday — Look Beyond Yourself • Luke 24:13-35
Wednesday — Show Me! • John 20:24-29
Thursday — Keep On Keeping On • John 21:4-14
Friday — Your Job, Should You Be Willing... • Acts 1:1-11
Saturday — You Win! • 1 Corinthians 15:3-4

Week Thirty-Six ☞ Whatcha Gonna Do?

Sunday — Doing Nice Stuff for Others • Acts 9:36-42
Monday — Doin' Little Things • Matthew 25:31-40
Tuesday — Giving Your All • Mark 12:41-44
Wednesday — Be a Little Flexible • Acts 8:26-39
Thursday — Brave Enough to Serve • Acts 6:8–15; 7:54-60
Friday — Gettin' a Second Chance • Acts 15:36-41; Colossians 4:10-11
Saturday — Your Serve • Galatians 6:2

Week Thirty-Seven ☞ The First Church

Sunday — Fill 'er Up • Acts 2:1-4
Monday — Passing the Torch • Acts 3:1-10
Tuesday — Trouble Won't Stop Us • Acts 5:17-42
Wednesday — What's Mine Is Yours • Acts 2:42-47; 4:32-37
Thursday — That's Impossible! • Acts 5:12-16

Friday – Come, See, Go, Tell • Acts 13:1-5
Saturday –What's Your Church Like? • Psalm 133

Week Thirty-Eight ☞ What Is Love?

Sunday – Show Some Kindness • 1 Corinthians 13:1-4
Monday – Do Unto Others • 1 Corinthians 13:5
Tuesday – Grudges Don't Help Anyone • 1 Corinthians 13:5
Wednesday – Whatever Happened to Fairness? • 1 Corinthians 13:6
Thursday – Shield with Love • 1 Corinthians 13:7
Friday – Stayin' Put There • 1 Corinthians 13:8
Saturday – No Excuses • 1 Corinthians 13:1-8

Week Thirty-Nine ☞ The Great Role Model

Sunday – "I Want to Be in the Theatre" • Luke 9:23
Monday – Playbook or Phone book? • John 8:31-32; 2 John 9
Tuesday – Can We Talk?• Matthew 7:7; John 14:13-14; 15:7
Wednesday – Actions Speak Louder Than Words • John 13:34-35; • 1 John 4:11-21
Thursday – Doing Your Job Well • John 15:5, 8, 16
Friday – A Hand Without an Arm • 1 Corinthians 12:12-31
Saturday – What Can I Do? • Review

Week Forty ☞ God's Special Agents

Sunday – Message Board • Genesis 18:1-15
Monday – Get Outta Here! • Genesis 19:1-3, 15-25
Tuesday – Don't Run the Roadblock • Numbers 22:1-35
Wednesday – Baby Announcement • Judges 13:2-5, 20
Thursday – Red Licorice • 1 Kings 19:3-9
Friday – A Saving Alibi • Daniel 6
Saturday – Rules and More Rules • Review

Week Forty-One ☞ Angel Helpers

Sunday – Passing the Test • Daniel 3:1-30
Monday – Great News • Luke 1:26-31
Tuesday – Newsbreak • Luke 2:8-14
Wednesday – Dream Talk • Matthew 1:20; 2:13, 19-20
Thursday – We Can't Be Stopped • Acts 5:17-20
Friday – Rescue! • Acts 12:1-11
Saturday – News Bulletins • Review

Week Forty-Two ☞ Hot Line to God

Sunday – Hot Doggin' • Matthew 6:5-8
Monday – Using a Model • Matthew 6:9-13
Tuesday – Point Out the Good Things • Ephesians 1:3-15; Hebrews 13:15
Wednesday – Say Thanks Once in a While • Mark 6:41; Rom. 7:25; Eph. 5:4; Phil.1:3
Thursday – Confess, You'll Feel Better • Luke 15:11-21; 1 John 1:9
Friday – If You Want It, Ask for It • Matt. 7:7-8; Phil. 4:6; James 1:5-8
Saturday – Just Like Talking to a Friend • James 4:2

Week Forty-Three ☞ Can't Keep Quiet

Sunday – Changing Teams • Acts 9
Monday – The Workhorse • Acts 4:36-37; 11:22-26
Tuesday – The Best Team • Acts 18:24-28; Romans 16:3-5
Wednesday – Too Young! • 1 Cor. 4:17; 1 Tim. 4:11-12; 2 Tim. 1:5
Thursday – Not a Shy Guy • Acts 2:14-41
Friday – Doing What's Right • Acts 16:16-34
Saturday – Don't You Want to Tell Someone? • Review

Week Forty-Four ☞ The Best Lessons

Sunday – Pay Attention in Class • Luke 11:28; Rom. 10:17; 1 Peter 2:2-3
Monday – Is Your Homework Done? • Acts 17:11; Revelation 1:3
Tuesday – Exam Time • Psalm 119:9, 11
Wednesday – Thinking in Spanish • Psalm 1:2-3; Philippians 4:8-9
Thursday – The Big Test • James 1:22; 2:14-20
Friday – You Be the Teacher • Matthew 28:19-20
Saturday – Secret Weapon • Psalm 119:98

Week Forty-Five ☞ The Evidence Is Clear

Sunday – A Special Gift • Matthew 7:16-20; Acts 1:4-5; Galatians 5:16
Monday – Are You a Prunepit? • Galatians 5:22
Tuesday – Peace or Pieces? • Galatians 5:22
Wednesday – Christian Snobbery? • Galatians 5:22
Thursday – U-Turn • Galatians 5:22
Friday – Self-controlled or Sin-controlled? • Galatians 5:23
Saturday – Copycat • Galatians 5:22-23

Week Forty-Six ☞ The Famous Apostle Paul

Sunday – Blasting into the Limelight • Acts 9:19-31
Monday – We're Just People • Acts 14:8-18
Tuesday – What Are You Missing? • Acts 16:13-15
Wednesday – God or gods? • Acts 17:16-34
Thursday – Can't Stop Talking • Acts 20:7-12
Friday – I Did My Best • 2 Timothy 3:10–4:8
Saturday – A Good Role Model • 2 Timothy 4:7

Week Forty-Seven ☞ Old Testament Role Models

Sunday – Noah Stands Out • Genesis 6–8
Monday – Team Leader • 2 Kings 11:21–12:16
Tuesday – New Mom • Numbers 27:18-23; Joshua 6
Wednesday – A Dangerous Job • Esther 2; 4–5
Thursday – Forgive and Forget • 1 Samuel 19:1; 26:9-12
Friday – Surely You Don't Mean Me? • Exodus 3
Saturday – The Hall of Fame • Hebrews 11

Week Forty-Eight ☞ Leaders from the New Testament

Sunday – Getting Things Ready • Luke 3:1-23
Monday – No Stereotypes • Acts 10

Tuesday – Hangin' In There • Acts 2:1-14
Wednesday – Choosing Your Team • Luke 6:12-16
Thursday – Best Friend • Matt. 17:1; John 13:23; 19:26; Rev. 1:9
Friday – A Great Teacher • 1 Timothy 4:11; 2 Timothy 3:10-17
Saturday – Stand Firm • 2 Timothy 1:6-14

Week Forty-Nine ☞ Bible Kids

Sunday – Do You Hear Something? • 1 Samuel 3
Monday – Listen to Me! • 2 Kings 5:1-15
Tuesday – A Kid Leads the Way • 2 Kings 22:1–23:3
Wednesday – Childlike Trust • Luke 18:15-17
Thursday – The Boy Who Shared • John 6:1-15
Friday – Eavesdropping • Acts 23:12-22
Saturday – Serving God • Review

Week Fifty ☞ We Can Do This

Sunday – Getting Along with Everyone • 1 John 3:18; 4:7-8
Monday – Great Job! • Rom. 12:18; 14:19; 15:2; Eph. 4:12
Tuesday – Working Together • Ecclesiastes 4:9-10; 1 Corinthians 9:19-23
Wednesday – Like You Never Blew It! • Matthew 18:21-22; Ephesians 4:32
Thursday – Don't Give Up • Acts 2:42; Hebrews 10:25
Friday – Be a Team • Jeremiah 32:39; John 17:21; Acts 2:42
Saturday – One Body • Review

Week Fifty-One ☞ Learning from the Book of James

Sunday – Tough Day • James 1:2-15
Monday – Get in the Game • James 1:16-27
Tuesday – Breathe or Die • James 2:1-26
Wednesday – Watch What You Say • James 3:1-18
Thursday – Quit Thinking About Yourself • James 4:1-17
Friday – Pray with Power • James 5:13-20
Saturday – Show Your Faith • Review

Week Fifty-Two ☞ What's Gonna Happen?

Sunday – He's Coming Back! • Luke 17:29-36
Monday – Here Comes the Judge • 1 Corinthians 3:12-15; 4:5
Tuesday – Never Give Up • Romans 8:38-39; Colossians 1:5; 1 John 2:28
Wednesday – Signs of the Times • Matthew 24:3-14
Thursday – What's the Most Important? • Matthew 6:19-24
Friday – Praise Forever! • Revelation 7:12, 19
Saturday – When Is He Coming? • Jude 25

How Did the World Get Here?

Read Genesis 1:1-10

Mark shook his head as he came out of the classroom. He was confused. The evolution stuff his teacher had been talking about really made sense. In fact, logically, evolution made more sense than believing God created everything by just saying some words. A lot of his friends believed evolution was true. He didn't want to look weird to them.

Whoa Mark, it's time to get back to basics.

The basics are found in Genesis 1:1. Mark believes in God. He has grown up going to church and reading the Bible. So now he can't pick and choose which parts of the Bible to believe. It's either true or it isn't. God's first gift to the world was . . . the world! God made something out of nothing. God just said the words and there was the world. The world was the first of God's many gifts.

What About You?

• Have you ever been confused by teachings on evolution?
• Does it matter what your friends believe? Why?

Talkin' About It

If evolution is confusing you, tell God about it. Ask him for help to resist any pressure to believe what you know isn't really true. Ask him to help your faith grow stronger. Thank him for the gift of the world.

In the beginning, God created heaven and earth.

Genesis 1:1

Read Genesis 1:11-13

The brilliant orange and red of the leaves was lost on Tim. He griped about the chill in the air as he angrily dragged the rake through the leaves. Tim was majorly ticked! "It's a beautiful Saturday afternoon, big football game at school—and I have to rake the stupid leaves! Maybe we should just cut down all these dumb trees. Then there wouldn't be any leaves to rake."

Can you imagine a world without trees?

Tim is so busy resenting the work he has to do that he isn't thinking about all that plants do for us. They are a gift from God. Think about it . . . do you like to eat fruit? Receive flowers? Sit in the shade? Are you thankful for medicine when you're sick? Some of that medicine comes from plants. Imagine a world with no grass or plants. Bottom line is, raking or no raking, God's gift of plants and trees makes our world a lot more pleasant.

What About You?

• Plants are definitely beautiful, but what are some things plants do for us?
• Even if cutting grass and raking leaves is a major pain, how would you feel about a world with no plants?

Talkin' About It

Thank God for the plants and trees he created, even for the work they make. Thank him for knowing exactly what we would need and providing for those needs.

Everything came into existence through him. Not one thing that exists was made without him.

John 1:3

"I Hate Leaves!"

Pour On the Sunscreen!

Read Genesis 1:20-23

One benefit (and there weren't many) of living in a crowded ocean front city was . . . the BEACH! And Kelly couldn't wait to get there. The absolute best way to spend a summer day was splashing in the ocean, surfing the waves, baking in the sun, playing volleyball on the sand—in other words just enjoying the beach.

The ocean is much more than a playground.

The ocean and all the creatures that live in it are valuable gifts from God. On the fifth day of creating, God made everything that lives in the ocean from tiny seahorses to huge killer whales. Also that day he made all the birds and flying creatures. Pretty busy day for God, huh? Want to know how creative God is? Look at all the shapes, colors, and sizes of ocean creatures and birds.

What About You?

• Have you ever spent any time near an ocean? What did you like best?
• If you live in, oh say, Iowa, why should you care anything about the ocean?

Talkin' About It

Thank God for all his creation. Ask him what you can do to help endangered animals. Consider the largeness and power of the oceans God created. Think about how important water is in our world.

> *The LORD's deeds are spectacular.*
>
> Psalm 111:2

Read Genesis 1:26-31

Gina hurried down the sidewalk. She hated walking past the corner where the "druggies" hung out before school. It wasn't so much that they looked grungy as it was the smoke from who knows what they were puffing on and the filthy language that poured out of their mouths. They all thought they were so-o-o-o cool.

Gina knows she is made in God's image.

That's a good reason to take care of herself and treat her body right. God created Adam, the first man, to be like himself. That meant Adam could think, make decisions, and know right from wrong. God even gave Adam a job to do right away. He trusted Adam to name all the animals.

What About You?

• How do you take care of your body?
• What could you do to take better care of yourself?

Talkin' About It

You're made in God's image. That's like being a copy of God! Ask God to help you remember that you are made in his image. Ask him to show you where you can improve in taking care of yourself.

So God created humans in his image. In the image of God he created them.

Genesis 1:27

Take Care of Yourself!

Everyone Needs Friends!

Read Genesis 2:18-23

Marcy was about as low as she could go. Being in a new town, new neighborhood, new school with no friends was no fun. Marcy had no one to giggle with, tell her troubles to, complain about teachers with.

God knows that we all need someone.

God looked at Adam and saw that he was lonely. And guess what? God cared. So he made a partner for Adam. Eve was the first woman. God cares when we are lonely, too. That's why he gave us families and friends. So even if your family gets on your nerves, or your friends are sometimes annoying, be thankful for them. Life would be mighty lonely without them!

What About You?
• Who is your best friend?
• How are you a good friend to others?

Talkin' About It
Thank God for your family and friends. Thank him that he cares when you feel lonely. Ask him to help you be a good friend to others.

Then the LORD God formed a woman from the rib that he had taken from the man.

Genesis 2:22

Read Genesis 2:1-3

Have you ever been so busy that you rushed from one thing to the next? That's what Doug was doing—he hurried from class to band then basketball practice to dinner to homework then fell into bed. That's when he realized he hadn't even noticed if the sun was shining that day or if Dad was gone on a business trip.

That's not good!

You just can't get any busier than God was during creation. Stop and think about all the work he did each day. Read the Genesis account of creation again, and you'll see that at the end of every day, God stopped to look over what he had made. Every night, he said, "Yep. That's good." After six heavy-duty days of creating everything from grass to man, God stopped. That's right, he just stopped on the seventh day and . . . he rested.

What About You?

• What things keep you really busy?
• How can you organize your life so you get everything done and still have time to rest?

Talkin' About It

Thank God for the reminder to stop and enjoy the world he made for you. Thank him for a day of rest when you can worship him.

By the seventh day God had finished the work he had been doing. On the seventh day he stopped the work he had been doing.

Genesis 2:2

Smell the Roses!

Doing My Part

Read Genesis 2:15

Almost every week there is a news report about some kind of terrible pollution or an oil spill or damage to the ozone layer. It sometimes seems like our world is falling apart. Every time there is a story about this, someone asks, "Why don't *they* do something about it?"

Guess what? We are they!

Yep, look back at Genesis 2:15. God told Adam to take care of the Garden of Eden. We are Adam's descendants and the world is where we live. So taking care of the world is our job.

What About You?

• What can you do to help take care of the world around you?
• What are some ways you can help save energy?

Talkin' About It

Thank God for the world. Tell him you want to do your part in taking care of it. Ask him to show you ways to help. Ask him to help you be an example to others of caring for his creation.

The LORD made the earth by his power. He set up the world by his wisdom. He stretched out heaven by his understanding.

Jeremiah 51:15

Read Exodus 4:1-5

Brian felt sick to his stomach. Today was his first speech in speech class. Standing up in front of the class was not his favorite thing to do. Brian asked God to help him, but he didn't feel much better. *Maybe a speech is too little a thing for God to care about,* he thought. *Maybe he only helps with big things.*

God cares about anything that is important to you.

Do you need an example? God told Moses to be a leader. But Moses was a little scared about how the people would feel about him. God turned a stick into a snake right in front of Moses. That showed Moses in no uncertain terms that he was not going to be alone. God asked Moses to do a job and by his power the people would follow Moses.

What About You?

• When has God helped you do something hard?
• Is there something you need to ask his help with right now? What?

Talkin' About It

It's OK to tell God when you are afraid. It's even OK to tell him that you don't really feel his presence with you all the time. Ask him for help to do hard things and to remind you of how he has helped in the past.

*T*he LORD *will give power to his people.*

Psalm 29:11

Will God Help Little 'Ole Me?

Read Exodus 7:14–11:10

"Zack is a major jerk. He's always pickin' on me and trying to embarrass me in front of the other guys," Matt complained. When Mom suggested that Matt pray for Zack, his response was, "Yeah right. Like a creep like Zack would care what God thinks."

God can make himself heard.

When God told Moses to lead the Israelites out of slavery and the Egyptian king got in the way, God made the king listen. It took ten terrible events, but the king finally realized God has the most power. Never underestimate God's power to make himself heard.

What About You?

• Do you know someone you think would "never" listen to God? Who?
• Do you listen to God? Do you do what you know he wants you to do?

Talkin' About It

Ask God to help you remember how important it is to listen to him and obey him. If you have a Zack in your life, pray for him.

Hallelujah! Salvation, glory, and power belong to our God.

Revelation 19:1

Read Exodus 14

*O*K, if I say no and get out of here, will they call me names? If I say I'm a Christian, what will they say? I never should have come to this party, I knew what kinds of things these guys are into. Rick's mind was racing. He was afraid to tell the other guys that he didn't want to try the beer they thought made them so cool.

Can God get Rick out of this mess?

Sure he can. Remember the Israelites? The Egyptian Pharaoh said they could leave Egypt. Then he changed his mind and sent his army after them. The Israelites were backed up to the Red Sea and the army was bearing down on them. It looked hopeless. Then God parted the waters of the Red Sea and the Israelites walked through on dry ground—and the water splashed down on the Egyptian army. No problem is too big for God's power.

What About You?

• When have you needed God's help to get out of trouble?
• Can you think of a time that God kept you safe? When?

Talkin' About It

Thank God for his power that protects you. Thank him for caring when you are in trouble and need help, even if the trouble is your own fault.

*W*hen the Israelites saw the great power the LORD had used against the Egyptians, they feared the LORD and believed in him and in his servant Moses.

Exodus 14:31

Just Say 'No'

Right Answer, Wrong Way

Read Joshua 6:1-21

*F*ollow directions, follow directions. Mike stuffed the paper with the big red F on it into his backpack. Mr. Smalley's written comments that Mike needed to follow directions only made the failing grade sting more. *Now my math grade is down the tube,* he thought. *It's not fair; I got the right answers, who cares if I didn't do it the way the instructions said?*

Following directions is very important.

Joshua followed God's instructions, doing exactly what God told him to do, even if it didn't make any sense to him. The end result was that the walls of Jericho fell down, and Joshua and his army captured the city. It seemed impossible, but because Joshua followed God's instructions, God's power helped him.

What About You?

• Have you ever been in trouble for not following directions? When?
• What directions from God do you need to follow more closely?

Talkin' About It

If following directions is hard for you, tell God about it. Ask him to help you have the patience to follow directions. Thank him for his power that is available to help you whenever you need it.

*L*ove the LORD your God, follow his directions, and keep his commands.

Joshua 22:5

Read Joshua 10:1-13

The district track meet was scheduled for Thursday afternoon. Unfortunately, a major spring storm was also scheduled for Thursday afternoon. Lisa was really looking forward to running in the track meet. *I wonder if it would help if I prayed for the storm to hold off for a day?* she wondered. *Oh yeah, like God is going to change the weather just because I pray.*

Well Lisa, stranger things have happened.

Joshua once prayed that God would make the sun stand still for almost 24 hours. Joshua and his army were fighting God's enemies and he wanted to win the battle before the fighting stopped because of darkness. God answered Joshua's prayer and used his power to hold the sun still until Joshua's army had won.

What About You?

• When has God answered one of your prayers?
• Do his answers cause you to trust God more?

Talkin' About It

When you think about all the power that is available to you through God, it's amazing. Thank God for his power and ask him to help you trust him more.

Will Begging Help?

The LORD is the strength of his people.

Psalm 28:8

Don't Be Fooled By Fakes

Read I Kings 18:16-39

Jennie slammed the door and threw herself on the bed. *Why do my parents insist on making me go to church? My friends don't have to, and I think it's wrong for me to have to go,* she thought. *I should be able to decide what's most important to me—and I choose my friends!*

Are your friends more important to you than God?

Elijah met up with some guys who thought they had found something with more power than God. So Elijah called for a contest and matched God up with the gods they thought were so powerful. Guess who won? No contest—hands down—GOD! Nothing should be more important to you than God. No person or thing has more power than God does. His is the power you want on your side!

What About You?

• What sometimes gets to be more important to you than God?
• Would a true friend try to pull you away from God?

Talkin' About It

It can be a daily struggle to keep God first in your life. Ask him to use his awesome power to help you stay true to him.

Be very careful to love the LORD your God.

Joshua 23:11

Read Deuteronomy 6:1-15

How many times have you seen God turn a stick into a snake? Has he ever sent plagues on someone who has been bugging you? Well, has he parted the waters of a big sea, or even the mysteries of science class for you? You've read six Bible stories this week about how awesome God's power is. But how does God help *you* with the tough things in life?

God's power is available to you.

The stories you've read this week show you how powerful he is and to what lengths he will go to help his people. It's like a fantastic new electrical appliance that can do anything you want—but it's no good at all if you don't plug it in. God is there for you. He cares about what's happening in your life, but you've got to talk to him, spend time reading his Word, and ask him for his help.

What About You?

• How much time do you spend with God every day?
• Have you ever seen God's power in your life? When?

Talkin' About It

Thank God for caring about you. Tell him you want to spend more time getting to know him, and ask him to help you schedule your time so you have time to be with him.

Plug In the Cord

I can do everything through Christ who strengthens me.

Philippians 4:13

When You Blow It

Read Genesis 3

*M*an, I really blew it! Why did I get so mad at Mom? I hate it when I yell like that. I don't even know what I'm so mad about. Craig lay across his bed as he thought about his behavior. *I'm gonna be majorly grounded for this. I haven't seen Mom so mad in a long time. Why do I do these things?*

It's called sin, Craig.

It all started back in the Garden of Eden. Adam and Eve had a perfect setup . . . a great place to live, a beautiful relationship with God, everything they could ever want. God gave them only one rule to keep: don't eat the fruit from this one tree in the middle of the garden. Doesn't seem so hard, does it? But Adam and Eve blew it. They broke God's rule and ate the fruit. That was the first sin. Since that time, all humans sin. We can't help it—we're doing what comes naturally. But, God can help us control our sinful desires and actions. All we have to do is ask him.

What About You?
• Be honest. Have you done something you knew was wrong?
• Do you do one sin over and over? Would you like to be able to stop doing it?

Talkin' About It
Tell God what you have trouble with. Don't worry, he won't be surprised. Ask him to help you break the sin pattern. Thank him for his help.

If we love each other, God lives in us, and his love has reached its goal in us.

1 John 4:12

Read Genesis 4:1-13

Moira slammed the door and threw her school books on the bed. "It's not fair! I can't help it if 'Perfect Peter' got all A's on his report card. So what if I got a few C's and D's? It's not fair that I'm grounded just for that. I'm gonna get that little twerp—if it's the last thing I do. He'll be sorry he got me grounded."

Moira, Moira, have you forgotten what happened to Cain when he was jealous of his brother?

Cain tried to get even with Abel because God accepted Abel's offering, but not Cain's offering. But the problem was not Abel's—it was Cain's. He didn't follow the rules God gave for offerings. Cain got so out of control that he killed Abel. God punished him big time for that. Cain had to wander around homeless; and the crops he had taken such pride in didn't grow for him after that. Watch your temper, no jealousy attack is worth the punishment it can bring.

What About You?

• When have you lost your temper and done something you were sorry for later?
• When have you been jealous of someone? For what?

Talkin' About It

The initial feelings of jealousy are not a sin—it's sin when you let it take over your thoughts and actions. Ask God to help you nip these feelings in the bud.

[Love] doesn't think about itself.

1 Corinthians 13:5

Watch Out for the Green-eyed Monster

Be an Individual

Read Genesis 6:5-8; 7:23

"Great news, Mal, Friday night we're all gonna meet at the movie theatre and after the movie we're going to Lauren's house. Some of the guys are coming over. Her parents never pay any attention to us –it's gonna be a blast!" Jessica exclaimed.

"Uhh. . . great." Mallory tried to sound excited. But there was a little alarm going off in her head. She wasn't super comfortable with these plans.

Then don't do it. It's OK to be an individual.

You don't have to go along with the crowd when they make you uncomfortable. Remember Noah? He lived at a time when everyone was knee-deep in sinful living.

Noah was the only one trying to live for God. He could have given up and joined everyone else. But he didn't, he was an individual. That paid off. When God had enough of the sinful living and decided to flood the world and start the human race over, he saved Noah.

What About You?

• Do you get pressure from your friends to do things you are uncomfortable with?
• How do you handle that?

Talkin' About It

What your friends think of you is important. It shouldn't always be, but let's be honest. Ask God to help you not to get involved in things you are uncomfortable with. Ask him to help you think of creative alternative activities to suggest.

You are light for the world.

Matthew 5:14

Read Genesis 11:1-9

"The hottest party of the year is Friday night!" Mara announced loudly. "Anyone who is anyone is invited. If you're not invited to my house Friday night, you are a nobody. We are the coolest!" Jenna listened to this proclamation with her friends.

"I'd give anything to be invited to that party," she said. "That group is the absolute coolest."

Watch out, Jenna. They aren't as cool as they think they are.

There were a bunch of guys in the Bible once who thought they were pretty cool. They started building a tower that was going to reach all the way to heaven. They thought they were almost as important as God. God didn't think they were so cool, though. He thought they were just full of pride. God stopped their building project and made all the guys speak different languages. Then they couldn't even talk to each other anymore. They weren't so cool then.

What About You?

• Is there a crowd at your school who thinks they are cooler than anyone else?
• How do you feel when you're around people who think they are better than everyone else?

Talkin' About It

Thank God for your friends. Ask him to keep you from being full of pride. That kind of pride always causes trouble.

Pride precedes a disaster, and an arrogant attitude precedes a fall.

Proverbs 16:18

You're Not As Cool As You Think!

Keep God First!

Read Exodus 32:1-10

Jeremy spent most of English class thinking of ways to convince Mom and Dad how much he needed a $125 pair of in-line skates: (1) his cheap pair wasn't sophisticated enough to let him do all the tricks he just knew he could do with the new pair, (2) all his friends had the new more expensive kind—surely Mom and Dad didn't want him to be weird, (3) these skates were all he wanted, (4) they would make him a happy guy.

Watch your priorities, Jeremy!

Remember the story of the people who put something ahead of God in their hearts? They had a golden calf made and worshiped that instead of God. They said they wanted a god they could see. God was very sad when he saw what they had done. He had done many things for these people, and they had forgotten everything. Their golden calf was destroyed, and they were punished.

What About You?

• Does anything sometimes become so important to you that it pushes God to second place? What is it?
• Are you happier when God is in first place, or when something else is?

Talkin' About It

Ask God to help you keep your priorities straight. That's not always easy; but he is a lot stronger than you are.

Never have any other god.

Exodus 20:3

Read Judges 13:3-5; 16:4-21

"Molly, do you know who Sara likes?" whispered Penny.

"Yeah, she told me, but I promised not to tell," answered Molly.

"O come on, I won't tell anyone. Sara wouldn't care if I know, too," Penny begged.

Caution Molly, remember what happened to Samson.

Samson was the strongest man who ever lived. He promised to serve God all his life. A sign of his promise was that he never cut his hair. Things were going along fine until Samson fell for a beautiful woman. She was paid by his enemies to find out why Samson was so strong. After she bugged him for a while, Samson told her that if someone cut his hair, his strength would leave. Sure enough, when Samson was sleeping, the woman made sure he had a haircut and that was the end of Samson's strength. He broke his promise, and God took away Samson's strength.

What About You?

• Have you ever broken a promise? What were the consequences?
• Has someone broken a promise to you? How did you feel?

Talkin' About It

It's so easy to let a secret slip out, especially if someone is pestering you about it. God knows that and he's willing to help you, just ask him for strength to keep your mouth shut.

You are my inheritance, O LORD. I promised to hold on to your words.

Psalm 119:57

Keep your Promises

I'm Doomed

Read Romans 3:23-25

The stories this week make two important points. Number one—everyone is a sinner. Number two—God punishes sin. That makes the future look a little grim, doesn't it? You're going to sin, you can't help it. That means you're going to be punished, right?

Before you give up, look at the rest of the picture.

God knew all people are sinners and that sin comes naturally. But he couldn't let people into his perfect heaven with sin all over them, so he came up with a plan. God's Son, Jesus, came to earth and died for people. That act of love paid for all sins. So, when you accept Jesus as Savior and ask him to forgive your sins, he takes your punishment for you. Quite a plan, huh?

What About You?

• Have you asked Jesus to be your Savior and forgive your sins? If you haven't, maybe you'd like to now. Talk to an older Christian about it.
• When you stop and think about it, how do you feel about what Jesus did for you?

Talkin' About It

Jesus' actions showed an incredible amount of love for you. Thank him for what he did. Thank God for his plan. This is definitely the best gift ever! Tell God you want to obey him for the rest of your life.

Whoever knows and obeys my commandments is the person who loves me.

John 14:21

Read Genesis 41:39-43

Just as Theo came around the corner, a spray paint can came flying at his head. He instinctively caught it, then was knocked into the wall as four or five guys came flying out of the locker room. When Theo looked up, he saw the words the guys had painted on the wall. Words so gross, he blushed. But then a bigger problem developed—Coach Grey came in. There was Theo with a spray can in his hands and there were the dirty words on the wall. This didn't look good.

God can help even in a situation that seems hopeless.

Joseph was accused of messing around with Potiphar's wife; but he didn't do it. No one believed him, and he was thrown into prison. But, Joseph loved God and God knew what was going on. He helped Joseph explain a confusing dream the king of the country had. The king was so impressed that he put Joseph in charge of the whole country.

What About You?

• Have you ever been accused of something you didn't do? What happened?
• When has God helped you out of a tough situation?

Talkin' About It

Thank God that nothing surprises him. He always knows what is happening to you. Thank him that he's there to help you when you ask him.

I will strengthen you. I will help you.

Isaiah 41:10

Honest, I'm Innocent

How Does It Feel to Be Hungry?

Read Exodus 16:1-16

"That's the last box of food," Nick said. He climbed in the van beside Pastor Dan. "It's hard to believe there are really hungry people around here who need to use the Food Pantry," Nick said.

"Yeah, I know what you mean. We don't usually see homeless or very poor people in our neighborhood," Pastor Dan said. "But, that doesn't mean they aren't out there. For some people being able to get this food is like manna from heaven. They often have no idea where their next meal will come from."

Manna from heaven.

That's another example of how God cares about our every need. When the Israelites were wandering in the desert and complaining about being hungry, God heard their complaints. He cared about their needs. God sent them food from the sky, which was about the only place it could come from in a desert. Every person had enough to eat every day.

What About You?

• What needs does God meet for you every day, without your even asking?
• Do you have any idea how it feels to be hungry?

Talkin' About It

Thank God for meeting your needs. Thank him for help he gives every day that you don't even think about.

My God will richly fill your every need in a glorious way through Christ Jesus.

Philippians 4:19

Read Judges 16:23-30

Molly followed Sara down the hall, careful not to attract attention to herself. A week ago Molly had broken a promise she had made to Sara. Now she couldn't even face her friend. *I don't deserve to be Sara's friend. I could never even ask her forgiveness. I feel like pond scum.*

Saying you're sorry can make a difference.

Take Samson, for instance. He broke a promise to God and the result was major punishment. But, Samson knew that blowing it once didn't mean God would turn his back on him forever. Samson told God he was sorry and asked for help one last time. God answered his request and even used Samson to defeat his enemies. If you feel you've disappointed God, tell him you're sorry. He's still there for you.

What About You?

• When have you disappointed someone? Did you tell that person you were sorry?
• Have you ever felt as if you didn't deserve God's help?

Talkin' About It

Tell God you need him in your life. Tell him you're sorry for times you have disobeyed or disappointed him. Thank him for his forgiveness.

It Ain't Over 'Til It's Over

The* LORD *is my strength.

Exodus 15:2

Never Give Up

Read 1 Kings 17:8-16

Sean threw his math book on the kitchen table in disgust.

"What's the matter?" Mom asked.

"I don't get this junk. I read the stuff and try to do the homework—but it's like I got a wall around my brain and none of it sinks in," Sean moaned.

"Why don't you ask the teacher for extra help?" Mom asked.

"Nah, he wouldn't do that," Sean answered.

You don't have what you need because you don't ask.

Think about the woman in the Bible who gave up because she didn't have any food. She sat down and waited to die. Elijah knew God would help her if she just asked. When Elijah asked for her, God made sure the woman had all the food she needed. God is always willing to help us. So often we miss his help just because we don't ask for it.

What About You?

• What do you need God's help with right now?
• Is it hard for you to ask for help? Why?

Talkin' About It

Think about what you need God's help with. Ask him for exactly what you need. Thank him for his help and for always being there for you.

Ask, and you will receive. Search, and you will find. Knock, and the door will be opened for you. Matthew 7:7

Read 1 Samuel 17:1-50

*W*hy *did I say yes to Pastor Dan? Why did I let him talk me into this? I'm gonna be sick; yeah, I'm gonna stand up behind the pulpit and throw up in front of everyone.* Cori's brain was in a panic attack.

You wouldn't think it would be this scary to stand up in front of your own church, people you have known all your life, and give your testimony. But I've never felt so alone in my whole life!

You don't have to feel alone, Cori.

There was once a young boy named David, and he had to do something a lot tougher than talk in front of his church. David took on the giant Goliath, something no soldier in the whole Israelite army was brave enough to do. But David knew he would not be fighting alone. He knew God would help him. Do you know who won?

What About You?

• When have you had a hard time and needed God's help?
• Have you ever felt completely alone? Why?

Talkin' About It

Think about it. God promised never to leave you alone. Thank him for that.

Never Alone

I will never neglect you or abandon you.

Joshua 1:5

You Don't have to Fight

Read 2 Chronicles 20:1-29

"I'm gonna punch your lights out, creep. You better be ready, 'cuz after school, you'll be roadkill," hissed Roger. Garth shivered as Roger walked away.

"What are you going to do?" Todd asked. "You're not going to fight that pit bull, are you? No offense, but you don't have a chance against him."

"What choice do I have?" Garth said. "If I don't fight him, Roger will think he can push me around any time he wants."

Logical conclusion, but there was one time when an army won without fighting a bit.

That's because God helped them. Jehoshaphat's army was up against a much bigger army. They didn't think they had a chance. But Jehoshaphat asked God for help. God told him not to worry, but just stand up to the big army and see what God would do.

So Jehoshaphat's army marched toward the big guys. Unbelievably, the other soldiers started arguing and fighting with each other. Pretty soon they had all killed each other! Jehoshaphat's army won without fighting a bit!

What About You?

• Think about how much power God has. How do you get that power in your life?
• Does God still help people like he did in Bible times?

Talkin' About It

Thank God for the miracles he does to help his people. He still does them today. Thank him for taking care of his children.

Don't be frightened or terrified. . . . the LORD is with you.

2 Chronicles 20:17

Review Scripture from past week

So God was available to help Joseph, Samson, David, the entire Israelite nation, and a hungry old woman. These people are like the superstars of the Bible, so of course God would help them. But, what about little old me? I'm just a regular kid living a regular life. You know, nothing spectacular. Am I supposed to believe that God will really help me with my piddly little problems?

In a word ... yes!

These stories are examples of how God cares about every part of your life—whether you're hungry, scared, facing a big problem, or whatever. God cares and he promises to be with you constantly, no matter what you are going through. He's available to help you and strengthen you, just ask.

What About You?

• What have you learned about God from this week's stories?
• Have your feelings about God's involvement in your life changed? How?

Talkin' About It

Tell God what you have learned about him. Start a daily journal of how God is involved in your life. Thank him for caring about what you care about. Thank him for his help.

The Lord is my helper. I will not be afraid.

Hebrews 13:6

It's Yours for the Asking

It's OK to Say No

Read Genesis 6:9-22

The gang had been bumming around the mall all afternoon. No special plans—just hanging out. Then someone suggested they take in a movie. The theatre was right there in the mall. Eric was all for it until he heard which movie they wanted to see. It was an R-rated movie that his folks had specifically told him to stay away from.

Tough call. If he says no to his friends, he'll catch some heavy-duty teasing. If he goes with them, he is directly disobeying his folks. What to do? What to do?

Noah is a good example of how to handle this situation.

Noah went against the crowd to obey God. Remember? God decided to wipe out all creation with a big flood. But Noah had always obeyed God so he would be saved. However, to be saved, Noah had to build a big boat—on dry ground—when there was no place to go sailing nearby. He must have taken some heavy duty teasing, but it paid off when he and his family were the only ones who survived the flood. When you gotta choose between obeying and disobeying—it's OK to say no to temptation.

What About You?

• When was a time you had to choose to obey or disobey?
• Do your friends ever pressure you to do something you don't want to do? How do you handle it?

Talkin' About It

God says to obey him. Bottom line—that means nothing makes a good argument for disobeying him. Ask God to help you stand up for what you know is right.

If you love me, you will obey my commandments.

John 14:15

Read Genesis 22:1-19

"Mom, I made it!" Lindsay screamed, running through the house looking for Mom. They bumped into each other in the laundry room. "I made the traveling soccer team!"

"That's great, I'm proud of you!" Mom said.

"Coach only picked 16. Practice is every day. Games are on Sunday," Lindsay gushed.

"Oh, I see. That's a bit of problem, isn't it? We go to church on Sunday, and what about your puppet team that performs so many Sundays?"

Obeying God can mean making hard choices.

Abraham had to make a tough choice, too. Abraham loved his son, Isaac, more than you can imagine. He had waited a long, long time to be a father. But now God asked him to sacrifice Isaac to him. Whew! Abraham started to obey when God stopped him. Abraham showed God that he was willing to give up something important in order to obey God.

What About you?

• Have you ever had to give up something important?
• Have you ever been sorry you obeyed?

Talkin' About It

Tell God what is important to you. Tell him what sometimes keeps you from obeying him. Be honest, you can't fool him anyway. Ask him to help you obey him.

I fall asleep in peace the moment I lie down because you alone, O LORD, enable me to live securely. Psalm 4:8

Whatcha Gonna Do?

Page 45

You Always Get Your Way

Read Deuteronomy 1:8;
13:27-33; Numbers 14:
26-35

"Micah, please clean your room before you go out tonight," said Mom.

"Oh man. Mom, you're always on my case. It's my room. Can't I keep it the way I like it? Why does it have to be the way you want things?" Micah complained for a longer time than it would have taken him to clean his room.

Complaining instead of obeying can have some serious consequences.

Take the case of the Israelites. God promised them the land of Canaan. They sent 12 spies to check out the land. Ten of the spies came back and said,

"The people are too big, we could never defeat them. We say to forget it." The other 2 spies said, "God will help us. He said the land was ours." The people listened to the 10 scaredy-spies and didn't take the land. God punished them by making them wander in the desert for 40 years.

What About You?

• Be honest. When do you usually complain instead of obeying?
• What happens when you disobey?

Talkin' About It

Complaining is not attractive. Ask God to help you get rid of this habit and just do what you gotta do. Thank him for his patience with you.

Be sure to obey the commands of the LORD your God and the regulations and laws he has given you.
Deuteronomy 6:17

Read Numbers 20:6-12;
Deuteronomy 3:23-29

Corey stepped up to the plate, determined to get a hit. He swung hard at the first pitch. Strike one. Two balls and another strike later, Corey took a deep breath. He looked over the next pitch. *It's high and outside,* he thought, so he let it go by.

"Strike three!" the umpire called. Corey threw his bat on the ground and shouted, "What? Do you need glasses? It was high and outside. You're crazy!" In a flash, Coach Myers was on his feet and Corey was on the bench.

Losing your temper only leads to trouble.

Just ask Moses. He was leading the Israelites to the land God had promised them. But they complained constantly and Moses got tired of it. When they started whining that they were thirsty, God told Moses to hold his shepherd's staff and speak to a big rock. Water would come from the rock. But Moses lost his temper and smacked the rock with his stick. He disobeyed God, and as punishment he didn't get to go into the new land.

What About You?

• When have you lost your temper?
• Do you think Moses had a good reason to get mad?

Talkin' About It

Tell God what makes you mad. Ask him to help you keep your temper in check. Thank him that he doesn't lose his temper.

*B*e careful to obey these laws. Then things will go well for you.

Deuteronomy 6:3

Temper Your Temper

Obeying Pays Off

Read Joshua 2; 6:22-23

I *know Mom won't let me go. She doesn't like how all the kids hang out at the mall on Saturday afternoon,* Kim thought. *Well, I haven't got anything to lose. I might as well ask.*

To Kim's incredible surprise her mom said she could go. "You've tried so hard to keep our rules and obey Dad and me. I think you've earned the right to do this. I've seen how responsible you are. You see Kim, obeying can mean rewards."

Rahab is a good example of the rewards of obeying.

She risked her life to hide two spies that Joshua sent into her city. Rahab knew they were Israelites and that their God was very powerful. So she hid them from the soldiers and the king of her country. Rahab obeyed God and she wasn't even a believer yet. Rahab was rewarded for her obedience by being saved when Joshua and his army captured the city. Rahab was glad she obeyed.

What About You?

• When have you been rewarded for obeying?
• Have you ever obeyed when it was a very hard thing to do?

Talkin' About It

Tell God what rules you find hard to obey. Ask him to help you. Ask him to make you brave when you need to be.

In the same way let your light shine in front of people. Then they will see the good that you do and praise your Father in heaven.

Matthew 5:16

Read the book of Jonah

Molly put her books in her locker and closed it. She turned around and saw Sara. *I miss being Sara's friend,* she thought. *But since I spilled her secret to the other kids, I can't face her.*

Suddenly Sara was standing in front of Molly. "Hey, I miss you, can we be friends again?" she said. Molly couldn't believe it. She was getting a second chance. She would definitely not blow it this time!

Once Jonah blew it. Then God gave him a second chance.

God told Jonah to go tell the people in Nineveh to start living for God. Jonah didn't want to, so he ran away. He tried to get as far away from Nineveh as possible, but God found him. Jonah ended up in the belly of a big fish for three day with nothing to do but think about his disobedience. When the fish spit him out, God gave him another chance to obey. Jonah went right to Nineveh and preached! When you get a second chance—make it count!

What About You?

• When have you disobeyed, then been given a second chance?
• How did you handle the second chance?

Talkin' About It

Thank God for the second, third, and fourth chances he gives you. Thank him that he doesn't say, "Enough!" and walk away.

Take Two

Obeying:

You, O Lord, are good and forgiving, full of mercy toward everyone who calls out to you.

Psalm 86:5

To Obey or Not to Obey

Review Scripture from past week

Obedience is a thorn in the flesh for just about everybody. No matter how old you grow to be, there is always someone to obey—God. And, as we have seen in the Bible stories this week, you don't really want to disobey God because he takes it seriously.

The most important thing to remember about obeying God is: God is love.

He knows you're going to blow it sometimes, after all you're human, and you're a kid. He cares about whether or not you obey, but he also cares about your heart attitude. He knows whether you are really trying to obey him or just blowing him off. God has an incredible amount of patience and he'll hang in there with you—and help you learn from your mistakes.

What About You?

• What lesson have you learned from a time when you disobeyed?
• Do you think about the consequences before you disobey?

Talkin' About It

Tell God how you feel when you have disobeyed him or your parents. Ask him to help you think before you act and be more obedient. Thank him for his patience.

I have clung tightly to your written instructions. O LORD, do not let me be put to shame. Psalm 119:31

Read Genesis 19:4-16

Not many things scared a tough guy like Dan. At least not many things he would admit to. That day was supposed to have been one of the coolest days of his life. Dan and Uncle Jerry were at a World Series game in Candlestick Park, waiting for Dan's beloved Giants to take the field.

So what happened? An earthquake hit! Everything shook, there wasn't anyplace safe. But Dan had someone to call on for help. "God," Dan cried. "Help!"

Can God help him when the whole city is going down?

Lot needed God's help when Sodom was in big trouble.

God was destroying Sodom because of all the sinful people that lived there. But God knew that in his heart Lot loved him, so he wanted to save Lot. God sent angels to lead Lot and his family out of Sodom before the whole city burned up.

What About You?

• When was a time God protected you from danger?
• Who has God put in your life that helps protect you?

Talkin' About It

Thank God for protecting you. Thank him for parents and other adults who care about you and do their best to protect you.

Turn to me and be saved, . . . because I am God, and there is no other.

Isaiah 45:22

This Is Scary!

Page 51

Please! Help My Brother

Read Exodus 2:1-10

When Matt heard his name called over the loudspeaker, asking him to go to the office, he couldn't figure out what he had done. It was unusual for him to get in trouble. Of course, nothing was impossible. When he got to the office, Mr. Jones told him that his little brother was very sick and had been taken to the hospital. Matt's dad would be picking him up to join the family there. As Matt packed his schoolbag he prayed with all his heart. "Please God, help my brother. Keep him safe."

That sounds like what Miriam might have prayed.

Her brother Moses needed protection from the Egyptian pharaoh who wanted all the Israelite baby boys dead. Moses' mother hid him as long as she could. When he was too big to hide, she put him in a basket and floated him down a river. Miriam watched until Pharaoh's daughter found him. The princess took him and raised him as her own son.

What About You?

• When have you prayed for someone else's safety?
• How do you know God hears prayers for safety?

Talkin' About It

Tell God what you are afraid of or what worries you. Be honest with him, even if you fear he will think it's silly. He won't. Thank him for his protection.

But let all who take refuge in you rejoice.

Psalm 5:11

Read Exodus 12:1-30

Mr. Morris droned on and on about the rules. *He acts like we've never had a science lab before,* Jerome thought. *Why can't we just get to the experiments? Who cares about the dumb old rules? It can't be necessary to know every single one of them!*

It very well might be, Jerome.

The Israelites had to follow God's rules very carefully—their lives depended on it. God had been using Moses and Aaron to convince the Egyptian pharaoh to free the Israelites from slavery. The fickle pharaoh said yes, then no, yes, then no. He just couldn't stick with a decision, even though God kept sending plagues on the people.

Now it was time for the last plague, and it was a biggie. The oldest child in every home would die. God told the Israelites what to do to protect themselves from this plague. They followed every single rule, and their families were safe.

What About You?

• What rules do you have that are for your safety?
• Have you ever broken a safety rule? What happened?

Talkin' About It

Having rules to follow can sometimes be a pain. Ask God to show you how rules are for your protection. Thank God for parents and teachers who care about your safety. Thank him for his protection.

You are my hiding place. You protect me from trouble.

Psalm 32:7

Safety Rules

Take a Stand

Read Esther 4–7

Cori was in love. She spent most English classes dreaming about Sean Morris—high school freshman. When Sean asked her to the Sweetheart Dance, Cori was thrilled. Of course, she didn't know Sean had a lot more than dancing in mind.

Cori had strong feelings about sex and virginity, which she tried to express to Sean. He wasn't interested, and Cori knew she had to be braver than she had ever been and take a strong stand with Sean. She prayed for God's help.

Be strong like Esther!

Esther took a stand in a really tough situation. She knew the right thing to do would be the unpopular thing because she would have to reveal that she was Jewish. Then she had to go up against Haman who wanted to have all the Jews in the land killed. Esther went to her husband the king for help. It worked! The Jews were saved and Haman got what he deserved.

What About You?

• Where did Esther get the courage to do such a brave thing?
• Have you had to do something that took a lot of courage? Where did you get the courage?

Talkin' About It

Thank God for lessons he teaches by making you take a stand for what you believe. Thank him that he is with you through everything.

> *The LORD knows the way of righteous people.*
>
> Psalm 1:6

Read Daniel 3

"I was put in prison because of my faith in God," the speaker said quietly. "I didn't see my family for many years. By the time I was released, my children were grown. I had missed their childhood. Even after my release soldiers followed me. My family had to be very careful. We could only have church services at night, in private. We couldn't talk publicly about the Lord."

Rob couldn't believe anyone would get in trouble just because he believed in God.

You want to hear about trouble? Listen to this:

Shadrach, Meshach, and Abednego were three Jewish boys who refused to worship a golden statue the king made of himself. They would worship only God. The boys faced terrible punishment, but Shadrach, Meshach, and Abednego trusted God. They were thrown into a blazing hot furnace as their punishment. God protected them. He sent an angel and the four of them walked around in the fire. When the boys came out, they were perfectly fine—they didn't even smell like smoke!

What About You?

• Have you ever been in danger because of your faith?
• Do you trust God to protect you in dangerous situations?

Talkin' About It

In some parts of the world people are persecuted daily for their faith. Thank God for freedom to worship him. Pray for those who need his protection in order to worship him.

My help comes from the LORD, the maker of heaven and earth.

Psalm 121:2

You Have No Choice!

You Can't Pray Here!

Read Daniel 6

"Did you hear about that school down south where some kids got in trouble for praying in school?" Jim asked. "It's so dumb. The school board sets aside 5 minutes every morning for 'meditation and thought' but the kids who want to pray can't."

"Yeah, I heard," Tim answered. "I can't believe anyone would get in trouble for praying."

Daniel got in trouble big time for praying.

He was a prisoner in Babylon, but he impressed the king so much that he was made a ruler. The other rulers were jealous of him and wanted to get him in trouble. They knew Daniel prayed to God every day, so they tricked the king into making a law that people could pray only to him. Of course, Daniel kept right on praying to God, so the king had to punish him. Daniel was thrown into a pit full of hungry lions. But, God knew Daniel hadn't done anything wrong, and he protected Daniel from the lions.

What About You?

• Do you think Daniel knew that God would protect him?
• Is your faith strong enough for you to take a stand like Daniel?

Talkin' About It

Thank God for the freedom to pray and go to church. Thank him for surrounding you with his protection.

Be strong and courageous. Don't tremble! The LORD your God is the one who is going with you. He won't abandon you or leave you.

Deuteronomy 31:6

Review Scripture from past week

Maybe you think you don't need to be protected. After all, you live a pretty regular life. It's unlikely that you have ever had to risk your life by taking a stand for your faith. This week's Bible stories were about some pretty scary situations. But doesn't it make you feel good that God protected his people in each of these stories?

God is involved in your life, too.

God protects you every day in ways you don't even think about it. He even puts other people in your life to protect you. Yep, those parents and teachers that drive you bonkers sometimes also help protect you. That's true of the rules in your life, too.

But remember that just because something bad happens to you doesn't mean God isn't protecting you. Sometimes you learn important lessons from bad things, just as you did from reading the Bible stories this week. God loves you and wants what is best for you.

What About You?

• Is there anyone who doesn't need protection at some time in life?
• What are some ways God protects you every day?

Talkin' About It

Thank God for his constant protection.

The eternal God is your shelter, and his everlasting arms support you.

Deuteronomy 33:27

Your Insurance Plan

Follow Your Leader

Read Exodus 20:3

Jenny and Mom were at it again. It seemed like Mom was always trying to get Jenny to think about her priorities. "Mom, why are you always on my case about priorities? It's not, like, something I really think about. Priorities are something for grown-ups to think about, you know, when the things you do really make a difference. I'm just a kid, who cares what my priorities are?"

God cares, Jenny.

God gave Moses a set of 10 easy rules to help people live in a way that pleases God. The Ten Commandments teach us how to live peacefully with each other and respectfully and lovingly with God. The first commandment is about priorities; specifically what is most important in your life. God wants that number one spot. If you put something in front of God, then that thing, activity, friend, sport, or whatever becomes your god. If that happens, you're going to have problems. Keep God number one!

What About You?

• Think about what is important to you. Is anything more important than God?
• What can you do to be sure that you keep God in the number one place?

Talkin' About It

Ask God to help you check out your interests and activities to see if anything is too important to you. Ask him to help you keep your priorities straight.

Worship the Lord your God and serve only him.

Matthew 4:10

Read Exodus 20:7

Jim bent over his math book at the kitchen table. The new chapter of algebra didn't make a lot of sense to him. Finally, Jim threw his pencil on the floor in frustration and said, "God, this is hard!"

Mom looked up from her dinner preparations in surprise. "Was that a prayer, Jim?"

Now it was Jim's turn to look surprised, "What?" he asked.

"You just called out God's name, were you talking to him?"

Jim thought for a minute, "No. I guess I hear other kids use God's name like that so often that it's slipped into my habits, too."

That's a habit you might want to break.

The second commandment God gave Moses is that God's name should never be used in vain. That means as a swear word, or even just for emphasis in conversation. God promises future punishment to any who use his holy name wrongly.

What About You?

• Where do you hear God's name used in the wrong way?
• How do you feel when you hear God's name used as a swear word?

Talkin' About It

When you hear something 100 times a day it's easy to let it become a habit for you too. Ask God to help you resist the habit of using his name wrongly.

The name of the LORD is a strong tower. A righteous person runs to it and is safe.

Proverbs 18:10

Watch Your Mouth

Too Tired Doesn't Count

Read Exodus 20:8-11

"Rise and shine, and give God the glory . . ." Dad's off-key singing made for a rude awakening to the day. "Come on, Meg, time to get up," he sang. "We leave for church in an hour." Megan mumbled a response as Dad went to get himself ready. He checked back in half an hour, and Megan was still in bed. "Megan, get up. We're leaving in half an hour!" Dad wasn't singing anymore.

"I'm too tired, can't I sleep in this once?" Megan moaned.

"Nope, staying up late on Saturday is no excuse for sleeping in Sunday," Dad said firmly.

Good rule Dad, but God thought of it first.

The fourth of God's Ten Commandments is that the day of the week he set aside as a holy day should be kept holy. His ideal was that no one would go to work or school on that day. It's a day to think about him and worship him. That means gathering together with others who love God, studying his Word, and worshiping him.

What About You?

• Do you ever try to get out of going to church? Why?
• If you do go to church, what is your motivation for going?

Talkin' About It

Tell God if it's hard for you to get up for church, or if you think it's boring. Maybe you go just to see your friends, not to worship God. Ask him to help you remember what the day is for and to have an attitude of worship.

Remember the day of worship by observing it as a holy day.

Exodus 20:8

Read Exodus 20:12

"You are totally unfair. You were a kid a hundred years ago, and you don't remember anything about what it's like!" Mason was literally spitting the words at his parents. All his friends were going on a hunting trip, but his parents wouldn't let him go. They didn't think his friend's high school brother was old enough to be in charge of six kids. Mason complained all evening.

Honor your father and mother. Mason missed that one by a mile.

This commandment means to obey your parents and treat them with respect. This isn't to make you miserable—honest—it's for your own good. Your parents really love you and they want what's best for you. It may be hard to believe, but since they have lived longer, their decisions are usually wiser.

What About You?

• Have you ever spoken to your parents like Mason did? How did you feel afterward?
• What is one way you can show respect to your parents?

Talkin' About It

Tell God if this isn't an easy commandment for you. It's true that parents are sometimes hard to understand. Ask God to help you do the right thing, even when it's hard. Surprise your parents and tell them you love them.

Children, obey your parents because you are Christians. This is the right thing to do.

Ephesians 6:1

You Gotta Have Respect

Treat Others As You Want to Be Treated

Read Exodus 20:13-16

Angela pulled on her sweatshirt and put her gym clothes away. Then she went back to the shower room to get her necklace and earrings. *They were gone!* Angela called her friends over and they searched the entire shower room—but they didn't find her jewelry. Someone had stolen her stuff. Angela felt pretty crummy the rest of the day.

Treat others the way you would want to be treated.

Some of the commandments say don't steal from others, don't lie to or about others, don't murder, and don't commit adultery. All four of these things hurt others and will make you feel rotten, too. You may think, *I'd never murder anyone or commit adultery.* Well, what about the thoughts that lead up to those sins? Thoughts lead to actions; so watch your thoughts.

What About You?

• Has something of yours ever been stolen? How did you feel?
• Have you ever been lied to? Have you ever told a lie? Did it lead to more trouble?

Talkin' About It

Talk to God about these four commandments, especially any you have trouble with. Ask for help to keep your thoughts pure. Ask for help to treat others the way you would like them to treat you.

Love your neighbor as you love yourself.

Matthew 19:19

Read Exodus 20:17

When Michael walked into the school, he could tell right away that something was wrong. He put his things in his locker and went looking for his friends. They were all talking quietly in a corner of the hallway. "What's up?" Michael asked.

"Man, haven't you heard?" whispered Jack. "Tim Burton was shot last night. He was at the mall and some guy wanted his Charlotte Hornets jacket. Tim wouldn't give it to him, so the guy shot him. He's in the hospital in bad shape."

Coveting—wanting what someone else has only leads to trouble.

That's probably why God made "Don't covet" one of the Ten Commandments. Coveting doesn't usually lead to shooting someone, but it takes a lot of energy and brain power—thinking how you'd look in that Hornets jacket, or how you could get it away from it's owner. It destroys friendships and generally makes for a person that's no fun to be around.

What About You?

• When have you coveted what someone else had?
• When you covet something, what other problems could develop?

Talkin' About It

Talk to God about something you really want and tell him if you spend too much time thinking about it. Ask him to help you get it out of your mind.

Be happy with what you have.

Hebrews 13:5

If It's Not Yours, Leave It Alone

Live By the Rules

Read Exodus 20:3-20

*T*he Ten Commandments. Never have any other god. Never make your own carved idols. Never use the name of the Lord in vain. Remember the Lord's day and keep it holy. Honor your father and mother. Never murder. Never commit adultery. Never steal. Never lie. Never covet what your neighbor has.

These commandments are to make your life easier.

Anything is easier when you know the rules. It's easier to live correctly when you have guidelines. Following the Ten Commandments helps you treat God and others the right way. You would certainly be happier if everyone around you followed them, and others will be happier when you do.

What About You?

• Which commandment gives you the most trouble?
• Which commandment do you most often see broken around you?

Talkin' About It

Tell God that you know the Commandments can make life easier, but there is one or two that are really hard for you to stick with. Ask his help in following those commandments.

My son, do not forget my teachings, and keep my commandments in mind.

Proverbs 3:1

Read Genesis 37

Jason had his whole future planned. Play high school basketball; earn a sport scholarship to college; then head for the pros.

Then, everything was changed—a sledding accident, a crushed leg, and a doctor who said no more basketball. Jason just didn't get it. *Why did God give me the talent to play basketball and now he won't let me play? What about my dreams?*

When it seems that God has slammed a door shut—look around.

Joseph's future looked pretty bright too. He was his father's favorite son. He had a couple of dreams telling him he was going to be an important guy someday. Life was good. Then, his jealous brothers decided to get rid of him. Suddenly he was hauled off to Egypt to be a slave. *What about his dreams?*

Joseph kept trusting God and found out that God knew exactly what he was doing—Joseph ended up being an important ruler in Egypt.

What About You?

• What plans and dreams do you have in mind for your future?
• How are you going to feel if God changes everything around, like he did with Jason and Joseph?

Talkin' About It

Thank God that he always knows what's going on. Ask God to show you what his plans are for your life. Ask him to help you keep on trusting him no matter what happens.

The LORD's plan stands firm forever.

Psalm 33:11

What about My Dreams?

Can Good Come from from Bad?

Read Genesis 42; 45

Jason didn't take the news of the end of his basketball career very well. But then something cool happened. Jason's dad brought a laptop computer to the hospital for him to do his homework on. Jason had never spent much time on homework because he was too busy playing ball, and his grades showed that But, suddenly homework was fun! He was good on the computer. Jason's grades went up and he really enjoyed working on the computer.

It is possible for something good to come out of a bad situation.

Remember Joseph who was shipped off to Egypt to be a slave? Well, he was such a good guy that he ended up a ruler in Egypt. Yeah, he went from slave to ruler. A few years down the road, his brothers were starving. They came to Egypt looking for food. Guess who they had to ask for it? Yep, Joseph. God had put Joseph in a place where he could help his family. When bad things happen, look for how God may turn it into to something great!

What About You?

• Have you ever had something good come from something bad?
• Do you believe God cares what happens to you?

Talkin' About It

Ask God to increase your faith to believe he's always working in your life and looking out for you.

Share what you have with God's people who are in need.

Romans 12:13

Read Ruth

"This stinks!" Mark yelled at his parents. "Why do we have to move now? I just made the basketball team and I'm even a starter. I've got lots of cool friends and my grades are OK. Are you trying to wreck my life? What am I gonna do in California?"

It would feel crummy to leave the only place you've ever lived. But if it's God's idea, it is definitely the best thing to do.

Take Ruth, for instance.

Ruth lived in Moab her whole life. When she was widowed, she moved to Judah with her mother-in-law, Naomi. It must have been a tough decision to leave home, but it was the right one.

When they got to Judah, Ruth and Naomi had no money. God took care of them by showing Ruth a field where she could pick up left-over grain for their food. Sounds glamorous, huh? The owner of the field noticed Ruth, and after a while, they were married. Ruth and Naomi never had to worry about food again.

What About You?

• Have you ever had to do something hard that later turned out for good?
• When life gets hard, do you wonder if God is still in control?

Talkin' About It

Everyone goes through tough things. Talk to God when you have a tough time. He doesn't put you in a new place or a hard situation then just leave you. He will help you.

Wait with hope for the LORD. Be strong, and let your heart be courageous. Yes, wait with hope for the LORD.
Psalm 27:14

Hang In There!

I Really Care about This!

Read Nehemiah 2

Carol and her friends walked down the sidewalk to their homes. "This is disgusting!" Carol said as she looked around at trash in the streets and graffiti on the buildings.

"Yeah, I wish I lived in Beverly Hills—big houses with beautiful lawns," Margo dreamed.

Suddenly Carol had an idea, "You guys, *this* is our home. Let's clean this place up and make it look nice."

Sounds like a big job, doesn't it?

But when you really care about things, you take on big jobs. Speaking of big jobs— how about rebuilding a broken-down wall that surrounds an entire city? That's the job Nehemiah took on. He thought it looked bad that God's holy city was wrecked. So Nehemiah took a group to Jerusalem and started the huge project of rebuilding the walls. People made fun of them and it was a lot of work, but Nehemiah didn't quit. He was the leader of the first step of God's plan to get Jerusalem back in shape!

What About You?

• What big job do you care enough about to work on?
• When you have a hard job, do you think about how it honors God?

Talkin' About It

You may see things that need to be done around you all the time. Ask God to show you where he wants you to get involved. Ask him to show you his plan for your life.

God, who began this good work in you, will carry it through to completion on the day of Christ Jesus.

Philippians 1:6

Read Daniel 2

Beth cranked up the volume on her tape player and sang along with the music as she did her chores. When Mom appeared in the doorway, Beth thought it was to tell her to turn the music down. Instead Mom said, "Beth, how about if I sign you up to sing a solo at church? You have a beautiful voice, you should be using it."

"I am using it. But I don't want to sing in front of a bunch of people," Beth answered.

If God gives you a talent, shouldn't you use it?

Daniel could tell you something about that. God gave Daniel the unusual ability to explain what dreams meant.

That came in handy when the king of the land where Daniel was a prisoner had a dream he didn't understand. God helped Daniel explain it and the king was so happy that he made Daniel a ruler. God's plan was in action—now that country had a ruler who believed in God. None of it would have happened if Daniel hadn't used the gift God gave him.

What About You?
• What gift has God given you?
• How can you use it for him?

Talkin' About It
Everyone can do something. Your gift might be that you listen well or you are a good helper. Ask God to show you what your gift is and how to use it for him.

Sing, Girl, Sing, Sing.

Teach me to do your will.

Psalm 143:10

Good Job, God!

Read I Samuel 16:1-13

Melanie, Kelly, and Lisa sat on the bleachers and watched the football team work out. "The best player on our team is Mike Reeves. He is so cute!" said Melanie

"He's OK, but not as good as Jess Hurley. He's awesome," countered Kelly.

"You mean the best football player is the cutest one?" questioned Lisa.

It's tempting to think a nice package means good contents.

But God cares more about what's on the inside. He once showed that by passing over the handsome, strong men and choosing a young boy to be king. God sent Samuel to anoint one of Jesse's sons to be king. Samuel naturally thought one of Jesse's older, handsome sons would be the new king. But God said, "I look at what is in a person's heart, not how he looks on the outside." God's plan was carried out and David became king.

What About You?

• When have you gotten caught up in outside looks instead of what a person is like on the inside?
• Do most people put a lot of emphasis on "packaging" and not what a person is really like?

Talkin' About It

Thank God that he looks at our hearts and sees past our mistakes. Ask him to help you see beyond other's looks and learn what they are like inside.

Humans look at outward appearances, but the LORD looks into the heart.

I Samuel 16:7

Review Scripture from past week.

Have you ever had a lot of stuff to do in a short amount of time? Say you have homework in every subject; and your mom wants you to clean your room; and your friends want to go to a movie; and . . . . Well, you get the picture. How do you get everything done?

The best way is to have a plan

You need a system of what to do first and how much time each thing is going to take. This week's Bible stories have shown how much God accomplished in the lives of people because he had a plan. He knew what was happening in the life of each person, and he knew where he wanted that person to end up. So he worked out his plan in each life. That meant people had to go through some hard times before they got to the good part of his plan. But when they trusted God and followed his plan, good things happened for them.

What About You?

• How have you seen God's plan working in your life?
• How can you plan to know God better and serve him more?

Talkin' About It

God knows your situation and he has a plan for you. Ask him to show you his plan, step by step. Ask him to make you willing to follow his plan, even if it leads through some tough times.

In all your ways acknowledge him, and he will make your paths smooth.

Proverbs 3:6

Have a Plan

Love My Family?

Read Genesis 4:1-2

"Jamie, I've got to run out and buy a baby gift for the Watkins. Will you watch your brother and sister for an hour?"

Jamie was confused, "I didn't know the Watkins had a new baby."

"Well, they don't yet," Mom said. "They've been waiting to adopt and just heard they're getting a baby. In fact, they get the little boy in a couple of days. So we're getting together a quick baby shower. They are so excited!"

Everyone loves babies!

Even though her brother and sister bugged her sometimes, Jamie was glad to be part of a family.

Families are a gift from God. When the first babies in the whole world were born, it was because God told Adam and Eve to have babies—to fill the earth with people. He knew families were a good thing.

What About You?

• What about your family are you especially thankful for?
• Why do they bug you sometimes?

Talkin' About It

Everyone is bugged by family members sometimes, that's part of living with other people. But, stop and think what life would really be like without them. It wouldn't be so great, would it? Thank God for each member of your family.

Children are an inheritance from the LORD. They are a reward from him.

Psalm 127:3

Live Life Well

Read Genesis 21:1-7

Abby and her friends were sitting around talking when someone said, "Hey did you hear that Teresa Smith is pregnant?" Well, that tidbit picked conversation up quite a bit.

"Is she gonna drop out of school?"

"She's way too young to get married."

"She could always have an abortion."

That stopped conversation cold.

Some women do opt for abortion when they don't want the child that's growing inside them. Others feel abortion is murder and is always wrong. There are some people who wait a long time for a baby, and it's hard for them to understand how anyone could have an abortion. Take Abraham and Sarah, for instance. They waited a long time for God to fulfill his promise that they would have a big family. They knew their little baby was a gift from God and the beginning of their family. Abraham and Sarah were very old when Isaac was born, and they praised God for their precious baby.

What About You?

• How do you feel about abortion?
• Do you know people who had to wait a long time before having a baby? How did they feel when their baby came?

Talkin' About It

Thank God for life. It's a gift. Thank him that you were born. Ask him to help you live life well—honoring him and serving him.

Every good present and every perfect gift comes from above, from the Father who made the sun, moon, and stars.

James 1:17

Am I Gonna Get Married?

Read Genesis 24

Myrna drifted off to sleep every night with the same thought in her mind. Something that girls talk about all the time but boys would never admit caring about. She thought about who she would marry someday and planned what her wedding would be like.

Having someone to love, and knowing you're loved in return feels good.

But, how would you like it if your parents chose your mate and told you when you would get married? Abraham decided all that for his son Isaac. He sent his servant back to their homeland to find the right girl. That was a big responsibility, wasn't it? God led the servant to a pretty girl named Rebekah. He brought her back to Isaac, and they were married. Isaac and Rebekah loved each other very much.

What About You?

• What kind of person do you hope to marry?
• How would you feel about the prospect of never getting married?

Talkin' About It

The gift of marriage is not given to everyone, and some who do marry, don't stay married. Start praying now for your future. Pray for your future spouse, for salvation, health, and a happy home life. Ask God to prepare you for whatever is ahead in your life.

The LORD grants favor and honor. He does not hold back any blessing from those who live innocently. Psalm 84:11

Read Genesis 25:19-34;
27:42-45

"Get away from me you little twerp!" Devon shouted at Ryan.

"Get away from me you little twerp," mimicked Ryan. Devon ran to his room and slammed the door. That didn't discourage Ryan. He stood outside the door singing at the top of his lungs and pounding on the door. He would do anything to annoy his brother. Fighting was their normal way of communicating with each other.

You wanna hear about a fight?

Listen to this: Esau and Jacob were twin brothers. Twins usually get along great, but not these two. Part of the reason was their dad liked Esau best and their mom liked Jacob best. Jacob played that for all it was worth when he stole something important from his brother. Esau was mad enough to kill his brother. In fact, Jacob had to run away from home for his own safety. Now, that's a fight!

What About You?

• Do you ever try to annoy your brother or sister on purpose? How?
• What makes you most angry with your brother or sister?

Talkin' About It

It may not feel like it sometimes, but brothers and sisters are gifts from God. Think about the good times you have had together. Tell God that you really love your brothers and sisters. Thank him for them, and ask his help in getting along with them.

Brothers!

Share the same attitude and live in peace.

2 Corinthians 13:11

Big Sister Blues

Read Exodus 2:4, 7

When Mom pulled in the driveway and two of the three kids ran out to meet her, she knew the babysitting had not gone well. Cori had tried to exercise her authority as babysitter over Ryan, and he responded by throwing the TV remote control at her. Now Cori's head was bleeding, Mallory was terrified, and Ryan was hiding. It would be a long time before Cori agreed to babysit her brother and sister again.

Babysitting is a big responsibility.

Just think about Miriam's job. Her baby brother Moses was floating in a basket on a river because the king wanted all Israelite baby boys killed. His mom kept him hidden as long as she could. Now she was hoping someone would find him who could help him. Miriam kept watch. When an Egyptian princess found him, Miriam ran up and offered to find a slave woman to care for the baby. She got her own mother! Miriam was a great babysitter!

What About You?

• What good thing can you say about a brother or sister?
• How do you feel about babysitting younger siblings?

Talkin' About It

Thank God for what you can learn by babysitting younger family members. Thank him for older siblings that help watch out for you. Ask him to help you take responsibility as seriously as Miriam did.

May God, the source of hope, fill you with joy and peace through your faith in him.

Romans 15:13

Read 1 Samuel 1

"I've never wanted anything so much in my life! Please, God, please, please, please!" Lately Marty's prayers had been begging sessions. Marty was totally consumed with making the basketball team. It meant so much to him that he was begging God and trying to cut deals with him.

Sounds a little like Hannah.

Only what Hannah wanted was a child. Being a mom was very important to her. She couldn't think about anything else. In fact, she promised to give her child to God to serve him. God answered her prayer—Hannah had a son whom she named Samuel. She kept her promise and sent Samuel to live in the temple where he served God.

What About You?

• If you got something you wanted a lot, would you be able to give it away?
• When has God answered a prayer that you prayed very earnestly?

Talkin' About It

Thank God for answering prayer. Hannah is a good example of how God listens to us. Praise God!

My heart finds joy in the LORD.

1 Samuel 2:1

I Want This More than Anything!

Read Psalm 100

Maybe you're saying, "Well, I could be thankful for my family if they weren't so totally uncool, and if they didn't pick on me, and devote their lives to making me miserable!" It is true that family members can sometimes get on your nerves and even make life a bit difficult. But, if you're really honest about it, you know you love each one of them.

The point of this week is to get you thinking about that love.

Thank God for each family member and for some special thing that person does for you. Maybe you could even do something nice for your family, maybe even tell them what they mean to you. Maybe.

What About You?

• What specific things are you thankful for when you think about your family?
• What's a positive thing about being part of your family?

Talkin' About It

God knows that your family sometimes bugs you, but he also knows that deep down inside you love each family member. Tell God what you love most about each one.

Let's come into his presence with a song of thanksgiving.

Psalm 95:2

Tell the Truth Now

Read Joshua 3

Coach Peterson walked into a silent gym. All the players sat quietly as their new coach walked across the floor. None of them knew what to think about this new guy. Everybody had loved Coach Williams—he brought out the best in his players and really cared about them too. That's probably why he had gotten a chance to coach for a college. This new guy had big shoes to fill.

That's the same situation Joshua had.

Imagine trying to fill Moses' sandals! Moses had led the Israelites for a long time and everybody loved him. Now the people were supposed to switch their trust to Joshua. They had to be wondering if God would help Joshua like he had helped Moses. God answered that question. He had Joshua send the priests into the Jordan River, then he rolled the water back on either side to make a dry path through the middle. Now everyone knew God's strength was with Joshua!

What About You?

• Have you ever lost a teacher or coach that you really liked? How did you feel about the replacement?
• When have you needed to know that God is with you as surely as he showed himself to be with Joshua?

Talkin' About It

God promised to be with us and help us. Ask him to help you remember that promise. Thank him that his awesome strength will help you.

God arms me with strength. His perfect way sets me free.

2 Samuel 22:33

Who's the New Guy?

Sick of Being Picked On

Read Judges 4:6-15

*E*ighth graders are a major pain! At least that's how it seemed to Raven and her friends because they were lowly sixth graders. Some of the eighth graders made a hobby out of picking on the sixth graders. It had gotten so bad that Raven didn't want to go to school anymore. She didn't know how to make them stop, and she didn't want to tell a teacher because then the eighth graders would really pick on her.

The Israelites knew all about being picked on!

They were slaves and the slavemaster treated them crummy! God told Barak to lead the Israelites to freedom, but he was too chicken to go without Deborah. She came along and the two of them led their little army against the bigger, more powerful enemy. God was with them. Remember it was his idea for them to lead, and guess what? They won!

What About You?

• Have you ever been picked on by someone bigger than you? How did it feel?
• What did you do to stop the persecution?

Talkin' About It

Thank God for taking care of his people. Thank him that you can call on him when you are in trouble.

The LORD is my rock and my fortress and my Savior.

Psalm 18:2

Read Judges 7:1-22

"Are you psyched for the game on Friday?" Dad asked.

Clarence put his science book down and thought for a minute before he answered. "I don't know why we are even showing up," he finally said. "We don't have a chance against Hudson. Their school is twice the size of ours, and they bring twice as many players. We are gonna get totally creamed."

Take a lesson from Gideon, Clarence.

Gideon was leading his army against the Midianites. He had 32,000 soldiers, but that wasn't even a fraction of how many the other army had. Even so, God thought Gideon had too many soldiers. He wanted to be sure that when they won the battle, they knew it was because of God's strength and not theirs. He trimmed Gideon's army down to 300 soldiers. Then he helped them win!

What About You?

• When have you felt outnumbered or too small for a problem?
• When have you known that God's strength helped you with a problem?

Talkin' About It

God can do anything he decides to do. Thank him for his strength that gets you out of tough spots and helps you through hard times.

Be strong, all who wait with hope for the LORD, and let your heart be courageous.

Psalm 31:24

Bigger Doesn't Mean Better

Friends Forever

Read Ruth 1

Mindy choked back tears as she hugged Alli. "I've known this day was coming ever since Mom said we were moving. I just can't believe it's here," Mindy whispered. "You're the best friend I've ever had. No matter what, we are gonna keep in touch. We'll take turns calling and we'll write letters, and we'll visit each other whenever we can." The two friends hugged again, then Mindy's mom said it was time to go.

If you've ever moved away from a friend, you know how hard it is.

Try to imagine how Ruth felt. She moved away from her family and her friends. Ruth knew that the right thing for her to do was to move to Judah with her mother-in-law, Naomi. She wanted to serve God as Naomi did. It must have been very hard for Ruth to go, but she depended on God's strength to help her.

What About You?

• Have you ever moved away from a close friend? Has a friend moved away from you?
• How have you done at staying in touch with a friend far away?

Talkin' About It

Being lonely for someone is a lousy feeling. But it helps knowing that God's strength is there for you. Thank God for his loving strength that helps you when you're hurting.

Wherever you go, I will go, and wherever you stay, I will stay. Your people will be my people, and your God will be my God.

Ruth 1:16

Read 1 Samuel 24

"Turn the other cheek. You'll be surprised at what good things can come from not losing your temper." Mom's advice wasn't exactly what Pete wanted to hear. He was sick of Jeff picking on him. Jeff made his life miserable, and he just wanted to get even! Pete didn't know if he had the strength inside to "turn the other cheek!"

Hang on! Listen to David's story.

King Saul made David's life miserable because he was jealous of David. He tried to kill David several times. Then one night, David found King Saul sleeping in a cave. No one was guarding him, and David could have gotten even with the king right then and there. But David knew it would be wrong to kill Saul. He believed in God, and God gave him the strength to walk out of the cave and leave Saul alone.

What About You?

• When have you wanted to "get even with someone" for the way you were treated?
• When have you turned the other cheek instead of getting even?

Talkin' About It

Keeping your temper when someone has been mean to you takes a lot of strength. Thank God that his strength is there to help you turn the other cheek. If you're having a problem in this area, ask his help.

Call on me in times of trouble. I will rescue you, and you will honor me.

Psalm 50:15

Turn the Other Cheek

Live By the Golden Rule

Read 2 Samuel 5:1-5

"Slam! Michael Jordan does it again. Look at him go!" The TV announcer was going crazy as Michael Jordan led the Chicago Bulls to victory.

When the game was over, Eric turned off the TV. "Wow, that Michael is the best."

"Yeah, and besides being so good at basketball, he seems to be a really nice guy. He set up a foundation to help people, and he spends lots of time with handicapped kids," Roy added.

Treating others the way you would like to be treated can bring wonderful rewards.

David did that. He had known since he was a little boy that he would someday be king, but he didn't let it go to his head and start acting better than other people. He treated others fairly and with respect. Sure enough, he became king one day—and the people were thrilled. They knew he was a fair and honorable guy.

What About You?

• Do you try to treat others the way you would like them to treat you?
• How do you feel about people that treat others fairly?

Talkin' About It

Ask God for the strength to be kind and fair to others. If there is some person you have particular trouble with, tell God about it.

Be courageous and strong.

1 Corinthians 16:13

Read Psalm 28:7

No matter how tough or cool you are on the outside, there are times when you need help. There's nothing wrong with that—everyone does. No one else may know when you are afraid or confused. It's probably not something you would talk to your friends about, and you may not be comfortable talking to your parents about it. So what do you do?

The source of all strength is available to you!

And he's waiting for you to realize that you need him. Whether you need help in controlling your temper, giving a new guy a chance, saying good-bye to a friend, dealing with a bigger guy, or maybe overcoming a bad habit—God is there for you. Ask him for help with whatever is getting you down. He loves you and he will do what is best for you. Believe it!

What About You?

• What do you need God's help with right now?
• Does it make you feel hopeful to know you can ask God for help?

Talkin' About it

You can admit stuff to God that you wouldn't tell another living soul. Go ahead—be honest with God. Wherever you're weak, ask for his help.

God our Father loved us and by his kindness gave us everlasting encouragement and good hope.

2 Thessalonians 2:16

Strength for Today

Alone in a Crowd

Read Genesis 8

Keith had never felt so alone in his life. A bunch of the guys were going to Rick's house after school. Rick's parents wouldn't be there so the guys were gonna try some marijuana cigarettes that Rick's older brother had given him. Keith didn't want to do it because he felt drugs were dangerous. But the guys all laughed at him and called him a baby; even his best friend Kyle.

You're not totally alone, Keith.

No one could have felt more alone than Noah. He and his family floated in the ark for months. Since the whole earth had flooded, he pretty much knew there were no people left out there. When the water started going down, Noah must have wondered if God remembered he was still in the boat. Never fear! God did remember that Noah was on his private cruise. When it was safe God told Noah to come out.

What About You?

• When have you felt totally alone? Why?
• Have you ever felt like God is right beside you?

Talkin' About It

We all feel lonely sometimes. That's not the same thing as feeling alone. You're never alone. God is always with you. Thank him for that. Thank him that he knows everything that's happening to you.

Give thanks to the LORD because he is good, because his mercy endures forever.

Psalm 106:1

Read Genesis 28:10-22

Dona went through the house and turned on every light. She turned on every television and found a baseball bat. Then she settled herself under a blanket in a chair against the wall. Dona started counting the minutes until Mom got home. Being home alone was scary.

Jacob was alone once.

He left home and family and traveled alone to a new land. He might have been afraid and anxious about the future, but something happened that made him feel less alone. Jacob had a dream. In his dream, God told Jacob some things that were going to happen in the future and that he would always be with Jacob. When Jacob woke up, he knew he didn't have to feel alone anymore.

What About You?

• Have you ever felt alone even when other people were around you? Why?
• Why is it scary to be alone?

Talkin' About It

Sometimes it's scary to think about the future 'cause we don't know what is going to happen. The good news is that God does know the end and he's always with you. Thank him for his presence and ask him to help you follow him.

The LORD is your guardian.

Psalm 121:5

Home Alone!

Expect Tough Times

Read Genesis 39:20-23

"Don't tell me how much God loves me when Dad is lying in a hospital bed dying of cancer," Justin screamed at his mom. "If God really cared, he wouldn't let this bad stuff happen to Dad. Dad is a good guy. He always tries to live for God."

Knowing God doesn't protect you from bad things in life.

Joseph sure learned that. It was totally unfair when he was thrown in prison; he hadn't done anything wrong. But God was with him and he made something good come from the bad. The head of the prison saw what a good and honest guy Joseph was. It wasn't long until Joseph was put in charge of the whole prison.

What About You?

• When have you felt you were treated unfairly?
• When has God helped you get through a hard time?

Talkin' About It

Everyone has to go through bad things at times. The wonderful thing is you don't have to go through them alone—God's strength will help you. Thank him for his strength and for caring about what happens to you.

The LORD reached out to Joseph with his unchanging love and gave him protection.

Genesis 39:21

Read Exodus 13:17-22

"My head knows that God hasn't forgotten about us, but my heart wants some proof," Annie admitted. Things had been tough since her dad left. Mom worked two jobs just to make ends meet. Sometimes Annie was afraid they were gonna lose their house and end up living in their beat-up old car.

That's how the Israelites felt.

They were walking through the wilderness to the new homeland God promised them. God knew they were scared so he sent a huge cloud pillar to lead them in the daytime. At night it became a pillar of fire. The Israelites only had to look at the cloud to be reminded that God was with them.

What About You?

• When have you wished you could see God?
• Is God always with you? How do you know?

Talkin' About It

Thank God that he knows everything that is going on in your life. Ask him for more faith to remember that he is always with you, no matter what.

Prove It!

Whoever lives under the shelter of the Most High will remain in the shadow of the Almighty. *Psalm 91:1*

It's HOT!

Read Exodus 15:22-25

"Man, it's hot!" Mandy sighed. She took a long drink of ice cold water from her thermos. It was so hot that Mandy and Beth didn't talk much as they walked down the street. But when Mandy noticed a ragged old man sitting under a tree, she wondered aloud where he could get a cool drink on a hot day.

The Israelites were once hot and thirsty.

They were also homeless and wandering through the wilderness. They complained quite loudly about their thirst and God heard them. He told Moses to throw a tree into some water that was too bitter to drink. Moses did and the water became sweet. So the Israelites drank all they wanted.

What About You?

• In what everyday things can you see that God is with you?
• What's happening in your life? Is there a specific area where you would like to know God is with you?

Talkin' About It

It's comforting to know God is with you when you have a need. Thank him for meeting your needs and taking care of you.

Our help is in the name of the LORD, the maker of heaven and earth.

Psalm 124:8

Read Joshua 1:1-5

"We've got 3 seconds on the clock. I want Smith to inbound the ball to Chris. You have to get rid of it quickly, Chris. Turn and shoot. It's our last chance to win the game." Chris' insides started shaking before the buzzer even started up the game again. What a big responsibility … what if he couldn't do it?

Wonder if Joshua felt like the job God gave him was too big?

Wonder if Joshua's insides shook when he was told that he was gonna replace Moses? Joshua and all the Israelites were big time Moses fans. What did Joshua have to offer as a new leader? Maybe

Joshua wanted to turn and run as far away as he could get. But, he didn't. He waited to see what God would do.

What About You?

• Have you ever had to take over someone else's job?
• When have you known that God helped you do something?

Talkin' About It

When God gives you something to do, he will help you with it. That's the great thing about him always being with you. Thank him that you don't have to handle anything alone.

Be strong and courageous! Don't tremble or be terrified, because the LORD your God is with you wherever you go.

Joshua 1:9

Your Job, Man

Don't Be Chicken!

Review Scripture from past week

Many different situations come up in life that are scary. New things you have to do, new places to go, new jobs and responsibilities given to you, loved ones getting sick . . . well, you can come up with your own list.

You may know in your head that God is with you through whatever happens.

But it wouldn't be a surprise if your heart wonders about that sometimes. That's where faith comes in. God told us in the Bible that he is with us, no matter what—that's the bottom line. You've read six examples this week of how God is with his people, helping them through hard times. These are in the Bible to encourage you to believe that God is with you too.

What About You?

• Be honest. Do you have trouble believing God is always with you?
• Choose a verse from the ones you read this week that reminds you God is with you. Memorize it.

Talkin' About It

Tell God that your faith is weak sometimes. Thank him for being patient with you, and for always sticking close to you.

I am always with you.

Matthew 28:20

Read 1 Samuel 20

Sandy burst into a big smile when she saw Teresa. "Hi ya!" she shouted.

"Hi ya yourself!" Teresa shouted back. "It's so good to see you. I thought you guys were never comin' back from vacation."

"It's good to see you, too. I've got so much to tell you about our trip." Sandy filled her friend in on every detail of their trip, from the sights they saw to the hottest guys west of the Mississippi. Friendship like theirs makes life a lot of fun.

David and Jonathan were best friends.

But they had a problem. Jonathan's dad, King Saul, didn't like David. In fact, he tried to kill him several times. One time Jonathan went to see if King Saul was still mad at David. He was, so David knew he had to leave. David and Jonathan promised to be friends forever!

What About You?

• Who is your best friend?
• Would you do anything for your best friend?

Talkin' About It

One way God shows his love for you is by giving you friends. Thank him for your friends and the love they show you.

Love each other.

John 15:17

Best Friends

Lovin' the Creeps

Read 2 Samuel 9

No one had ever been more mean to Keith than Kevin was. It seemed like Kevin was constantly on his case about one thing or another. So, when a bunch of guys in the locker room started making up jokes about Kevin, it would have been understandable if Keith joined right in. But he didn't. Do you know why?

Because of David's example.

Yep, David was a good example of God's love. Remember how King Saul chased David and tried to kill him? After King Saul died, David became king. Then, instead of punishing King Saul's relatives, he brought the only living relative of King Saul to his palace and shared everything he owned with him.

What About You?

• How do you treat people who have been mean to you?
• Do you think you would be able to do what David did? Why?

Talkin' About It

Getting even is sure a human approach to problems, but not a godly one. Tell God the name of people you have trouble loving. Ask for his help.

Love your enemies, and pray for those who persecute you.

Matthew 5:44

Read 2 Kings 2:1-11

Mark plopped down in a chair and took off his tie. "Man, this stinks!" he said. Mom sat down on the arm of the chair and waited for him to go on. "Carl was my age. Most of life was ahead of him. We were gonna go to college together, and he wanted to be an architect. Carl was a Christian. Why didn't God keep him from dying?"

There is another way of looking at it, Mark.

Death for a Christian can be seen as a reward. It's a time to see God's love very clearly. Elijah spent his life serving the Lord. When it was time for him to go to heaven, God sent a chariot that was made of fire. It took Elijah to heaven in a whirling wind. Joining God in heaven is truly a reward.

What About You?

• When have you been angry because someone you loved died?
• Why is joining God in heaven a reward?

Talkin' About It

Not many people have gone to heaven in a chariot of fire. But it's nice to know that heaven is a future reward. Thank God that he rewards those who serve him.

Rejoice and be glad, because you have a great reward in heaven!

Matthew 5:12

Sometimes Life Stinks

Sweat It Not!

Read 2 Kings 4:1-7

The house at 513 Ashley was a junk heap. The grass was always tall, the shutters were falling off, the paint was chipping. When the neighbors found out that a sickly old widow lived there, they all pitched in and fixed up the place. They showed love without expecting anything in return.

God helped another widow with a problem.

This widow owed a man lots of money, but all she had was a little oil. He was going to take her sons into slavery as payment. God told Elisha to send the woman to gather jars and then start pouring her little bit of oil into them. She poured and poured until every jar she had was full. Then she sold the oil and paid the man.

What About You?

• When have you shown love to someone without expecting something in return?
• What does God do for you every day that shows he loves you?

Talkin' About It

Thank God that he cares about your everyday needs. Thank him for all he does for you.

Turn your burdens over to the LORD, and he will take care of you.

Psalm 55:22

Read 1 Chronicles 22:6-7;
2 Chronicles 3–4

Leonard's heart raced. His palms were sweaty, he couldn't concentrate, and his stomach was churning. Why? . . . Janet. Yep, Leonard had his very first girlfriend. He thought about her all the time. And, he couldn't do enough for her. He wanted to give her presents, carry her books, do homework with her, be with her every minute.

Have you ever felt that kind of love for God?

Have you ever wanted to give God gifts and do things for him? David did. He wanted to build a temple for God. God said David could make the plans, but his son Solomon should build the temple. It was made with special wood, gold and silver, and beautiful cloth. The temple was a love gift to God.

What About You?

• How can you show love to God?
• How do you feel about your church being a love gift to God?

Talkin' About It

Tell God ways that you want to show love to him. Ask him to help you remember these things every day.

Feelin' Sick

The LORD's glory filled God's temple

2 Chronicles 5:14

Nah! It Can't Be

Read Ezra 1:1-11

You could've knocked Matt over with a feather. Really, he had never been more shocked. The very last thing he expected to hear come out of Jack's mouth was that he was a Christian. Can you blame Matt? Jack hangs with a tough crowd, has long oily hair, wears ratty clothes. He sure doesn't *look* Christian!

Guess you can't judge a book by the cover!

People probably thought King Cyrus didn't care anything about God. But God had shown him that everything he had was a gift from God. So Cyrus wanted to do something for God. He helped the Israelites rebuild God's temple in Jerusalem. He even gave them silver and gold and other things to use.

What About You?

• When have you judged someone before you got to know him or her?
• How would people looking at you know that you love God?

Talkin' About It

Ask God to help you not judge people before you get to know them. Ask him to help you live so that others can see you love him.

God is love.

1 John 4:8

Read 1 Corinthians 13

There doesn't seem to be anything more important than showing love—to God and to others. You have read six stories this week telling how God shows love to his children and how we can show love to others. It really isn't enough to say that you love someone if your actions don't back it up.

1 Corinthians 13 tells specific ways that love acts.

It's not always easy to love others because some people are not at all lovable. But anyone can love their friends. A Christian shows God's love by being able to love even his enemies. It's not easy but it helps to think about how much God loves you and all that he has done for you. Then it is easier to share love with others.

What About You?

• Is there one specific thing in 1 Corinthians 13 that you have trouble with? What?
• Is there a person you feel is not lovable? Why?

Talkin' About It

God makes no secret how important love is to him. Thank him for the love he freely shows to you. Ask him to love others through you.

Stay Close to the Source

We must show love through actions that are sincere, not through empty words.

1 John 3:18

It's Greek to Me

Read Genesis 41:1-40

$X = 2y + 4z - 4$ m-o-u-s-e. "What kind of equation is that?" John asked Meg.

"That shows how much algebra I understand," she answered. "I wish the heavens would open and algebra knowledge and understanding would spill down on me. That's the only way I'm ever gonna get this stuff."

Don't give up.

One time the king of Egypt didn't understand a dream he had. He asked all his wise men and counselors. None of them could explain it. But God told Joseph what it meant, and Joseph told the king. Joseph didn't just happen to know all about dreams, God gave him that wisdom. So don't give up on stuff you don't understand. Ask God for wisdom.

What About You?

• What are you having trouble understanding?
• What are different ways God could help you understand this?

Talkin' About It

Tell God what you don't understand and ask for his help. He may choose to explain it to you through a friend, a book, a teacher, or a blast of wisdom. Thank him for whatever he does.

God's riches, wisdom, and knowledge are so deep that it is impossible to explain his decisions or to understand his ways!

Romans 11:33

Read Deuteronomy 11:19-21; 32:47

Jamie keeps having this horrible nightmare that she is talking with a bunch of really cool kids. They are impressed with her self-assurance and wisdom. But she unknowingly blows the whole thing when she quotes some bit of wisdom that she picked up from . . . her parents!

Do parents really know anything?

Moses certainly thought they did. He even thought that a really good way for kids to learn about life and living for God could come from parents. They can teach values and lessons from the Bible just by how they live their everyday lives. Not a bad idea. Maybe you should give them a chance!

What About You?

• What are three things you really like about your parents?
• What are three things you have learned from your parents?

Talkin' About It

Parents and teens don't always get along, that's no secret. But if you're honest about it, you will admit your parents have some good points. Thank God for your parents and all you learn from them.

Learning from My Parents?

Love the LORD your God, follow all his directions, and be loyal to him.

Deuteronomy 11:22

Choose Smart!

Read I Samuel 25:1-35

Jackie didn't know what to do. Her friends wanted to crash a high school party. Jackie knew there would be drinking and other stuff going on there. She didn't want to get involved in that junk. But she didn't want her friends to dump her.

What should she do? Fitting in with your friends is of major importance, right? So if all your friends decide to do something totally dumb, do you go along, just to keep fitting in; or do you choose smart and let them go their merry way?

Choosing smart means making good choices.

Abigail showed good judgment, and she kept David from making a terrible mistake.

David was so mad at Abigail's husband Nabal that he wanted to kill him. Abigail brought gifts to David and begged him to calm down. She told him it would be wrong to kill Nabal. Smart woman. She kept David from making a big mistake.

What About You?

• What can you do to get out of going along with your friends?
• How can you be an example to others of smart choices?

Talkin' About It

Ask God to help you choose good friends, then the other choices won't be so tough. Tell him you want to be an example of choosing smart to others.

The fear of the LORD is the beginning of knowledge.

Proverbs 1:7

Read 1 Kings 3:5-13

Andrea and her friends lounged around on the floor of the family room, sipping diet colas and talking. They had just finished watching *Aladdin*. "What if there really were magic lanterns?" asked Allison. "What would you wish for, if you could have anything in the whole world? Beauty, brains, money?"

Believe it or not, Solomon actually got to do that.

And it wasn't a genie who granted his wish. God said he would give Solomon anything his heart desired. He could be rich or famous or powerful. Solomon made a wise choice— he asked God to make him wise so he could tell the differ-ence between good and evil. God thought that was a good choice, so he made Solomon wise—and rich and famous as a bonus.

What About You?

• What would you ask for if God said he would give you anything?
• Why did Solomon's choice please God?

Talkin' About It

Being a kid and making wise choices aren't always easy. Ask God to help you think things through before you make choices. Ask him to help you choose wisely.

The LORD gives wisdom. From his mouth come knowledge and understanding.

Proverbs 2:6

Make A Wish; Any Wish

Use Your Brain

Read 1 Kings 3:16-28

Anna and Gloria were shouting at each other so loudly no one would know they were really best friends. "Why do we always have to do what you want?" shouted Anna.

"What are you talking about? You always get your way." responded Gloria.

Suddenly in the middle of a shout, they both turned to Janet and asked, "Who's right?" Gulp. What should Janet say?

God gave Solomon wisdom, and it wasn't long before he got to use it.

Two mothers came to him, fighting for all they were worth. They each had a baby, but during the night one of the babies died. Now they were arguing over whom the living baby belonged to. Solomon knew what to do. He said to cut the baby in half and give half to each mom. He knew the real mother would rather give up her baby than have it killed. That's wisdom at work!

What About You?

• Who do you go to for advice when you have a problem?
• Why do you choose that person?

Talkin' About It

Having to take sides when friends fight is no fun. Ask God to give you wisdom to know right from wrong. Ask his help when friends come to you for advice.

Whoever walks with wise people will be wise.

Proverbs 13:20

Read Daniel 5

For a solid hour Cori complained about her parents. "They bury me in rules; they don't remember what it's like to be young; they don't like my boyfriend" . . . on and on. Suddenly she stopped and asked Sara, "What should I do?" Sara thought Cori was too hard on her parents. But if she said that, Cori might get really ticked. What should she say?

That could be the same question Daniel asked himself.

Daniel was dragged out of jail to read some handwriting on the wall. The king wanted to know what it said. Well, it was bad news about the king being punished because he didn't obey God. Daniel might have been scared to pass along that message. But God gave him the wisdom to understand it, so he told the king the truth.

What About You?

• When have you been able to explain something to someone?
• When have you been afraid to tell someone the truth?

Talkin' About It

Did you know that when you need help understanding something, God is there for you? Ask him for help.

If any of you needs wisdom to know what you should do, you should ask God, and he will give it to you. God is generous to everyone and doesn't find fault with them. James 1:5

Now What Do I Say?

Wise Guys

Review Scripture from past week

So, can you just sit back in your chair and turn your mind away from the tube or video game and say, "OK God, hit me with some wisdom?" Sorry, it doesn't work that way. It's not that easy.

It's true that God has incredible, unlimited wisdom.

It's also true that he wants to share it with you. But, you have to do your part. Don't get discouraged, it's not hard. It just takes time. You don't realistically expect to just sit back and have him pour his wisdom into your head, do you? In order to absorb God's wisdom, you gotta spend some time with him. Read his Word, pray, hang out with people who have known him longer than you have. Above all else, be quiet once in a while. In order to hear God talk to you, you gotta listen.

What About You?

• How much time do you spend alone with God each day?
• When was the last time you knew that God was speaking to you?

Talkin' About It

If you haven't been spending time with God, tell him you're sorry. Ask him to help you make a devotional schedule and stick to it. Thank him for his wisdom and his willingness to share it with you.

Help me understand so that I can follow your teachings. I will guard them with all my heart.

Psalm 119:34

Read Genesis 17:15-19; 21:1-2

"Mom, you said you'd drive me to the mall a half-hour ago. Let's go. My friends are waiting." Roberto said impatiently.

"I said I would drive you when Dad got home to stay with your brother. Tiento is asleep. I can't leave him home alone, can I?" Roberto really didn't care about Tiento as long as he got what he wanted.

Waiting is so-o-o-o hard.

Even when you really believe a person is going to do what he says, it's hard to wait. Abraham and Sarah knew all about that. God told them they would have a child. They waited and waited, and it didn't happen. Didn't God mean what he said? Of course he did. Even though it took a long time, God did what he said he would do.

What About You?

• How good are you at waiting for people to do things for you?
• Have you ever felt like God wasn't going to keep his promises? What made you feel that way?

Talkin' About It

Tell God about doubts and fears you have. Ask him to help you believe that he means what he says and that he keeps his promises.

*G*od faithfully keeps his promises.

1 Corinthinas 1:9

Show a Little Patience, Will Ya?

Promises, Promises

Read Genesis 9:8-17

Everytime Rob ran up the basketball court his eyes scanned the crowd looking for his dad. This was Rob's last home game, and Dad promised he would come. It was the fourth quarter now, and he still hadn't shown up. *Well, he just won't see me play at all this year,* thought Rob. *Guess work wins out again. Another promise broken.*

Broken promises are totally useless.

God made a promise to Noah that he would never destroy the whole earth by a flood again. That was after the earth had been wiped out by a flood because everyone except Noah was so rotten. God hung a rainbow in the sky as a sign of his promise. When you see a rainbow, remember God keeps his promises.

What About You?

• How do you feel when someone breaks a promise to you?
• Do you think people feel you can be trusted to keep your promises? Why?

Talkin' About It

Read through some of God's promises in the Bible. Thank him that he means what he says. Ask him to help you keep promises you make.

Whenever I form clouds over the earth, a rainbow will appear in the clouds. Then I will remember my promise to you and every living animal. Never again will water become a flood to destroy all life.

Genesis 9:14-15

Read Exodus 16:1-15

A. J. heard muffled voices coming from his parents' room. They were talking about money again. Since Dad started his own business, money had been tight. Mom and Dad had prayed about starting the business. They were sure God led them to do it. A. J. wondered why it was so tough for them. Had God led them to the business then forgotten about them?

The Israelites felt a little forgotten one time.

"Did God free us from slavery, just to let us die of hunger in the desert?" they asked. God doesn't work that way. Even though the Israelites were in the middle of a desert, he sent food. Birds came from nowhere and bread fell down out of the sky. When God says he's gonna do something, whether it's leading you somewhere or taking care of you — believe him.

What About You?

• Why is trusting God sometimes so hard?
• For what specific thing is it hardest for you to trust God?

Talkin' About It

Thank God that he cares about every need you have. Thank him that he can be trusted to finish what he starts and to do what he says.

Hurry Up, God!

[God is] going to send you food from heaven like rain.

Exodus 16:4

Who Ya Gonna Call?

Read Numbers 21:4-9

Michael was in shock—and worried sick about his best friend. Mark was sick—very sick. He might even die. One minute he was fine, the next he was flat out sick. Michael went back and forth between praying and worrying. He begged God to make Mark well. He wanted a miracle.

When someone we love is sick, we all want a miracle.

What if you could be healed of a serious illness by looking at a statue? Right. Well, it really happened. God once told the Israelites to look at a bronze snake statue to be healed from snake bites. Sounds pretty wild, huh? But when the people looked at the statue and were healed, they knew God meant what he said.

What About You?

• When have you asked God to heal someone?
• Do you trust God to take care of your loved ones?

Talkin' About It

Thank God for healing the Israelites. Thank him that you can talk to him and tell him what you need or who you are concerned for. Thank him for meaning what he says.

You are my hope, O Almighty LORD. You have been my confidence ever since I was young. Psalm 71:5

Read 1 Samuel 8:6-22

"**M**om, I need $75!" Jeremy said. "I want to get a sweater like all the guys are wearing." He didn't really think Mom was going to hand him the money, but he was planting a seed. It didn't work, though. Mom thought $75 was a lot of money—and Jeremy didn't need a new sweater. "Yeah, but everybody has one. Do you want me to look weird?" Jeremy whined.

Just because everybody has something doesn't mean you need it too.

For example, God governed the Israelites with a loving hand. But, all their neighbors had a king, so they wanted a king, too. God told them they would regret it, but they insisted. So God said they could have a king. They should have listened to God. They got a king, and they were soon miserable.

What About You?

• When have you begged for something, but not liked it so much when you got it?
• Why would you want to have what everyone else has?

Talkin' About It

Ask God to help you be brave enough to be different from everyone else, if it's the best thing.

Leave the Crowd Behind

Live by my standards, and obey my rules. You will have life through them. I am the LORD.

Leviticus 18:5

Show Me!

Read Judges 6:11-23

"I'm gonna stand with my back to the goal, 3/4 of the way down the court, throw the ball over my shoulder with one hand, bank it off the right side of the backboard and—nothing but net!" bragged Mikey.

Laurie wasn't buying it. "Show me," she said.

Sometimes you just need proof.

Gideon sure did. God's angel told Gideon that God would use him to save the Israelites from their enemies. But Gideon needed proof. He was from a poor family and he didn't think God could use him, especially for something so important. So Gideon put some food on a rock. The angel touched the rock and the food was burned up. That was proof enough for Gideon.

What About You?

• When have you needed proof that something was true?
• Is there someone you always believe without asking for proof?

Talkin' About It

Thank God for his patience when you question something he has said in his Word. Thank him that you can always believe what he says.

The Messenger of the LORD appeared to Gideon and said, "The LORD is with you, brave man."

Judges 6:12

Read 2 Timothy 3:16

Would you like to be able to pick and choose what parts of the Bible to believe? That would make living the Christian life pretty easy, wouldn't it? Just choose the things that are easy for you as true, and the things that are hard for you as not true.

Uh, uh. It doesn't work that way.

God said that everything in the Bible is true, even the things that are hard to swallow. And it's all put there for a reason, whether it's teaching or correcting. When God says something—he means it. But, if that scares you, remember this too: God also says in the Bible that he loves you!

What About You?

• OK, be honest. What command from the Bible would you just as soon wasn't true?
• When do you have trouble believing what God says?

Talkin' About It

Tell God what things in the Bible are hard for you to believe or obey. Ask him to help you understand and obey. Ask him to help you always believe he means what he says.

All or Nothing

Blessed is the person who places his confidence in the LORD.

Psalm 40:4

Read Your Mind

Read Genesis 37:5-10

Tia tried to concentrate on science, honest, she did. But her mind kept wandering to the TV show she saw the night before, even though she knew that the plot wasn't stuff that was good for her to think about.

It's hard to have good, clean thoughts when your mind is filled up with rotten stuff. What if God wants to use your thoughts to talk to you? Would he be able to get through the junk in your mind?

He spoke to Joseph in his thoughts.

Joseph was asleep and in his dreams God told him things that would happen to him in the future. Joseph found out he was going to do important work for God someday. God couldn't have spoken to Joseph in his dreams if his mind was filled up with junk.

What About You?

• When has God spoken to you in a dream or a thought?
• How can you keep your mind clean?

Talkin' About It

Ask God for help in keeping your thoughts on pure things. Ask him to help you listen for what he has to say to you.

Keep your thoughts on whatever is right or deserves praise: things that are true, honorable, fair, pure, acceptable, or commendable.

Philippians 4:8

Read 1 Samuel 3

M*an, I don't know what to do.* Tyler was struggling with the decision of whether or not to try out for the soccer team. It doesn't seem like such a big decision, but with all the other things in his schedule, Tyler didn't know if he wanted to give up a couple of hours every night for practice. *I wish God would just tell me right out loud what I should do. Aaahhh, he doesn't do that.*

Well, he did do that for a kid once.

Samuel got confused when he heard his name called out in the middle of the night. He thought it was the priest he worked for calling his name. But, after being awakened three times, the priest told him it must be God waking Samuel up. Sure enough, the next time he heard his name, Samuel asked God what he wanted. God wanted to talk to Samuel about the future.

What About You?

• How would you feel if you heard God call your name out loud?
• Why would God talk to a kid about the future?

Talkin' About It

God doesn't usually speak aloud anymore. But we can know what he has to say by reading his Word and spending time in prayer. Tell God you want to hear what he has to say to you. Tell him you will spend time reading his Word and praying.

Did You Hear Something?

The LORD will continually guide you.

Isaiah 58:11

Open Your Ears

Read Daniel 2

"We need to talk, Katy," Mom and Dad looked quite serious as they sat down. "We're concerned about you and your choice of friends. Your grades are falling, and you don't seem happy anymore. Maybe we can help if you'll talk to us."

Katy stiffened without realizing it. *Why should she listen to her parents? Could she learn anything from them?*

There is a one word answer to that question: Nebuchadnezzar.

Quite a word, huh? Here's the story. King Nebuchadnezzar of Babylon had a strange dream. None of his advisors could explain it to him. He knew that Daniel served God and might be able to explain it. Even though the king didn't serve God, he listened to Daniel's explanation. He was so thankful for Daniel's help that he made him a ruler.

What About You?

• When have you been stubborn about listening to someone's instruction?
• What person has God used to help you?

Talkin' About It

Even if you think people are too different from you to help you, give them a chance. Ask God to help you be open to parents or teachers who can be God's spokespeople to you.

Open your ears, and come to me! Listen so that you may live!

Isaiah 55:3

Read Genesis 18:1-15

Sometimes Laura didn't know if she was coming or going. Between keeping up with school and friends, keeping her parents happy, and figuring out where God fit in, she felt like she was running as fast as she could but not moving an inch. She tried praying, but her words bounced off the ceiling right back at her. *How do I find out why I'm on this planet or what I'm supposed to do with my life?* she thought.

Read the Bible.

The examples of how God spoke to his people in Bible times can be an encouragement—like when he spoke to Abraham about the son he and Sarah would have. God sent three angels to deliver that news to Abraham..

Abraham and Sarah couldn't believe they would have a baby because they were so old. Instead of talking to them in a dream that they could question, or as a voice in the night, God sent three angels to talk directly to Abraham. They spent some time with Abraham and answered his questions.

What About You?

• When have you known God was talking to you?
• How did God communicate with you?

Talkin' About It

If you find the Bible hard to understand, get a modern translation. Ask God to make his Word clear to you. Thank him for the guidance and instruction it contains.

Come close to God, and he will come close to you.

James 4:8

Bible Messages

Dream Time

Read Genesis 28:10-22

When Alfred looked out the window, he couldn't believe what he saw. Trees were laying on the ground, the sky was pink, and the grass was orange. Dogs and cats were walking upright dressed in suits, and people were crawling on all fours. He ran to find his mom. He looked everywhere, his heart was pounding and he couldn't breathe; then—he woke up. Whew! It was all a dream. Alfred stared into the darkness, wondering what this dream meant.

Not all dreams have some fantastic message.

But Jacob's dream sure did. He ran away from home because he stole some things from his brother and Esau was really ticked. Jacob was afraid Esau would kill him. Jacob walked a long way then lay down to sleep for the night. When he fell asleep, he had a strange dream in which God told him that everything would be all right and he shouldn't worry. That was a relief. That was a dream with good news!

What About You?

• When have you wanted assurance everything was going to be all right?
• How do you know God cares when you are worried about something?

Talkin' About It

Thank God that he cares about what you fear. Thank him for helping you know everything

I am with you and will watch over you wherever you go.

Genesis 28:15

Read Exodus 3:1-10

"Come on, Molly. We'll tell our folks we're going to sleep over at Maria's house, then we'll go down the street to Raven's house. Her folks aren't home and a bunch of guys are coming over. It'll be a blast!"

"No way," Molly said. "My parents always find out. The last time I lied to them I was grounded for a month. It isn't worth it."

Experience is a great teacher, isn't it?

We can learn from others' experiences, too. Like when God spoke to Moses from a burning bush that never burned up. Pretty dramatic, huh? God wanted to be sure Moses paid attention to this message because it was very special. God had an important job for Moses to do. He wanted to use Moses to free the Israelites from slavery. The dramatic way the message was delivered left no doubt as to it's importance.

What About You?

• What would be the best way for God to get your attention?
• Would you be willing to do whatever God asked you to do?

Talkin' About It

Thank God that he does talk to us and that he has different ways to communicate to different people. Thank him that he knows which ways speak to individual people.

Learn From Experience

Those who love me will do what I say.

John 14:23

If You Wanna Hear, You Gotta Listen

Review Scripture from past week

Think about all the ways God could speak to you: a book, friends, parents, a song, minister, dreams, inner voice, the Bible, experiences—ways too numerous to mention. The point is that he does want to speak to you.

Are you willing to listen to what God has to say?

If you're gonna hear him, you gotta be listening. That means being quiet sometimes, spending time with him, reading his Word and praying, listening to your parents or minister or older Christians. Be willing to spend time quietly thinking about God and waiting to hear him speak.

What About You?

• How much time do you spend alone with God every day?
• Do you feel you are ready and willing to listen, however he may speak to you?

Talkin' About It

Be honest with God about how often you "listen" for his words. Ask him to help you improve on listening. Thank him for caring enough about you to communicate with you.

Pray in the Spirit in every situation. Use every kind of prayer and request there is. For the same reason be alert.

Ephesians 6:18

Read Genesis 21:14-21

"I feel crummy. No, I feel worse than crummy, I feel like the pond scum of life," Rusty moaned. 'Course it did seem like everything was going wrong lately—he lost a $50 science book, did the wrong page of math homework, missed the winning shot of the basketball game—well, you get the picture. "Doesn't anybody care how crummy I feel?" shouted Rusty.

You bet. God cares.

He comforted Hagar when things seemed hopeless. Abraham and Hagar had a son even though they weren't married. Things were going along OK until Abraham's wife, Sarah, became jealous of the boy. She insisted that Hagar and Ishmael be sent away. They wandered in the desert until their food and water ran out. When Ishmael began to cry, Hagar put him down and went off alone because she couldn't watch her son die. God heard Hagar and Ishmael crying. He sent an angel to tell her that God would take care of them. Then he sent water for them.

What About You?

• What makes you feel crummy?
• What makes you feel better?

Talkin' About It

Thank God that he cares when you feel crummy, no matter what the reason. Thank him for the examples of his care that are in the Bible.

Let your mercy comfort me as you promised.

Psalm 119:76

Feelin' Crummy

This Hurts

Read 2 Kings 4:8-37

Cindy had never felt pain so sharp or deep down in her gut. She felt betrayed and angry and confused. Mary was dead. Cindy and Mary had been best friends since 1st grade. Mary got sick in 4th grade and fought for her life for 3 years. But, she lost the fight and now she was dead. *God, where are you? Kids aren't supposed to die.*

God cares when you hurt.

Death is a natural part of life, but God knows that it hurts us when loved ones die. One time a woman's only son died. She went to find Elisha, a man of God who stayed at her home when he was in town. Elisha hurried to the boy. He lay on top of the boy and prayed for God's help. Soon the boy sneezed seven times and opened his eyes. God gave the woman back her son.

What About You?

• Have you ever lost someone you cared about? How did you feel?
• How does God comfort you when you're grieving?

Talkin' About It

God doesn't always bring people back to life, but he does care about the pain we feel. Thank him for sharing your grief.

He certainly has taken upon himself our suffering and carried our sorrows.

Isaiah 53:4

Read Job 1

Matt and his mom shuffled through the ashes of their home, looking for something—anything—to keep. They lost everything they owned in the fire. Matt's dad and little brother were seriously burned, too. *Why do bad things like this happen?* Matt wondered. *Does this mean that God doesn't love us anymore?*

It doesn't mean anything like that.

Bad things just happen and being a Christian doesn't protect us from those bad things. Job knew that. He lost everything—his wealth, children, and health. But, Job never stopped trusting God. He never even thought that God had stopped loving him. God knew that Job loved him more than anything. In Job's case, God gave him more children, more wealth, and renewed his health.

What About You?

• How do you feel when bad things happen?
• Why didn't Job get mad at God?

Talkin' About It

It is sometimes easier to deal with bad things when we can blame someone. But, blaming God isn't right. Ask him to help you keep trusting him regardless of what comes along. Thank him for helping you through tough times.

Praise the God and Father of our Lord Jesus Christ! He is the Father who is compassionate and the God who gives comfort. He comforts us whenever we suffer. 2 Corinthians 1:3-4

Digging Through the Ashes

Doesn't God Care?

Read 2 Kings 5:1-15

Ryan left the hospital room feeling pretty rotten. It hurt to see his grandpa like this. Grandpa was a big, strong man who loved fishing and laughing. At least, he used to be. Now he looked thin and sad; just breathing in and out seemed to take all his strength. Ryan slumped down in the waiting room and thought about Grandpa. *Why doesn't God make him better? I've prayed and prayed. Doesn't God care about Grandpa?*

God cares more than you can ever imagine.

God hurts when we hurt. Sometimes he even heals the people we pray for. He helped Naaman who was sick with leprosy. A little slave girl told Naaman to go to Elisha the prophet. She knew that he could help Naaman get better. Naaman went to see Elisha, and God helped Elisha heal Naaman. God doesn't always heal the people we pray for, but he is always with us, helping us through hard times, giving us the strength to deal with whatever comes along.

What About You?

• Has God ever healed someone you prayed for?
• When have you felt God's comfort at a time of loss?

Talkin' About It

Thank God that he sometimes chooses to heal people. Thank him for his comfort and strength that helps when you are grieving for someone.

The Almighty LORD will wipe away tears from every face.

Isaiah 25:8

Read 2 Kings 20:1-6

Coach Simmons was a totally cool guy. All the guys liked him because he treated them with respect, and he made practice fun. Chris was close to him because Chris' dad lived out-of-state and Coach was sort of a fill-in dad to him. Two days ago Coach had a car accident; he was badly hurt. The doctors didn't know if he was even going to live or not. Chris was a Christian, and he prayed constantly and sincerely for Coach Simmons, asking God to heal him and bring him back to school.

Prayer changes things.

God hears our prayers and cares about the things that make us sad or hurt. King Hezekiah prayed to God because he was told he was going to die. God's prophet Isaiah had passed along that bit of news to Hezekiah. The king reminded God that he had always tried to obey God. He didn't want to die yet. God heard King Hezekiah's prayer and healed him.

What About You?

• What prayer has God answered for you?
• How do you think King Hezekiah felt about God when he was healed?

Talkin' About It

Thank God for hearing your prayers and caring about what troubles you.

Ask for Life

This is what the LORD God of your ancestor David says: "I've heard your prayer. I've seen your tears. Now I'm going to heal you."

2 Kings 20:5

Don't Give Up

Read 1 Kings 19:1-18

Eric felt like a black cloud was hanging over his head and following him everywhere he went. He felt so rotten about himself that sometimes life didn't seem worth living. *School stinks; my family doesn't have a clue; my friends can't be trusted; I'm not good at anything . . . .*

Eric needs to know that someone loves him.

Eric sounds a lot like Elijah did one time. Elijah had a king and queen so mad at him that they wanted to kill him. He ran away and sat down under a tree. Elijah felt like he was the only person left in the entire world who still cared about God, and he didn't want to deal with it. He was ready to just give up and die. But, God comforted him, sent him food and water, and let him rest. Then he told Elijah there were still other people who served God. Elijah felt much better after that.

What About You?

• What makes you sad? Have you told God about it?
• Do you feel better about things when you talk to God about them?

Talkin' About It

We all feel depressed sometimes. Talk to God about things that get you down. Thank him for caring and helping you.

I'm leaving you with peace. I'm giving you my very own peace.

John 14:27

Read Philippians 4:6-7

If I blow this Spanish test, I'm gonna fail the class. Lois was so worried about not passing the test that she couldn't concentrate on studying. Every time she tried to focus on studying, her mind would freeze up and she would start thinking about the consequences of failing a class. It wasn't a pretty picture!

Worry can paralyze!

A normal, rational person can turn into a non-moving piece of stone because of worry. When your mind gets caught up in all the "What if's" you can't concentrate on things and a chain reaction begins: "I'm worried that I might fail–so I can't concentrate to study–so I probably will fail–so I'll worry that I might fail ......" It doesn't have to be this way. God wants us to give our worries to him. Picture in your mind just putting them in his hands. Then brush your hands off and get on with life, 'cause God is gonna take care of those worries now.

What About You?

• When you give worries to God, can you forget about them?
• Does God care about whatever worries you?

Talkin' About It

God cares about anything that worries you, no matter how big or small it may be. Tell your troubles to God and believe that he will handle them for you. Thank him for taking care of you.

Don't Let Worry Paralyze You

Turn all your anxieties over to God because he cares for you.

1 Peter 5:7

Take a Good Look at Yourself

Read Romans 3:23

*O*ooh boy, what have I gotten into? Robin wondered. She had agreed to go to a youth group meeting at Carlie's church. Robin thought it would be fun because some cute guys would be there, and they would play games and have food. She sure didn't expect to have to sit through a Bible study. *I don't need to hear this stuff. Sin is just big things like robbing banks or killing someone,* she thought.

Sorry Robin, you're not getting off the hook that easy.

The Bible says that everyone sins. You see, sin is more than robbing banks and killing people. Sin is anything you do that displeases God: being selfish, cheating, getting angry, being proud, being disrespectful to your parents. Not one person in the entire world can live every day without committing a sin. Some sins can be hidden from other people, but you know in your own heart what you have done. More important, God knows.

What About You?

• What habits do you have that might be sin?
• Why is sin wrong in God's eyes?

Talkin' About It

Be honest with yourself and God—you're not perfect. You do sin, even when you don't want to. The way to handle sin is to admit it to God, ask his forgiveness, and ask his help not to do it anymore.

I don't realize what I'm doing. I don't do what I want to do. Instead, I do what I hate.

Romans 7:15

Read Romans 6:23

Robin's mind wandered away from the Bible study. She thought about what to wear to school tomorrow, how cute that blond guy in the third row was, if her volleyball team could beat South. But then something caught her attention, "God doesn't allow sin in heaven. If you are a sinner, bottom line is you won't get in." *Well, that doesn't make any sense,* she thought. *You just said everyone sins, now you say sinners don't get into heaven. Guess, it's not very crowded up there.*

Hang on Robin, there's a second chapter to the sin story.

God is perfect, he doesn't sin at all, period. Heaven is perfect, too; and he doesn't want any dirty sin messing it up. So, sin-ners can't get in. But, that doesn't mean no one goes to heaven. God made a plan that allows people into heaven. His sinless son, Jesus, came to earth and lived as a person like us. He was treated badly and eventually died for us. Choosing to believe in Jesus is choosing eternal life in heaven. Deciding not to believe in Jesus is choosing eternal death in hell.

What About You?

• What do you know about Jesus?
• Have you made a decision to believe in Jesus?

Talkin' About It

Now you know the first two steps of God's plan. Tell God you know you are a sinner and that you're sorry for your sins. Thank him for sending Jesus to die for your sins.

You Gotta Choose: Death or Life

> *A righteous person's reward is life. A wicked person's harvest is sin.*
>
> *Proverbs 10:16*

Who Loves Ya, Babe?

Read John 3:16

So everyone sins; sinners don't get into heaven; God has a plan to help that problem which involves his son, Jesus, going through some tough things. What's the plan? Robin wondered. And, why did he do it? Why would God want his son to go through hard things? Why would Jesus do it?

The answer is simple—love. God loves everyone.

God wants everyone to have the chance to live in heaven with him someday. In order for that to happen, our sin had to be paid for. Remember, people started out perfect with Adam and Eve. Since then, we have chosen to be sinners. Jesus came to earth. He was beaten and made fun of and eventually nailed to a cross. His death was the payment for our sins. It gave us the chance to be clean in God's sight, so we can be allowed into heaven. Jesus was willing to go through these horrible things because he loves us

What About You?

• How does knowing what Jesus went through make you feel?
• Do you understand that Jesus went through all those things for you?

Talkin' About It

Thank God for his awesome love. It's hard to comprehend love that great, isn't it? Tell him that you love him, too.

Christ died for us while we were still sinners. This demonstrates God's love for us.

Romans 5:8

Read John 14:6

Robin's attention snapped back to the speaker as he was closing. "The story doesn't end here," he said. "Understanding and believing what Jesus did for you is the next step. This is a personal decision. Not one that you make because your buddy does or to impress someone. If you want more information, I'm here. Come and talk to me after the meeting. If you came with a friend, he or she will wait a few minutes." Robin took a deep breath and glanced at Carlie.

"I'll wait," Carlie said, smiling.

It's a simple plan, based on love.

Let's review what we know. The Bible says everyone sins; God doesn't allow sin in heaven; God's son, Jesus, died on the cross, paying the price for all sin. Now what? It's sorta like when someone offers you a gift—it isn't yours until you take it. You must receive the gift of what Jesus did for you. You do that by believing that Jesus is the Son of God and that he died for your sins.

What About You?

• Do you believe that Jesus is the son of God and that he died for your sins?
• Is there any other way to get to heaven besides believing this?

Talkin' About It

Tell God that you believe Jesus is his son and that he died for your sins, though he had never sinned himself. Thank him for his wonderful plan and incredible love.

I am the way and the truth and the life. No one goes to the Father except through me.

John 14:6

You Gotta Believe

Confession Is Good for the Soul

Read 1 John 1:9

Pastor Dan sat down with Robin and asked, "Do you understand what I've been saying tonight?"

"Yes, I think I do. It's just that I never thought that I sinned. I thought sin was just terrible things that bad people did. I've heard about Jesus before, you know, like at Easter time. But, when I listened to you it seemed so, I don't know, personal. Like all that Jesus did was just for me. I want to receive Jesus. What do I do?"

Believe in Jesus and confess your sins.

Believe that Jesus is the Son of God, and that he died for your sins. Aaahhh, your sins. Yep, you gotta admit that you sin, that's confession. You know what? Confession actually feels good because then you're not trying to hide things from God anymore. He knows what your sins are anyway, but when you confess them—admit them to him—he knows you realize what they are, too. When you tell God you're sorry for your sins, he will forgive them because Jesus paid for all sin.

What About You?
• What sins do you need to confess?
• Are there some things you've been trying to hide from God?

Talkin' About It
You don't have to tell anyone but God about your sins. Be honest. Ask God to show you things in your life that you may not realize are sins. Tell him you're sorry. Thank him for his forgiveness.

If we love each other, God lives in us, and his love has reached its goal in us.

1 John 4:12

Read Acts 3:19

Pastor Dan gently continued explaining God's plan to Robin. "OK, you believe in Jesus and have confessed your sins. Now there is one more step. It's called repentance. Big word, huh? But it can be explained like this: When you're driving down the road and suddenly realize you're going the wrong way, what do you do? You turn around and go the right way. Repentance is turning away from sin and heading toward God's way of doing things right."

Turn around and walk with God.

Now granted, if you haven't been doing big, noticeable sins, this turning around may not be really obvious. But, you'll know in your heart because you'll be trying to live for God. Your family may notice a difference in your attitude, too. Don't worry though, you don't have to do this turning around all on your own. God will help you. Read the Bible to find out how he wants you to live. Talk to him and ask him for all the help you need. He's there for you.

What About You?

• When have you tried to change yourself without God's help?
• How does God help you turn around and live for him?

Talkin' About It

Tell God you want to change the way you've been living. Ask him to help you—to point out things that need to be changed in your life. Thank him for his forgiveness and help.

So change the way you think and act, and turn to God to have your sins removed.

Acts 3:19

Turn Around

Your Turn

Review Scripture from past week

This week, you've read about Robin's journey to salvation. Could you identify with her? Have you made the decision to receive Jesus' gift of salvation? Are you positive that you will enter heaven when the time comes for you to leave this earth? This isn't a decision to be put off until you're old. It needs to be made now.

God is waiting.

If you don't understand God's plan, or have questions, talk to your parents, or Sunday school teacher, or minister— anyone you know who has accepted Jesus. They will answer your questions or find someone who can. Remember, God loves you so much that he sent his son, Jesus, to die for your sins.

What About You?

• Honesty time. Are you expecting to go to heaven just because your parents are Christians?
• What have you learned this week about God's plan?

Talkin' About It

The decision to receive Jesus is one that each person must make. If you haven't done so before, tell God you know you are a sinner, that you're sorry for your sins, that you believe Jesus died for all sin, and that you want Jesus to come live in your heart.

Christ Jesus came into the world to save sinners.

1 Timothy 1:15

Read Psalm 1

**Week 18
Sunday
Good Guys
Versus Bad
Guys**

Mark has two close friends, Jack and Zack. When Mark hangs out with Jack and they do the things that Jack plans, Mark always gets in trouble. But, when he goes with Zack and does what Zack suggests, they have a great time. Same thing happens when he takes advice from Jack—it always turns out that someone gets hurt, or Mark gets in trouble.

Do you think there's a lesson to be learned here?

When you follow the advice of guys who don't care a hoot about God, you're gonna have problems. It's much better to spend your time with friends who care about God and want to serve him. You won't be tempted to do things that get you into trouble. Choose your friends wisely, and you'll avoid a lot of punishment, both now and in the future.

What About You?

• Do you have any friends who sometimes get you in trouble? Who?
• Why do you keep being friends with them?

Talkin' About It

Thank God for Psalm 1, it's got a great message. Ask him to help you choose friends wisely so your friends can help you know him better and serve him more.

You Win or Lose by the Way You Choose

Blessed is the person ... who delights in the teachings of the LORD.

Psalm 1:1-2

Page 135

Take Control of Your Mind

Read Psalm 36

Will was digging around under his older brother's bed looking for a baseball mitt. Boy, was he surprised to find a couple of porno magazines. *Wow. Mom would have a fit if she knew about these,* he thought. He considered telling her, but then he started looking at the pictures. Soon, without really planning to, Will found he was spending most of his time looking at those pictures or thinking about them. They began to take more time than anything else in his life.

Sin is happy to push it's way in front of God.

Don't kid yourself by thinking you can do something bad—just once. Sin has a way of worming itself into your mind.

You think: *No one knows what I'm doing, it's my little secret.* But, sin wants total control, it'll try to push God out completely. To fight it, think about how much God loves you. His love reaches beyond the clouds, it's as solid as a mountain. God's love is constant. Make that the most important thing in your life.

What About You?

• What is there in your life that tries to push God out?
• Can you think of a time when you actually felt God's love? When?

Talkin' About It

This is important. Don't let anything push God out. Thank him for his constant love. Ask him to give you strength to keep him in first place in your life.

This is love: not that we have loved God, but that he loved us and sent his Son to be the payment for our sins.
1 John 4:10

Read Psalm 37

Sherrie jumped for the rebound just as Rayla did. Sherrie didn't get to touch the basketball because Rayla slammed into her and she hit the floor, sliding almost all the way to the bleachers. Sherrie pulled herself up, expecting to hear Coach nailing Rayla for the foul. Instead, Coach was shouting, "Great, Rayla, keep up the good work and you'll be starting on Friday." Sherrie couldn't believe it—why did that creep get praised for playing dirty?

Don't sweat it. The bad guys may win for awhile, but good wins out in the end.

Does it seem like the bad guys always win? Does it bug you to see creeps with lots of money and important positions? Does it seem to you that Christians should have the best of everything? Well, just wait. Psalm 37 tells us that the bad guys will get the punishment they deserve someday, and God's people will get their reward. Trust God. He's in control, and he knows what's going on.

What About You?

• What incidence of a bad guy winning really bugs you?
• When the psalm says the good guys will get their reward, what is it talking about?

Talkin' About It

Don't get hung up on what you don't have. Instead, thank God for how he takes care of you, live the way that makes him happy, and thank him that he is in control of the future.

Why Do the Bad Guys Win?

The victory for righteous people comes from the LORD. He is their fortress in times of trouble.

Psalm 37:39

Stay Focused

Read Psalm 73

Lisa could see the finish line ahead of her. The ribbon glittered in the sunlight. She was in front of the other runners so she concentrated on keeping up the pace. With only a few feet to the finish, Lisa glanced back to see where the other runners were. That little break in concentration cost her the race. Another girl shot past Lisa and broke the ribbon. Lack of focus meant second place.

Stay focused on your goal.

What is your goal? Serving God and getting to know him better? Then stay focused on it. Don't get caught up in comparing the good things that happen to people who don't love God with the bad things that happen to those who do love him. When you take your eyes off your goal—loving and serving God—you'll have problems. Trust God to take care of what is fair or unfair. Make him the foundation of your life.

What About You?

• What kinds of things pull your focus away from God?
• How can you keep your focus on God?

Talkin' About It

Ask God to help you keep focused on him and not be jealous of non-Christians' success. Thank him that his children have a reward waiting for them in the future.

My body and mind may waste away, but God remains the foundation of my life and my inheritance forever.
Psalm 73:26

Read Psalm 112

"Here's the plan. We all go in the store together, then split up and spread out all over. The old lady working there can't watch all of us. So everybody try to grab something and slip it under your shirt. Meet back here in fifteen minutes," Vince instructed the guys.

Doug didn't feel good about the plan. "Shoplifting is wrong," he said. "If we get caught it'll go on our permanent records."

Stand up for what you believe, Doug.

Doing good has it's rewards. Psalm 112 tells us that fearing God and obeying his commands brings good things in the future. The person who fears God doesn't ever need to be afraid. He has God on his side, and he knows God will always take care of him. People who don't love God will be angry when they see someone doing good. They know that in the long run, their dreams will never come true.

What About You?

• When are you tempted to do things that are disobedient to God?
• How can you learn what is pleasing to God and what isn't?

Talkin' About It

Even if some guys make fun of you, it's better to obey God 'cause he promises a forever with him to those who obey him. Ask for the strength to resist temptation to "go along with the gang."

Blessed is the person who fears the LORD and is happy to obey his commands.

Psalm 112:1

Good Things Come to Those Who Do Good

You Gotta Read the Book

Read Psalm 119:1-8, 90-96

"But I got the right answers," Carol complained, holding a math paper with a big red *F* on it.

Mr. Shook wouldn't budge on Carol's request to improve the grade. "You do have the right answers. But you didn't arrive at the answers using the correct procedure. Procedure is important."

Carol disgustedly asked, "How am I supposed to know what the procedure is?"

Mr. Shook firmly answered, "Read the book!"

The answers and the procedures are in the book!

God gave his children a textbook that has all the answers and procedures for living for him. What is it, you ask? The Bible! It's not a book to be blown off because just about everything we need to know is written there. Reading the Bible helps us know what God is like and what he wants us to be like. Spend time every day reading the Bible, and you'll have a better handle on life.

What About You?

• Honesty time. How much time do you spend reading the Bible every day?
• How does that amount of time compare to the time you spend watching TV?

Talkin' About It

The Bible is God's special message to you. Get a version you understand. Then promise God that you'll spend time reading the Bible every day.

I have treasured your promise in my heart so that I might not sin against you.

Psalm 119:11

Review Scripture from past week

The bottom line is: there are good people in the world and there are bad people. Sometimes good things happen to the bad people. Sometimes it even seems like the bad guys are winning and will soon be in control of everything. But fear not.

God is in control.

The bad guys may have their day right now, but they will also have their judgment day in the future. People who love God and try to do right and live for him will get their reward someday. So don't get caught up in why the bad guys have so much good stuff. Just keep going along, doing good, reading God's Word, living for him. Leave the reward and judgment stuff up to God. He can handle it.

What About You?

• What part of the bad guy/good guy thing is hardest for you to swallow?
• Do you ever get so caught up in wanting the bad guy to get creamed that you forget to get on with your life?

Talkin' About It

Thank God that he is in control—all the time. Thank him that nothing escapes him; he knows everything that everyone does. Thank him for his Word that teaches about him.

Bottom Line

Mercy belongs to you, O Lord. You reward a person based on what he has done.

Psalm 62:12

Hide Here

Read Psalm 18

"Great game tonight," Coach Smith said, slapping Marcus on the back. "Thanks," Marcus said. He felt like a million bucks. It wasn't easy to get a compliment from Coach Smith. But, Marcus had been practicing extra hard. He had the basketball skills down, and now he was learning how to execute. It was nice to get the reinforcement from Coach Smith that he was being successful.

It feels good to hear nice things said about you.

It's good to say nice things about God, too. Some of the psalms were written as songs of praise to God, thanking him for the wonderful things he does. Psalm 18 praises God for his protection and strength. He's like a fort for his people to hide in and a shield to protect them. God is always ready to help his people. Praise God! He is faithful, trustworthy, and holy!

What About You?

• What nice thing has been said about you?
• What nice thing would you like to say about God?

Talkin' About It

Don't take God for granted. Thank God for his strength and protection. Thank God for who he is and what he does for you.

God arms me with strength and makes my way perfect.

Psalm 18:32

Read Psalm 33

"Why are you always so happy?" Katie asked.

Mindy stopped humming and looked surprised. "I don't know. I didn't realize I was always happy."

"Well, you are always singing or humming. You sure sound happy," Katie replied.

Music makes a happy sound.

One way to praise God for all he does is to sing joyfully to him. You don't have to sing well, just sing praise. When you think about all God does, you should be so full of joy that it bubbles out of you. For instance, think about the world he created. All he had to do was speak the word, and there was the world. Also think about how he protects his children. No one can say they are saved by any army or their own strength—it is God who protects! You can put your trust and hope in God because he will never fail!

What About You?

• What is your favorite praise song or chorus?
• For what one part of God's creation are you most thankful?

Talkin' About It

Sing a song of praise to God. Tell him how wonderful he is and that you appreciate all he does for you. Thank him for creating the world and all that is in it.

We wait for the LORD. He is our help and our shield.

Psalm 33:20

Safety Insurance

Read Psalm 66

Walking alone along a dark city street at night is pretty dumb. Desi knew that, but that didn't help him much now. He had to get home, and this was the only way. He took a deep breath and whispered a prayer that God would keep him safe. Then he started sprinting down the street, glancing around as he ran.

God does protect his children.

Think back over the stories in the Old Testament that tell how God has protected his people. Remember when he turned water into dry land? God's enemies turn chicken when they think of his mighty power. God hears the prayers of his children, and he does not turn away from them.

What About You?

• What is your favorite Bible story about God's protection?
• When have you been protected?

Talkin' About It

Thank God that he is always there for you. You can talk to him anytime you want and tell him anything you need. Thank him that he loves you and knows what is best for you.

I, the LORD your God, hold your right hand and say to you, "Don't be afraid; I will help you." Isaiah 41:13

Read Psalm 107

Rosa felt betrayed, angry, sad, hurt—a zillion things all at once. Bren had dumped her. They had been best friends for as long as Rosa could remember. Bren had always been there for her, when she was sad, when she needed encouragement, and when things were going great. But now Bren thought Stephanie would make a better best friend. Now what? Rosa wasn't sure she could ever trust anyone again!

God is always there for you.

God will never dump you. He took care of people wandering in the wilderness when they were hungry and thirsty. Even when the people were full of sin and evil, when they called on God for help, he was there for them. No matter what terrible messes people get into, when they call to him, God helps them. Praise God—nothing is too hard for him!

What About You?

• When have you felt deserted by a friend?
• What can you thank God for?

Talkin' About It

Thank God that he is always there, waiting for you to turn to him. God never moves, even when you move away from him.

I call to God Most High, to the God who does everything for me.

Psalm 57:2

Spiritual 9-1-1

Love Never Fails

Read Psalm 118

Steve stomped around the kitchen, slamming cupboards and sloshing milk from his glass. "You have too many rules. You don't trust me!" he yelled at his mom.

"It may seem like a lot of rules, to you, Steve. But Dad and I made them because we love you. No matter how grown up you think you are, you're still a kid. Our rules are to protect you until you can make mature decisions."

Rules may seem like limits, but they show love.

Praise God because his love surrounds you. His lovingkindness is forever! Whenever you call to God, he answers by helping you. His love is full of power, and his strength protects you. Praise God for his goodness. Praise God that you can hide in him and be protected from all your enemies. Praise God for his rules and guidelines that help you learn how to live.

What About You?

• How have God's rules and guidelines helped you?
• What can you praise God for?

Talkin' About It

Thank God for his love that lasts forever. Thank him that one way he shows his love is by setting rules and guidelines. Thank him for giving you parents who love you and protect you.

The LORD is my strength and my song. He is my savior.

Psalm 118:14

Read Psalm 139

Jameel thinks he can do just about anything he wants without getting caught. He is of the opinion that his parents are too dumb to know what he's up to. So Jameel hangs out with a gang of older guys who are into shoplifting, drinking, and who knows what else. *As long as no one knows what I'm doing, I'm safe,* he thinks.

There is "someone" who always knows what you're doing.

God knows everything about you. He knows when you slide into things you shouldn't be doing, and he knows when you are doing the best you can. He even knows what you are thinking, sometimes before you realize it yourself. God is all around you, he knew you before you were even born. Praise God that he knows everything there is to know about you, yet he loves you and helps you anytime you ask.

What About You?

• When have you thought you were doing something that no one would ever know about?
• How does it feel to know that God knows all about you—even your thoughts?

Talkin' About It

Thank God that he knows all about you and still loves you. Thank him that he helps you learn how to live for him.

Examine me, O God, and know my mind.
Test me, and know my thoughts.

Psalm 139:23

Got No Secrets

Just Say Thanks

Review Scripture from past week

There are two things that almost everyone learns from their parents. One is, if you can't say something nice, don't say anything. Two is, say "thank you." These are two things found in many of the psalms. Psalms were originally songs of praise and thanks to God for the ways he helped his people.

Thank God for all he does!

God is pleased when you take time to think of ways he helps you and shows his love for you. It is good for you to think of all the good things God does. That will encourage you if you get discouraged. Thank God for his loving care.

Thank him that he knows all about you and he is always with you.

What About You?

• What would you like to thank God for?
• How does it help you to remember God's past help?

Talkin' About It

Just as you like to hear "thanks" and "good job," it is good to say those things to God, too. Thank him for specific ways he helps you. Tell him "good job" for his creation and his protection.

I will make music to praise you.

Psalm 138:1

Read Proverbs 1:8-19

"The hardest thing about going to junior high is friends," moaned Jill. "It's a bigger school with tons more students, and there are suddenly a lot more choices for friends." Jill is working through this right now. Her old friends from elementary school are OK, but she has noticed some older girls who are pretty cool. *I know they do things that Mom and Dad wouldn't like. But, they seem to have a lot of fun, and they really stick up for each other.*

Choosing friends is a big decision.

When you hang out with people who don't care about God and do stuff that isn't right, you get sucked into that, too—whether you want to or not. Say your new friends smoke pot, and you think drugs are wrong. You can fight it for a while. But, if you are with them every day and they smoke pot every day, pretty soon it doesn't seem so bad so you try it, too. It's better to choose friends who share your values then you will be choosing wisely.

What About You?

• What group at school looks attractive to you?
• What about that group is so cool?

Talkin' About It

Ask God to help you choose good friends who won't get you into trouble. Ask him to help you not be concerned with the "in crowd" but instead with friends you can enjoy.

If sinners lure you, do not go along.

Proverbs 1:10

Be an Original

Make God #1

Read Proverbs 3:5-6

Who can you trust? Dee didn't know anymore. She thought she could trust her friends, but they let her down. Then she thought she could trust her parents, but they didn't understand her anymore. So she was trying to make decisions on her own, without anyone's advice or help. But, if she told the honest truth—she wasn't doing a very good job. Dee just didn't know who to turn to for help.

The only one who knows the answers is God.

God is the only one you can completely trust. He is the only one who will never disappoint you and never let you down. Don't think you know more than God or that he needs your advice on what is best for you. That's not trust. Put God in the driver's seat of your life. Make him number one, and he will guide you.

What About You?

• Do you want God to guide your life?
• What decision do you need to trust God to help you make?

Talkin' About It

Tell God where you need his help. Try to give your whole heart over to him, not holding back any part. Thank him for leading and guiding you. Thank him that he will never disappoint you.

Trust the LORD with all your heart and do not rely on your own understanding.

Proverbs 3:5

Read Proverbs 4:10-27

Jered bobbed and swerved and gritted his teeth as he played his video game. But suddenly, in the middle of the game the screen went black. *Bummer, dead batteries,* he thought. The game wouldn't work without batteries to give it power.

Your body has a power center too.

Your heart is the power center of your body. God says in the Bible to guard your heart and keep it clean. Choose to fill your heart with God's Word and his instruction. Keep evil and dirty things away from your heart. God says a good person views each new day as an exciting adventure, but a bad person has constant trou-bles. Your heart-power center should draw it's energy from God and stay on the path that pleases him.

What About You?

• Has it ever been hard for you to choose between right and wrong?
• How can you guard your heart against evil?

Talkin' About It

Thank God for reminders to keep your heart clean. Ask him to show you anything in your heart that needs to be cleaned up.

Pack a Punch

Guard your heart more than anything else, because the source of your life flows from it.

Proverbs 4:23

Get Movin'

Read Proverbs 6:6-11

Mom sent Jean to clean her room and do her homework. She turned on the CD player, then stretched across the bed to pick up some dirty towels. It felt good to rest on the bed, so she stayed for a minute. Before she knew it, Jean was sound asleep. She slept the whole afternoon, all the time Mom thought she was cleaning and doing homework. It didn't even bother Jean that she didn't get her work done.

Lazy people don't accomplish anything.

This proverb warns against laziness. If you got down on the ground and watched a little ant doing it's work, you would see that it's always busy, especially when storing food for a long winter. No one has to tell the ant what to do, he just does what he knows he should do. Does your mom or dad have to keep on your case to get you to take care of your room, do your homework, or help around the house? Maybe you need to take a lesson from the ant.

What About You?

• Honesty time. Do you wait for your parents to get on your back before doing your work?
• What kinds of jobs do you have to do?

Talkin' About It

It's hard to get motivated to work sometimes, but you're always up for fun, right? Ask God to help you learn to be disciplined to do jobs and homework.

Lazy hands bring poverty, but hard–working hands bring riches.

Proverbs 10:4

Read Proverbs 13:24; 22:6

"You're grounded for two weeks. No telephone or TV," Dad said firmly. "I know you won't believe this, Ray, but this really hurts me more than it does you. I don't like to have to punish you."

Dad was right, Ray didn't believe it. So what if he blew off his curfew a couple of times? This punishment seemed pretty harsh.

Punishment is no fun.

But, did you know that punishment is one way your parents show how much they love you? It's true! If your parents let you do anything you wanted to do, would you feel like they cared what happened to you? They want to teach you the right way to live and how to be a responsible grown up.

What About You?

• When is the last time you were punished?
• How do you know your parents love you?

Talkin' About It

Thank God that your parents love you enough to punish you. Thank him that they teach you the right way to live.

This Hurts Me More Than It Does You

*T*rain a child in the way he should go, and even when he is old he will not turn away from it.

Proverbs 22:6

Show Your Smarts

Read Proverbs 8:12-36

Dan made one of his typical sarcastic slams against Mr. Collins. Something about class being so dull that a funeral was more fun. "You're not as smart as you think you are, Mr. Big Shot," Mr. Collins snapped. Dan almost snorted out loud. *I'm not smart? I've had straight A's for the last 3 years. You can't get much smarter than that, can you?*

Being smart doesn't mean you live smart.

Wisdom comes from God, not books. God's wisdom teaches good judgment. It gives good advice and helps you make good choices. God's wisdom has been around since time began, and it's available to anyone who asks God for it. Knowledge is important, but the best thing you can find in life is wisdom.

What About You?

• How can you describe God's wisdom?
• How does God share his wisdom with you?

Talkin' About It

Thank God for his wisdom and for sharing it with you. Ask him to help you listen closely to him.

Listen to the discipline, and become wise. Do not leave my ways.

Proverbs 8:33

Read Proverbs 1:1-6

Just when I think I've learned a lesson and got my head on straight, I turn around and mess up again! Ever feel that way? Listen to this news flash—we all have. Grown ups and kids alike. We're all human so we all make wrong choices and silly mistakes.

The good news is God still loves us.

He knew we were gonna need constant help and specific instructions for certain areas of life. So he gave us the Proverbs. When you buy something new that has to be assembled, it comes with an instruction book. The book explains, step by step, how to assemble the new item. That's kind of how the Proverbs are. They give specific instructions on how to live. God realizes that the process of becoming a mature person takes time. We learn in stages, and some lessons we have to learn over and over again. He doesn't give up on you, so don't give up on yourself.

What About You?

• Which of the Proverbs from this week helped you the most?
• In what area of your life do you mess up over and over?

Talkin' About It

Don't give up on yourself! Ask God to help you work on the area of your life where you have the most trouble. Tell him why it is hard for you. Thank him for his patience.

Don't Give Up

Whatever you do, do it wholeheartedly as though you were working for your real master and not merely for humans.

Colossians 3:23

Watch your Mouth!

Read Proverbs 11:12-13

Jeremy was sprawled on the floor listening to music while Mike tossed darts at the dartboard. They weren't talking much—until Jim's name came up. Just the day before Jim had told Mike about a problem he was having. Of course, Jim believed Mike would keep this news to himself—and Mike meant to. But, when Jim was mentioned, Mike felt important because he knew a secret. He spilled it to Jeremy. Soon they were making up all kinds of stories to go along with it.

That's how gossip starts.

Imagine how Jim is gonna feel when he hears partially true stories about himself, that grew out of a secret he told Mike. Your mouth can cause so much trouble! Friendships can be totally wrecked because of words slipping out, even when you don't mean to spill the beans. No good comes from gossip—reputations are wrecked, trust is broken, and friendships are lost. When a friend trusts you with a secret, keep it. Don't share it.

What About you?

• What experiences have you had with gossip about you or someone else?
• Can your friends trust you?

Talkin' About It

Ask God to help you be a good friend. Ask God to help you keep secrets and be trustworthy.

> *Whoever gossips gives away secrets, but whoever is trustworthy in spirit can keep a secret.*
> Proverbs 11:13

Read Proverbs 15:16; 16:8

"If only I had those basketball shoes, I'd be happy," Todd said.

"If I had more money, I'd be happy," moaned Rick.

"All it would take for me to be happy is a girlfriend," John admitted. Each guy feels pretty sure about what it would take to make him really happy. Their ideas range from cooler parents to the most up-to-date fishing pole.

Sorry guys, you're missing the boat here.

Real honest to goodness happiness doesn't come from how much "stuff" you accumulate. The guys with the biggest and best toys are not necessarily the happiest. You can have all the "stuff" in the world; but if you don't know God, deep happiness that comes from the inside out just isn't possible. The stuff you get makes you happy for awhile, but that happiness doesn't last too long. You may look happy to everyone around you, but deep down inside, in that place that only you and God can see, you know you're not happy.

What About You?

• When have you thought some "thing" would make you happy?
• Why does knowing God bring real inside-out happiness?

Talkin' About It

Ask God to help you keep your head straight so you don't get caught up in "things." Thank him for the happiness that knowing him brings.

Better to have a little with the fear of the LORD than great treasure and turmoil.

Proverbs 15:16

Inside Out Happiness

Learn from the Best

Read Proverbs 15:31-33

Janna flew through the air doing round-offs and flips. She was good because she worked hard. Coach Debbie watched Janna's routines closely. "Keep your head tucked down," she advised. "Otherwise you'll hurt your neck on those front flips."

Wise people accept advice.

It may be hard to admit, but we can all learn from good advice. It's hard to take advice from some people, parents or older siblings, for example. But, it's smart to listen to people who love you because they care about you and want the best for you. Ignoring advice means you may make mistakes or not learn the best or easiest way to do things. Following advice helps us learn to be wise, and wise people want to learn as much as they can.

What About You?

• What was the last good advice you got?
• How do you respond when someone tries to give you advice?

Talkin' About It

Ask God to help you let go of your pride and be willing to take advice from others. Ask him to help you learn.

> Give advice to a wise person, and he will become even wiser. Teach a righteous person, and he will learn more.
>
> *Proverbs 9:9*

Read Proverbs 22:1

Martie spills secrets like water through a sieve; Lynn would do anything to get a guy to like her; Sara is always gentle and fair; Jenna is hilarious, but her jokes can be cutting and crude; Linnie is a great athlete, but dumber than a rock; Cori is smarter than Einstein . . .

A reputation is a title we hang on people.

Reputations aren't always fair, sometimes you get one for the dumbest single incident. Then you are stuck in a box with that title—*Big-time lier* or *Loose with Guys*—and it's very hard to get out of that box. That's good motivation to be careful who you hang out with and what kinds of things you do. A good reputation is better than wealth and fame. A reputation that reflects what is in your heart is the best kind to have.

What About You?

• What kind of reputation do you have?
• Does your reputation reflect who you really are?

Talkin' About It

Ask God to help you choose friends and activities wisely so your reputation is a good reflection of who you are.

Make a Good Rep

A good name is more desirable than great wealth.

Proverbs 22:1

How to be Popular

Read Proverbs 25:17-20

Carol glanced out the window and saw Marcia coming up the sidewalk. As she ran for her bedroom, she called out, "Mom, tell her I'm not here." The problem is that Marcia assumes that any time she is bored or doesn't have anything special to do, Carol is in the same boat. Since she lives across the street from Carol, she just drops in, any time she feels like it. It's getting to the point that Carol's entire family is tired of Marcia.

You can wear out your welcome.

How do you like people to treat you? That answer is a tip for how your friends would like to be treated. Some tips from Proverbs are: Don't wear out your welcome—don't try to be with a friend every single minute. Your friend will get sick of you. Another thing to remember is that telling lies about a friend is almost the same as beating him up with a stick. It hurts! Third, be smart in where you put your trust. Depending on someone who will let you down causes lots of pain. Also, when a friend is very sad, don't feel like you have to cheer him up, just sit with him and be a friend.

What About You?

• Which of these things do you need to work on?
• Who is a really good friend to you?

Talkin' About It

Tell God you want to be the kind of friend that others like to have around. Ask him to help you put these proverbs into practice.

A friend always loves.

Proverbs 17:17

Read Proverbs 31:10-31

Karen was pooped! Mom had been out of town for a whole week so, as the oldest girl, Karen was filling in. By Wednesday Karen was sick of hearing, "What's to eat? Where's my homework? I need clean underwear." From now on Karen would definitely appreciate all Mom did for the family.

Appreciate your Mom.

It's true that if there are both a mom and dad in a family, they work together to keep things going and get everything done. But, much of the housework and emotional support falls on mom. She kissed your hurts when you were little; she stretches the grocery dollars to make room for snack food; she listens to your sorrows and your joys. Proverbs 31 says a mom who serves the Lord deserves to be praised.

What About You?

• Why do you sometimes give your mom a hard time?
• Does someone other than a mom take care of your family? Who?

Talkin' About It

First thank your mom, or major care-giver for all he or she does for you. Then thank God for that person.

Her children and her husband stand up and bless her.

Proverbs 31:28

This Is Lots of Work!

Fortune Cookies

Review Scripture from the past week

Did you ever pop open a fortune cookie and read the little nugget of information on the paper inside? Sometimes it gives a suggestion on what kind of person you are or how you should live your life. Did you ever wish you could have little nuggets of information on how to live life God's way?

You do—Proverbs are nuggets of truth.

Short little phrases or sentences say "Do this" or "Don't do this" in order to be a better person and live more like God wants you to. Proverbs is full of advice to take to heart on how to treat others, what things to stay away from, when to listen to others, and how to be wise. Paying attention to the Proverbs can make life a lot easier.

What About You?

• Which of the six lessons from this week is hardest for you?
• Why is it hard to take advice from other people?

Talkin' About It

Thank God for the nuggets of truth and help found in Proverbs. Try to memorize a Proverb a day.

Those who take advice gain wisdom.

Proverbs 13:10

Read Luke 1:26-38

The news spread around school like wildfire: "Did ya hear? Gloria is pregnant. Yeah, fourteen years old and she's gonna be a mom. The worst part is, she doesn't even know for sure who the father is."

It's a good thing Gloria's folks had already shipped her off to a special home in another state. She wouldn't have been able to face the humiliation and sarcasm from people who were supposed to be her friends. It wouldn't be easy to be an unwed mother.

Imagine how Jesus' mother, Mary, felt.

Mary was a teenager engaged to Joseph when an angel appeared to her one night and told her she was going to have a baby. Mary was a good girl who loved God. She had never had sex with anyone, even Joseph. God knew Mary loved him. That's why he chose her to be the mother of his son, Jesus. Mary loved God so much that she would do anything he asked her to do. She was his humble servant.

What About You?

• How do you think other people reacted to the news of Mary's pregnancy?
• Would you be willing to do anything God asked of you?

Talkin' About It

Thank God for Mary's example of a willing servant. Ask God to help you trust him enough to make you a willing servant.

Anything You Say

Brothers and sisters, because of God's compassion toward us, I encourage you to offer your bodies as living sacrifices, dedicated to God and pleasing to him. Romans 12:1

A Plan Comes Together

Read Luke 2:1-5

"I hate family meetings," moaned Ross. "It usually means that we're gonna get yelled at for not doing our chores."

Roy shook his head, "I don't know, this one came up pretty suddenly. Let's see what's going on."

Actually, this family meeting was good news. Dad had a business trip to Florida, and he wanted to take the whole family. But, several things had to be done before they could go, so this meeting was to hand out jobs to everyone. Two days later, everything done, the family buckled into their airplane seats.

"I like it when a plan comes together," said Dad.

Mary and Joseph must have wondered about God's plan.

They knew from the Scriptures that the Messiah was to be born in Bethlehem. But they lived in Nazareth, and Mary's child was supposed to be God's Son. When the governor called for everyone to go back to the cities of their ancestors to be counted in a census, guess where Mary and Joseph had to go? You got it—Bethlehem the home of Joseph's ancestor, David.

What About You?

• When have you questioned if God's plan was being carried out?
• How do you think Mary and Joseph felt about God's plan when they found out they had to go to Bethlehem?

Talkin' About It

Trust, that's what it's all about. Ask God to help you learn to trust him to carry out his entire plan.

A child has been born for us. A son has been given to us.

Isaiah 9:6

Read Luke 2:6-7

Annie wrapped the yellow sleeper set in pink and blue paper and put a white bow on the package. She and Mom drove to the hospital to see Aunt Kelly and her new baby. Annie pressed her nose against the glass and looked at the rows of newborn babies in shiny bassinettes with clean white sheets. Nurses moved around the nursery caring for the babies. Down the hall, Aunt Kelly rested in a soft, clean bed. She had everything she needed, and she knew the nurses would take care of her baby.

That's nothing like the birth of Jesus!

Wouldn't you think the Son of God should be born in a fancy palace? He wasn't. When Mary and Joseph arrived in Bethlehem, every hotel was full. The baby was about to be born, so one innkeeper let them stay in his stable. That's where Jesus was born, wrapped in strips of cloth, and laid in a feed trough. Not a fancy beginning. Still, it was the right one for him.

What About You?

• What do you know about where and when you were born?
• Why was it right for Jesus to be born in a stable instead of a palace?

Talkin' About It

Jesus came for everyone, not just "important" people. Thank God for his perfect plan that even included where Jesus was born. Thank him for the gift of Jesus.

You will find an infant wrapped in strips of cloth and lying in a manger.

Luke 2:12

A New Baby!

All Right!

Read Luke 2:8-18

Miss Sanders was droning on and on about nouns and gerunds when the loudspeaker crackled and popped to life. The voice of Principal Schultz came blasting into the room. "I regret to inform you that we are having a problem with our heating system. Therefore, we will have to dismiss school one hour early today and cancel tomorrow's classes." No one heard the end of the sentence because about 15 voices yelled, "Great news! Best news ever! Hurrah! All right!"

That is great news, but it's not the best news ever!

The greatest announcement ever was made by an angel to a bunch of shepherds. Doesn't sound too impressive, does it? But when the stillness of the night was broken by an angel announcing that the Savior had been born in Bethlehem, you can bet the shepherds were impressed! Then the angel was joined by a whole skyful of angels praising God. When the angels disappeared, the shepherds hurried to Bethlehem to see the new baby.

What About You?

• What is the best news you ever received?
• Why was this great news given to shepherds instead of kings?

Talkin' About It

Thank God that Jesus came for all people. Thank him that Jesus came for you.

Today your Savior, Christ the Lord, was born in David's city.

Luke 2:11

Read Matthew 2:1-12

"We're lost, why don't we stop and ask directions?" Mom asked.

"Stop where?" Dad asked in frustration. They had been driving through these thick, dark woods for two hours. Mark noticed that the needle on the gas indicator was getting very low.

"The store keeper back on the main road said this was a shortcut back to the city," Dad said, "but the forest is so thick I can't even see the moon or stars to check directions. I hope we get out of here soon."

They need a bright star to lead them.

That's how the wise men found Jesus. A bright star appeared in the sky and the wise men knew that probably meant the Savior had been born. The wise men traveled many miles across a desert, following the star to Bethlehem and the home where young Jesus lived with his parents. The wise men brought gifts for the young king, too. They were excited that he had been born.

What About You?

• When has your family needed directions?
• Why do we give and receive gifts at Christmas?

Talkin' About It

Thank God for the special star that led the wise men. Thank him for the ways he leads you. Thank him for Jesus.

They saw the child with his mother Mary. So they bowed down and worshiped him.

Matthew 2:11

Rollin' with the Punches

Read Matthew 2:13-18

Carrie had a plan. She would clean her room, 'cause Mom insisted she do that before she could do anything fun. Then she would wash her hair, dress in some really cool clothes, meet her friends at the mall where they would hang out for a while, catch a movie, grab a pizza, then go to Julie's house for a sleep-over. But, her plans came crashing down around her when Mom got called in to work. Then Carrie had to stay home and take care of her brother. Carrie was disappointed, and she didn't care who knew it.

How do you feel when your plans are changed?

Joseph's plans were once changed suddenly. He and Mary were living in Bethlehem with their son, Jesus. Perhaps things had just settled down since Jesus' birth. Then one night, an angel came and told Joseph to take Mary and Jesus and leave the country because the king wanted Jesus dead. Joseph didn't question the plan or fuss about it. He got Mary and Joseph up and they left town.

What About You?

• What is usually your attitude when your plans are changed?
• Why did Joseph respond so quickly, with no argument?

Talkin' About It

Thank God for keeping Jesus safe. Thank him for guiding your life and changing your plans when it is necessary.

You make the path of life known to me.

Psalm 16:11

Read Luke 2:1-20

Did the stories this week help you realize that the people involved in the Christmas story were real people? Mary may have been a frightened, teenaged girl, but she trusted God and was willing to serve him as he asked. Joseph obeyed God's instructions two times without ever asking why he should do what the angel said. Little Jesus was born in a stable and the first announcement of his birth was given to shepherds out in a field.

Jesus came to be the Savior of all people.

That means you! Have you accepted Jesus as your personal Savior? Christmas is more than presents and fancy deco-rations. It is a celebration of the birth of God's Son. Jesus is God's gift to us. He made eternal life possible for each of us. All we need to do is accept his gift.

What About You?

• What does Christmas mean to you?
• What's your favorite Christmas tradition?

Talkin' About It

Thank God that there is more to Christmas than just presents. Thank him for the incredible gift of Jesus.

Real People

A virgin will become pregnant and give birth to a son, and she will name him Immanuel [God Is With Us].

Isaiah 7:14

Parents Make Me Nuts

Read Luke 1:31; 2:33, 41-52

"My parents are driving me nuts!" shouted Janet.

Carla peeked out from behind her locker door and smiled. "Age–old problem," she said. She continued stacking books in her arms as she asked, "What's happened now?"

Janet dropped her backpack on the floor. "They're always on my case about my grades. Just 'cause Craig got good grades, they think I should. They don't want me to have any life except doing homework. I wish they would just back off."

Jesus had parents to deal with, too.

Mary and Joseph were Jesus' earthly parents. They had the awesome responsibility of raising and caring for God's Son.

One time when Jesus was a young boy, Mary and Joseph couldn't find him. He was in the temple talking with the teachers. Jesus went home with his parents and obeyed them even though he might rather have stayed in the temple talking about God.

What About You?

• How do you get along with your parents?
• What do you wish they understood about you?

Talkin' About It

Getting along with parents is tough. Ask God to help you see things from their point-of-view. Ask him to help them understand you. Ask God to help you be obedient.

Then [Jesus] returned with them [his parents] to Nazareth and was obedient to them.

Luke 2:51

Read Luke 2:7

Mike ran top-speed down the gym floor. "I'm open! Throw me the ball," he shouted to his team-mate. Tom hurled the basketball through the air toward Mike. Just as Mike jumped to grab the ball, he tripped over his own big feet and tumbled to the floor. As Mike watched the ball bounce out of bounds, he wondered when his body was going to stop growing so he could get his coordination back. He had grown four inches in the last year, and it seemed like his legs and feet were always getting in his way.

It's hard to imagine Jesus being a gangly boy.

But he was. Jesus came to earth as a human baby and grew to manhood. That means he had to pass through those years of growth spurts and physical awkwardness. He knows how it feels to walk along and trip over your own feet. Talk to Jesus about your feelings. He understands how you feel about your changing body.

What About You?

• How has your body changed in the last year?
• What is the hardest part about these changes?

Talkin' About It

It helps to know Jesus has been through this, doesn't it? Tell him how you're feeling. Ask him for strength to get through until you're finished growing.

Don't you know that you are God's temple and that God's Spirit lives in you?

1 Corinthians 3:16

Tripping Over Your Own Feet

You Don't Know How Hard It Is!

Read Luke 4:1-13

"If I don't get a *B* on this science test I have to drop out of all sports," Bob told Steve.

"Says who?" Steve asked. It wouldn't be good news for any of the sports teams if Bob was cut.

"Says the school—and my parents. I'm failing science, it's gonna take a *B* to get me up to passing," Bob said with disgust.

"I'm doing good in science. How about if I keep my test paper on the edge of my desk. You're right behind me, just look at my answers. We need you in sports, man," Steve was totally serious.

"You mean I should cheat?" Bob wasn't sure what to do.

What would Jesus do?

Jesus! What does he know about being tempted to do wrong? He is the perfect Son of God. Actually, Jesus was majorly tempted by the devil himself. Satan offered some wonderful things to Jesus if Jesus would just worship him. Jesus didn't give in. No temptation was enough to make him worship someone other than God.

What About You?

• What temptation do you struggle with the most?
• How can you resist giving in?

Talkin' About It

Jesus always answered Satan by quoting Scripture. Thank God for his Word, and ask him to help you memorize verses to help you when you are tempted.

We have a chief priest who is able to sympathize with our weaknesses. He was tempted in every way that we are, but he didn't sin.
Hebrews 4:15

Read John 11:5

Mallory and Kara laughed so hard that they both fell on the floor. "Remember when we . . ." Mallory started to ask a question but Kara jumped in and finished it for her, ". . . dropped water balloons on our little brothers?" They both exploded in laughter again. Kara and Mallory had been best friends since kindergarten. They had shared many experiences, good and bad, and they knew each other well enough that they could finish each other's sentences.

Good friends are like frosting on a cake.

They make a good thing even better. Jesus had good friends. Besides his disciples, he was good friends with Mary, Martha, and Lazarus, two sisters and their brother. He spent time with them when he was in their town. One of his most famous miracles involved Lazarus.

Good friends make happy times happier and sad times easier to take because they understand what you feel and how you think.

What About You?

• Who are your best friends?
• Do you consider Jesus to be a friend?

Talkin' About It

Thank God for good friends. Thank him that Jesus had friends so that he can understand how important friends are to you.

Jesus loved Martha, her sister, and Lazarus.

John 11:5

Enjoy Your Friends!

Sorrow!

Read John 11:33-38

"Did you ever feel like you just can't go on? Like you want to crawl into bed, go to sleep, and never wake up?" Claudia was being very honest about her feelings.

"Yes," Mom said, "I've felt that way myself lately. But we can't do that. We have to go on with our lives. Dad wouldn't want us to give up." This was the first time Claudia and her mom had really talked since her dad's death almost four months ago. Claudia hurt so badly—some days the ache in her heart was so deep that she could hardly function.

Jesus knows about that kind of sorrow.

Jesus felt great pain when his friend Lazarus died. Everyone told him that if he had been there, Lazarus wouldn't have died. Mary and Martha, Lazarus' sisters, were full of sorrow. It hurt Jesus to see them in so much pain. He broke down and cried. Yes, Jesus knows how sorrow feels. He's been there himself.

What About You?

• When have you felt the most sad?
• What do you do when you are sad?

Talkin' About It

Does it help to know that Jesus felt sorrow? Tell God if it does. Thank him for putting this story in the Bible. Thank him for caring when you are in pain.

Jesus cried.

John 11:35

Read Luke 23:44-49

Jeff and T. J. were stretched out on the floor watching the Daytona 500. The cars zoomed around the track at incredibly high speeds. Midway through the race one of the cars was bumped by another car that was trying to pass. The bumped car spun around on the track and slammed into the wall. Flames shot up immediately and soon the whole car was engulfed in flames. "Look at that," shouted Jeff. "There's no way in the world that driver is coming out alive!"

Death is part of life.

You're born, you live a while, and you die. It's not the death part that's scary to most people; it's whether or not it's going to hurt. When it was time for Jesus to leave earth, he could have just ascended into the sky or left in a flaming chariot. But he didn't. Jesus faced death just like we do. He knows how it feels to look death in the face. So you can talk to him about how facing death makes you feel.

What About You?

• How do you feel when you think about death?
• Why did Jesus choose to die as we do?

Talkin' About It

Death is scary. Thank God that you don't have to face it alone if you know him. Thank him that leaving this earth means being with him.

After Jesus had taken the vinegar, he said, "It is finished!" Then, he bowed his head and died.
John 19:30

Death Is Part of Life!

Just Like Me

Review Scripture from past week

I'm sure you've heard someone say, "Jesus knows just what you're going through." Did you think *Yeah right! He's the perfect Son of God. He could have a zillion angels waiting on him or protecting him. How could he really know how I'm feeling?*

Don't forget, he has been through the same stuff you face.

After this week of devotions, you hopefully know that he does know how you feel. Jesus went through all that is involved in living with a family, obeying parents, and having good friends. Jesus was faced with temptation to do wrong. He felt sorrow and the agony of facing death. Because Jesus went through all these human experiences, he understands us much better.

What About You?

• Do you feel any differently about Jesus now that you've thought about his human side?
• What thing are you glad to know Jesus understands about you?

Talkin' About It

It's easier to try to be like Jesus when you know he has been through the same stuff you face. Thank God that he understands everything about you. Thank him that he can help you with any problem that comes up because he has been there.

God can guard you so that you don't fall and so that you can be full of joy as you stand in his glorious presence without fault.
Jude 24

Read Matthew 5:4

Jim was downright miserable. He had a knot the size of a volleyball in his stomach. He couldn't eat, couldn't sleep, couldn't concentrate—all because he lied to his dad. Crazy isn't it? Some kids lie right and left and never feel a twinge of guilt. But, Jim's dad trusted him, and Jim had never given him any reason not to—until now. Jim went to his dad and asked, "Can we talk?" Then he confessed the lie. Jim's dad could see that Jim was truly sorry for what he had done.

Jesus promised comfort to all who are truly sorry for their sins.

Many of Jesus' teaching sessions were to tell people how to live. One of Jesus' most famous sermons began with the Beatitudes, which explained some ways God wants his people to live. One thing Jesus said is that when you are really sorry for the things you do that are disobedient to God, you will be comforted. In other words, when you are sorry, God forgives. Then it's over—he won't throw that wrong thing back in your face.

What About You?

• What have you done that you were truly sorry for later?
• Is it harder to forgive yourself, or to believe that God forgives you?

Talkin' About It

Thank God for his forgiveness. Ask him to help you forgive yourself when you sin. Thank him that he never stops loving you.

The LORD has comforted his people and will have compassion on his humble people.

Isaiah 49:13

Livin' with Yourself

Hidden Strength

Read Matthew 5:5

Most of the students in the school love Mrs. Denney. Oh, some of them wouldn't admit it, but there's a whole bunch of them that like to hang around her room and talk to her about whatever is on their minds. Mrs. Denney doesn't look like the kind of teacher that junior high kids would like. She's short and old and very soft-spoken, but she doesn't try to push her opinions on the kids. Some of the other teachers who think they are so cool, dress like the kids, are loud and pushy, and are not nearly as popular as Mrs. Denney. She has a gentle, quiet strength.

Meekness is a quiet strength.

Jesus said the whole earth and everything in it will belong to the meek. Meekness doesn't mean wimpiness. A meek person is not pushy or loud, but has a gentle, quiet strength inside. A meek person stands up for what is right, doesn't question God, and is willing to let God lead.

What About You?

• Who do you know who is meek?
• Would you rather be around a meek person or a loud pushy person?

Talkin' About It

If you have a problem with being loud and pushy, tell God about it. Ask him to help you learn to be meek and gentle. Thank him for his love.

Oppressed people will inherit the land and will enjoy unlimited peace.

Psalm 37:11

Read Matthew 5:6

The last game of the season and Lance's team is undefeated. But they're down now, 46–48 and there are only twenty seconds left in the game. Coach Barber has called a time out and the players come straggling over. "Don't give up!" Coach encourages them. "This is the first time all year that you've been challenged by a good team. We've got the time to win. But let me tell you something. This game is going to be won by the team that wants it most. The team who is really hungry for the victory. You guys can do it—but you gotta want it."

Jesus said to have that kind of hunger for righteousness.

What did he mean by that? Jesus was saying that people who spend their energy trying to find happiness and contentment in things or fame and the praise of others are in for a big disappointment. The only way to be truly happy—deep down inside—is to have a real hunger to do what is right. That hunger will push you to learn more about Jesus and to live for him.

What About You?

• What do you "hunger" for? Righteousness or something else?
• Do you care enough about doing right to read the Bible daily? Why or why not?

Talkin' About It

Maybe you need to ask God to make you hungry for righteousness. Ask him to help you make that your number one goal!

Jesus told them, "I am the bread of life. Whoever comes to me will never become hungry, and whoever believes in me will never become thirsty." John 6:35

You Gotta Want It!

Getting Even

Read Matthew 5:7

Kelly and Sean had gone out for over a year. They were the envy of everyone in school. Then Laura came along, and she liked Sean's looks. She flirted shamelessly with him. Sean liked knowing that another girl thought he was cute, so he flirted back. Before long, Kelly and Sean were history and Sean was going out with Laura. Kelly was determined to get even with Laura for stealing her guy. She started rumors about Laura and made every effort to ruin Laura's reputation.

Nobody will win when you try to get even.

Jesus said to forgive anybody who wrongs you. When you hold a grudge or try to get even, you'll end up feeling worse. God will forgive you for all the wrong things you do. So you should forgive others for any wrongs they do to you. You receive mercy by showing mercy.

What About You?

• When have you wanted to get even with someone?
• When has someone forgiven you for a wrong thing you've done?

Talkin' About It

You may think getting even will feel really good, but it doesn't feel good to hurt someone else. Tell God if you need his strength to forgive someone. Ask him to help you.

Don't pay people back with evil for the evil they do to you, or ridicule those who ridicule you. Instead bless them, because you were called to inherit a blessing. 1 Peter 3:9

Read Matthew 5:8

Rick stretched out on the floor with a giant glass of soda and a big bag of peanuts salted in the shell. He was set to watch the baseball game on TV. About the third inning, Rick broke open a peanut and popped it in his mouth. "Ugh," he shouted. "This peanut is rotten!" He spit it on the floor and took a big swig of soda. That was weird. That peanut looked just like all the others from the outside.

Big lesson here— lookin' good on the outside doesn't mean bein' good on the inside.

Jesus said the condition of the heart, whether or not you are pure on the inside, is more important than how you look on the outside. You can fool people with your looks or behavior, but God knows what you're like on the inside. You can pretend to be a nice, kind person until you're blue in the face, but you can't fool God.

What About You?

• Honesty time. Are you pretending to be nice, but inside you've got some rotten spots?
• What can you do to make your heart clean and keep it clean?

Talkin' About It

You can't keep your heart clean by yourself, so ask God to help you. Admit any secrets to him that you've been trying to hide.

Create a clean heart in me, O God, and renew a faithful spirit within me.

Psalm 51:10

Keep the Peace

Read Matthew 5:9

"Gillie loves Matthew. Gillie loves Matthew," sang Michelle. What could be more irritating than a little sister? Especially when you are on the phone with the guy of your dreams.

"Mom," called Gillie. "Will you get this geek away from me?"

After she hung up the phone, Gillie descended on Mom. "You gotta do something. Michelle is totally ruining my life."

Mom sighed and said, "Honey, she's not trying to ruin your life. She's trying to get your attention. She really admires you and wants you to pay some attention to her."

Mom is being a peacemaker.

When someone irritates you, the easiest thing to do is get mad and strike back. Then a big fight develops and feelings, if not bodies, get hurt. More good will come from trying to keep the peace. Jesus said that peacemakers will be called the children of God. That means peacemakers are showing what God is like. Peacemakers know that it's more important to try to get along with others than to be right or first.

What About You?

• Can you be a peacemaker or is it more important to you to always be right?
• Who do you know who is a peacemaker?

Talkin' About It

Ask God to help you put your feelings aside when necessary and be a peacemaker. Ask him to help you put others before yourself.

A harvest that has God's approval comes from the peace planted by peacemakers.

James 3:18

Read Matthew 5:4-9

Have you ever heard people refer to the "School of Hard Knocks"? Do you know what they are talking about? The "School of Hard Knocks" is the lessons you learn in life from making mistakes, making bad choices, and having bad things happen to you.

Jesus wants you to be able to skip that school.

Jesus taught the lessons in these verses to the students in his school. He knew that if you study in his school, you won't have to go through the "School of Hard Knocks". That doesn't mean you won't have to learn hard lessons in Jesus' school. It does mean that when you are trying to obey him and be more like God, he will help you through the hard lessons. And, when you "graduate," you'll be a living example of God's love.

What About You?

• Some of the lessons you will learn in Jesus' school could make you unpopular, are you willing to risk it?
• Why would non-Christians be uncomfortable with the lessons in Jesus' school?

Talkin' About It

Time to make a decision. Are you serious about becoming more like Jesus? Are you through living on the fringe of his school? Talk to him about it.

I will find joy and be glad about you. I will make music to praise your name, O Most High. Psalm 9:2

School of Life

Salt Shaker Livin'

Read Matthew 5:13

The four letter words flying around the locker room would make a sailor blush. Most of the guys seemed to favor the "F" word. Rich doubted if these guys could say a complete sentence without using it. Jeff came over to Rich and said, "Hey, you played a f---in' good game tonight. Did ya ever see such a f---in' tall guy as the center on the other team?" Jeff went on and on with his limited vocabulary. Rich had to make a decision. Should he say something about Jeff's language, or should he ignore it?

Shake some salt out of the shaker.

Jesus said that Christians should be like salt in the world. You know what salt does? It flavors foods. When food is salted, the flavor changes; it's made more exciting. Jesus meant that Christians should be noticed because they are different from other people. Having Christians in the world should make people think about the things they do and say.

What About You?

• Do your friends know you are a Christian? Do you try to hide your Christianity?
• Who do you know who is salt? Why?

Talkin' About It

Ask God to give you the courage to be salt in your world for him. Tell him you want to make a difference.

You are salt for the earth.

Matthew 5:13

Read Matthew 5:14-16

C. J. couldn't see her hand in front of her face because the room was so dark. She felt along the wall for the doorway. She was careful not to make any noise. The whole point of the game of Sardines was to hide in the totally dark church and not be found by anyone. That was all well and good—but in the totally silent darkness, C. J. was getting a little nervous. How would she know when the game was over? What if no one found her? But just as C. J. was about to panic, she saw the tiniest sliver of light off to the right. C. J. stared at the light as it grew brighter and brighter. Soon it glowed in the darkness.

Light in the darkness is easy to see.

People who don't know Jesus are living in darkness. They can't see the light because they don't know its source. Jesus wants his children to be like a light in the darkness. The people in darkness will be able to see what God is like by looking at someone who knows him.

What About You?

• How can you show others what God is like?
• Why do some people try to hide their light?

Talkin' About It

Ask God to help your light shine brightly. Ask for his strength not to be afraid to let others know of your faith.

Don't Hide Your Light

I am the light of the world. Whoever follows me will have a life filled with light and will never live in the dark. John 8:12

Cut to the Quick

Read Matthew 5:21-26

Mark felt his temper rising from his gut right up through his head. He thought the top of his head was going to blow off. He turned and blasted Jim with angry words. "You creep. You've got the brains of a rock . . ." and on and on he raged. Jim looked like he had been hit with a Mack truck.

Angry words cut right to the heart.

That's one reason Jesus said not to get angry. Anger ruins friendships and hurts people. The words you spit out when you're angry can never be taken back. Even if you apologize for them, the pain they caused remains. When you want to tell God you love him, be sure that none of your friends are angry with you. If anyone is, you'll have to settle that first, then you can come back to God.

What About You?

• Have you ever lost a friend because of anger? Over what?
• Are you often angry without really knowing why?

Talkin' About It

Lots of changes are happening inside of you now. Sometimes you might feel confused and angry without really knowing why. Talk to God about it, ask him to help you control your temper and think before you speak.

Everyone should be quick to listen, slow to speak, and should not get angry easily.

James 1:19

Read Matthew 5:33-37

Mom finished washing dishes as Andrea finished her phone call. "Yeah, I swear on the Bible that I'll call you at 9:00," she laughed.

"Andie, you gotta watch your language," Mom said.

"What do you mean? I don't use swear words." Andrea said.

Mom slowly shook her head, "I know but promising to do something on the Bible is not necessary. Your word is good enough."

That's nothing compared to the language at school.

It's true that some kids swear a lot, but that doesn't make it right. Jesus set standards for Christians. He said not to swear by God's name or anything God made. God's name is precious and holy so don't cheapen it by using it to make a point. When you make a promise say a simple yes or no—that's all you need. Anything else you use comes from the devil.

What About You?

• What slang terms of God's name do you need to get out of your vocabulary?
• Do your friends use wholesome language? Do they notice that you do?

Talkin' About It

This is tough. If you hear swearing all day, it easily slips into your habits. But, pure speech is a good way to let others know you honor God. Ask him to help you keep your speech clean, and to get the bad words out of your mind.

Be Careful Little Mouth

Do not take an oath on anything in heaven or on earth. Do not take any oath.

James 5:12

Love My Who?

Read Matthew 5:43-48

Marcie and her gang of friends started laughing as Anna walked by. Suddenly, Anna felt like her clothes were all wrong, and her hair was on crooked. She wished she could just go home. *Oh well, what do I care what those creeps think anyway?* she thought. *They're just a bunch of self-centered Barbie dolls. None of them have a brain cell anywhere near their heads.* Anna definitely felt better after she ran the other girls down in her mind, but was that the right thing to do?

Jesus said, "Love your enemies."

It's not really any big deal to love your friends. We all love our friends, that's why they are friends. But can you love your enemies? Can you wish for good things to happen to them? Can you say kind things about them and even do kind things for them when the opportunity comes up? If you can love your enemies, you will be showing God's love to everyone around you—your enemies as well as the people watching you.

What About You?

• Do you have any enemies? Who? Why are they enemies?
• How could you show love to your enemies?

Talkin' About It

OK. This is a biggie. You probably can't show love to people who have been mean to you without God's help. Ask him to help you, and really mean it. You'll be amazed at what happens.

Do for other people everything you want them to do for you.

Luke 6:31

Read Matthew 6:1-4

Paul literally had to drag the box of canned goods into the gym because it was too heavy to lift. Since Pastor Dan had offered a ski trip to the five kids who brought in the most food for the Food Pantry, Paul had been consumed with winning. As he waited in line to have his box weighed, John came and got in line behind him. He was holding a couple of cans of green beans. Paul smugly moved his big box in front of him so John would be sure to see it. Then when it was Paul's turn to have his donation weighed he grunted and groaned lifting it up on the scale.

This is a case of doing the right thing for the wrong reason.

Giving is good. Any time you share what God has given you, whether it's money, possessions, or talents, it's good. But Jesus said to watch what your motivation is. Giving to get the attention and praise of others is wrong. If that's what you're hoping for, then that's your reward. Don't expect a pat on the back from God.

What About You?

• What good thing have you done, hoping others would notice?
• What good deed could you do secretly, just to help someone else?

Talkin' About It

Ask God to help you have the right motives for giving of your time, money, and abilities. Ask him to show you ways to help others.

Be careful not to do your good works in public in order to attract attention. If you do, your Father in heaven will not reward you.

Matthew 6:1

Yo! Look At Me!

Read the Instructions

Review Scripture from past week

When you have a really tough math project to do, how do you know how to do it? When you buy a new model airplane, how do you know how to put it together? If you're going to sew a dress, how do you know what to do? Instructions! Reading the instructions makes any job easier, even though we sometimes don't read them until we've tried to do it on our own.

Life is easier with instructions, too.

In the Sermon on the Mount, Jesus gave some instructions that will make life easier. Treat others the way you would like to be treated. Always remember that you are representing God in your world. Be generous with your time and money—but only to help others—not for praise from others.

What About You?

• Are you going to try putting any of these lessons from Jesus to work in your life? Which ones?
• What talents or abilities can you share with others?

Talkin' About It

Choose one lesson at a time to work on. Ask God to help you set your goals and desires. Then ask for the strength and wisdom to work on them privately.

Give your contributions privately. Your Father sees what you do in private. He will reward you. Matthew 6:4

Read Matthew 6:25-34

Megan couldn't concentrate on anything except what was worrying her. *I wonder if Linnie is my friend today? I never know from one day to the next if she's gonna be my friend or Kayley's friend for that day. What am I going to do if she's not my friend today? Who will I eat lunch with? Who will I talk to? I'll look like a total loser if I'm all by myself. Linnie and Kayley will sit across the room and make fun of me, then no one will want to be seen with me.*

Is all this worry going to help?

You can't change a thing by worrying. Jesus said that there isn't any reason to worry about anything. Trust God—

he is in control of everything. He takes care of the beautiful flowers and the birds. They never worry about what to wear or what to eat. You can waste a lot of energy worrying about things that may never happen or that you can't change anyway. Just live your life to please God and trust him to take care of everything.

What About You?

• What do you find yourself worrying about the most?
• Why do you worry?

Talkin' About It

Thank God for taking care of all your needs. Ask him to help you depend on him and not worry.

But first, be concerned about his kingdom and what has his approval. Then all these things will be provided for you.
Matthew 6:33

What Are You Worried About?

Take a Good Look at Yourself

Read Matthew 7:1-6

"You just don't get it. You want me to live like a kid out of the '60s. You don't care how I feel!" Todd shouted at his parents. He went on and on accusing his parents of being totally unreasonable and unfair. He said they were never willing to compromise on anything and that they always wanted things done their way. Todd let his parents have it. When he was done, they felt crummy and so did he. What Todd didn't realize was that most of the things he was accusing his parents of were things that he was guilty of.

Check out your own life before you bombard someone else.

It's so easy to criticize and judge other people because it's easy to tell others how they should be living. Is it hard to understand why others don't take your advice immediately? The things about other people that bother you the most may be things that you do yourself. Weird, huh? Jesus said to take care of your own life before you judge someone else.

What About You?

• What things about your friends are you most critical of?
• What do you need to clean up in your own life?

Talkin' About It

Thank God that he always judges you fairly. Ask him to help you not be judgmental of others. Ask him to give you a kind and fair heart.

You will be judged by the same standard you use to judge others.

Matthew 7:2

Read Matthew 7:7-12

Jane lay across her bed looking at the advertisement for a gymnastics exhibition. Many of the current and former Olympic athletes were going to be there. "This is so awesome. I'd love to go to this. So many stars are going to perform, and there's this autograph session afterwards if you buy the VIP tickets. But, the tickets are too expensive. I'm sure Mom and Dad would never go for it. I'm not even gonna ask."

God. He loves you and wants to give you good things, too. If you are a Christian and trying to live for him (there's the key), you can ask God for anything and he will do it for you.

What About You?

• What's the key to this promise?
• How do you "live for God?"

Talkin' About It

If you don't ask, you'll never know!

When you ask your parents for things, they do the best they can for you. But, if you don't ask, you'll never know what you missed. Same with

If your life is right with God, you can ask him anything. Tell him exactly what's on your mind. Ask him to do specific things for you.

If you live in me and what I say lives in you, then ask for anything you want, and it will be yours. John 15:7

Will Ya?

Just Ask,

Stick to the Rules

Read Matthew 7:13-14

"The ball can bounce twice before you have to hit it back over the net," Louis said firmly.

"It cannot, that's not in any of the rulebooks. You can hit it in the air, or it can bounce once," answered Dennis, waving his tennis racket in the air. "You can't just make up your own rules to play by. The rules are already written!"

That's true in bigger things than a tennis game.

Take for example, the way to get to heaven. There is only one way. You can't bend the rules and not pay any attention to God, burying yourself in sex, drugs, lying, alcohol, and all other kinds of junk, and still expect to go to heaven. Jesus said the way to heaven is such a narrow opening, that many people miss it, and some people don't choose it because it seems to have so many rules. It may seem like you have more freedom by living the other way—but since it keeps you out of heaven, is it really so great?

What About You?

• Are you happy with the way your life is going?
• Have you made a choice for or against heaven?

Talkin' About It

There are only two choices—for God or not for God. If you haven't made your choice yet, talk to God about it. Ask him to help you understand.

I can guarantee this truth: Those who listen to what I say and believe in the one who sent me will have eternal life. John 5:24

Read Matthew 7:15-23

"My dad knows Michael Jordan. They play golf all the time," bragged Scott.

"Yeah right. Your dad works in a factory. I'm sure he knows the greatest basketball player of all time." Scott's friends were not buying his story .

"He does! I'm not lying!" Scott shouted.

"Right, if he knows M.J. prove it!" they challenged.

Time to put up or shut up!

You can say a million words, but that won't make what you say true. Some things you just can't fake. Like whether you are a member of God's family. You can know all the "Christian" words to say, but the proof that you're a Christian shows up in your life. It's called "fruit." A Christian can't produce any kind of fruit but Christian fruit —such as love and kindness. And a non-Christian can't produce Christian fruit, in the same way that an apple tree can't grow oranges.

What About You?

• What fruit shows you are a Christian?
• How long can a person fake good fruit?

Talkin' About It

You may be able to fool other people, but you can never fool God. Come clean with him right now. Admit what you've tried to fake. Confess and ask his forgiveness.

Good people do the good that is in them.

Luke 6:45

Produce the Goods!

You Gotta Live With Your Choices

Read Matthew 7:24-29

What a day, thought Gina. *I'm beat. All I want to do is get something to eat, crash on the sofa, and veg out in front of the TV.* That's exactly what she did. The only problem was that she never got up. Gina knew she had quite a bit of homework to do, and that she needed to practice clarinet. But, she chose to continue veggin' out in front of the TV. Bedtime soon rolled around and there sat Gina, with several hours of homework yet to do and clarinet to practice. Now what?

Good or bad, you have to live with your choices.

In fact, Jesus made a point of teaching that truth. He told a story of a man who built his house on sand where there was no good foundation. Bad choice. When the storms came, the house fell down. Another man built his house on rock. Good choice. His house stood during the storm because it had a good foundation.

What About You?

• How do you build your life on a good foundation?
• Have you made that choice?

Talkin' About It

Thank God for the good foundation he provides when you put your faith in him. Confess any bad choices you have made and ask him to help you gain a stronger foundation by trusting more.

Do what God's word says. Don't merely listen to it, or you will fool yourselves.

James 1:22

Review Matthew 7:1-6

Let's be honest, the hardest part of this Christian-living thing sometimes is getting along with other people. After all, God stays the same and he's perfect, so how could you not want to please him? But, other people can be a pain in the neck sometimes—especially when they don't agree with what you think is important, or when they hurt your feelings.

It's easy to be critical and judgmental.

But, that's taking a big chance. Jesus said you'll be judged by the same standards you use to judge others—especially if you ignore "pain in the neck" actions in your own life and then criticize those same things in your friends. How you get along with others can show what God's love is like to people watching you. In the words of an old chorus, "They'll know we are Christians by our love."

What About You?

• What is your reputation like regarding getting along with others?
• Think of one person you have trouble getting along with. Talk to God about it.

Talkin' About It

There's always at least "this one guy" who rubs you the wrong way. Pray for him, asking God to show you ways to love him.

Forgive and you will be forgiven.

Luke 6 :37

No Double Standards

Oh Yeah? Prove It

Read John 2:1-11

The major league baseball strike of 1994–95 dragged on forever. Mitchell and his friends were having severe baseball withdrawal. But one day Ben ran to Mitchell's house. "It's over," he shouted. "I heard on the radio that the strike is over. Baseball is back!"

Mitchell didn't buy it. "I won't believe it until I see it," he said.

Do you need proof before you believe something?

The disciples left their homes and jobs to follow Jesus. But, it wasn't until after he did his first miracle that they finally knew who he was. Jesus and his friends were at a wedding. His mother was there, too. When the host ran out of wine to serve, Jesus' mother asked him to help. He told the servants to bring six jugs of water then dip some out and have the host taste it. It wasn't water anymore—it was now fine wine. When the disciples saw this, they knew he was the Messiah!

What About You?

• Do you totally believe who Jesus is or are you waiting for proof?
• How do you think the disciples felt about Jesus after this?

Talkin' About It

Jesus' power is able to help you with any problem you have. Thank him for his power. Thank him that he cares about whatever is going on in your life.

Although you have never seen Christ, you love him. You don't see him now, but you believe in him. I Peter 1:8

How Can You Sleep?

Read Mark 4:35-41

Carla had heard it over and over. "You're no good, stupid, ugly, a loser. No one will ever want to marry you!" Most of the time her dad was in a drunken stupor when he shouted these things. But, when you hear things so often, you start to believe them. Carla knew deep inside that God loved her, even if no one else did. But when she tried to talk to God, it felt like he was asleep or worse— maybe he agreed with her dad. She needed God's help, but he didn't seem to be listening.

Don't give up, he's listening.

The disciples panicked once when Jesus was sleeping. They were on a boat going across the Sea of Galilee and a big storm blew up. Their boat was being tossed around on the water like a toy. They were scared that they were going to die. Jesus was asleep so they woke him and asked, "Don't you care that we are going to die?" Jesus stood up and told the wind and the waves to be quiet—and they did! It was awesome! Even the wind and the waves obeyed Jesus!

What About You?

• When have you felt that God wasn't listening to you?
• How has he shown you in the past that he is listening?

Talkin' About It

Thank God that he is in control of everything. Thank him that his awesome power protects and cares for you.

Even the wind and the sea obey him.

Matthew 8:27

That's Not Important Enough

Read   Mark 6:35-41

"Good night, honey," Mom said as she kissed Ruthie.

"Oh, I'll be up for awhile," Ruthie sighed.

"Don't you have a big history test tomorrow? What's keeping you up late?" asked Mom.

"That big history test," Ruthie said. "I want to study more."

Mom smiled and said, "You've studied plenty. You won't learn any more at this late hour. Just ask God to help you remember what you've learned, then get some sleep."

"I'd feel silly praying about something as little as a test. God doesn't care about that!" Ruthie said.

He cares about everything.

He even cares when people are hungry. Thousands of people were sitting on a hillside, listening to Jesus teach. When the disciples said the crowd was getting hungry, Jesus took five loaves of bread and two small fish that were offered by a boy and turned that into enough food for over 5,000 people. There were even leftovers! He cared about hungry people.

What About You?

• What have you skipped praying about because you thought it was too little?
• How would you feel about a God who didn't care about the little things?

Talkin' About It

Tell God how it makes you feel to think he cares about every little thing, not just big things. Thank him for his care and his power.

Then he took the five loaves and the two fish, looked up to heaven, and blessed the food. He broke the loaves apart and kept giving them to the disciples to give to the crowd. Luke 9:16

Read Matthew 14:22-27

Camping out was great! Jade and her friends had fished and hiked in the woods all afternoon. Miss Hardy cooked dinner over the campfire and after dinner they told ghost stories. As the fire grew lower, the stories got scarier. When it was bedtime, everyone laughed about how great the ghost stories were, then they zipped their tents shut and climbed in their sleeping bags. But, Jade couldn't go to sleep. There were strange sounds in the woods and weird shapes showing on the sides of the tent. The ghost stories were bouncing around in her mind.

One time Jesus' disciples thought he was a ghost!

It happened late one night. The disciples were rowing their boat across a lake. It was a stormy night and Jesus wasn't with them. But suddenly in the middle of the stormy lake, they saw a man walking on top of the water! *It must be a ghost,* they thought. But, it wasn't a ghost, it was Jesus. He called out to them, "Don't be afraid. It is I." This was one more proof to the disciples that Jesus was the Son of God.

What About You?

• Why do you think Jesus came to the disciples this way?
• Have you ever wanted proof of who Jesus is? Would this kind of experience make you believe?

Talkin' About It

Thank God that he seriously wanted the disciples to know who Jesus is. Thank him that he wants you to know the same thing. Ask him to help you believe.

Jesus said, "Calm down! It's me. Don't be afraid!"

Matthew 14:27

It's a Ghost!

Try Again

Read Luke 5:4-11

Shannon ran down the mat at top speed. She jumped on the springboard and flipped over the vault. When she landed, her feet slid right out from under her, just like the last 10 times. She ended up sitting on the mat. "You almost have it. Your timing is getting better, but it's still a little off. Try again," Shannon's coach said.

Jesus told Peter to try again.

Peter didn't want to. After all, he and his partners had fished all night and not caught a single fish. But, there was something about Jesus when he said, "Drop your nets again." Peter tried one more time. It was worth it. The nets came up so full of fish that they nearly broke. Now Peter knew that Jesus was the Son of God. Jesus said, "From now on you will catch men, not fish." Peter left his boat and followed Jesus.

What About You?

• Are you willing to do whatever Jesus asks you to do?
• What did Jesus mean by catching men not fish?

Talkin' About It

Do you get discouraged when you have to do things over or learn the same lessons over? Tell God about it. Ask him to be patient with you and to use you in his work.

From now on you will catch people instead of fish.

Luke 5:10

Read John 11:1-44

Letitia cried for three days before the funeral, and she cried through the whole service. *My brother, my baby brother is just a statistic now,* she thought. *One more good boy who was killed in a drive-by shooting. He didn't deserve it. He shouldn't be dead!* As the minister was closing the service, he told everyone that Martin was a Christian and that he was in heaven now with the God he loved, and who loved him. Then he asked if anyone in the church wanted to know more about God. Three of Martin's friends raised their hands.

Sometimes good things come from bad things.

Like when Lazarus died. His two sisters sent word to Jesus when Lazarus got sick. Jesus was their good friend, and they thought he would hurry to Bethany to heal their brother. But when Jesus came, Lazarus was dead and buried. Jesus went to the tomb and called for the dead man to come out. Lazarus walked out of the tomb, still wrapped in his graveclothes. Many people believed in Jesus that day!

What About You?

• Why did Lazarus' sisters think Jesus could have saved their brother?
• When has something good resulted from a bad situation for you?

Talkin' About It

Death is a scary and hard part of life. Thank God that sometimes good comes from it—like someone accepting Jesus because of a death.

I am the one who brings people back to life, and I am life itself.

John 11:25

The Glory of God

Seein' Is Believin'

Review your favorite miracle of the week

Jesus did miracles so that the people who saw them would know who he was. Some people wouldn't believe until they saw the fantastic things he did. The power of his miracles attracted people to him, then they would listen to his message of love.

Reading about his miracles still encourages people today.

Have you trusted Jesus as your Savior? When you read about the miracles he did, you know how much power is available to help you with the tough things in life. Trust him with your whole life. Believe that his miracle-working power is available to you!

What About You?

• Has Jesus done any modern-day miracles that you know about?
• How has Jesus shown that he loves you?

Talkin' About It

Thank God for his power. Thank him for loving you and taking care of you.

*T*rust the LORD.

Psalm 37:3

Read Mark 10:46-52

"Everyone choose a partner. Now blindfold one of the partners. You'll go through half of the class period as a sightless person. Then we'll switch and the other partner will experience sightlessness," instructed Mr. Collins. Katy was the first of her twosome to be blindfolded. Even with the guidance and help of her partner, she kept walking into doorframes and desks. By the time her turn was over, she had major bumps and bruises on her legs.

What would life be like if you were blind?

Bartimaeus knew. He spent his days sitting beside the road because he couldn't see to work. When Bartimaeus heard that Jesus was passing by, he called to him for help. Jesus heard him and asked to see Bartimaeus. "What do you want me to do for you?" Jesus asked.

"I want to see," Bartimaeus answered. "Go on home," Jesus said, "your faith has made you well." Immediately, Bartimaeus could see.

What About You?

• How do you think Bartimaeus felt about Jesus after he was healed?
• How can having faith heal someone?

Talkin' About It

Thank God for your eyesight. Thank him that he cares about a single voice calling out in the crowd.

Go, your faith has made you well.

Mark 10:52

I Can See! I Can See! I Can See! I Can See!

Talk, Talk, Talk, Talk

Read Mark 7:31-37

The noise level on the bus was deafening. What do you expect when you put sixty middle school students in a cracker box sized bus? Anyway, the sponsors and the teachers sat huddled in the front seats, like they thought they could escape the noise. Finally, Mr. Samuels stood up, waving his arms and shouting over the noise, "You guys are too loud. We can't hear ourselves think up here. Stop shouting and just speak normally to each other."

What if you couldn't speak at all?

A man was brought to Jesus who couldn't speak or hear at all. This guy really believed Jesus could help him. Jesus had a warm spot for people who had faith in him. So he put his fingers in the man's ears, and he spit on his finger and touched the man's tongue. Jesus looked up and said, "Open up!" Suddenly, this guy who had never heard a sound or spoken a word before, could hear and speak clearly!

What About You?

• Why did Jesus care so much about people who thought he could help them?
• In what way would you like Jesus to help you?

Talkin' About It

Jesus just touched the man and prayed, and the man was healed. Thank him for his awesome power. Talk to him about what you need.

Have faith that you will receive whatever you ask for in prayer.

Matthew 21:22

Read Luke 8:43-48

When the main band, Shoe Laces, started playing, the noise level rose to a zillion decibels. All the kids in the audience stood up and danced to the music. The girls screamed and shouted at the band members. Some of the kids with seats near the stage went nuts, leaning over the stage, just trying to touch their idols' clothing.

All they wanted to do was touch them.

One time when Jesus was walking along in the middle of a big crowd, the whole group came to a screeching halt because Jesus asked his disciples, "Who touched me?" Right, Jesus—there were hundreds of people around you, how could anyone know who touched you? But, then a woman admitted to touching him. She had been sick for many years, and she thought if she just touched Jesus' robe, she would be well. Jesus was moved by her faith, "Go in peace," he said, "your faith has healed you."

What About You?

• How much power do you believe Jesus has?
• Was the woman healed just because she touched his robe? What healed her?

Talkin' About It

Ask God to help you have the kind of faith this woman had. Ask him to help your faith grow stronger.

Groupies!

What you have believed will be done for you.

Matthew 9:29

Thank You, Thank You, Thank You, Thank You, Thank You

Read Luke 17:11-19

Lionel didn't really want to, but he took a can of spray paint and wrote on the building wall, just like his friends were doing. When the owner showed up with the police, all ten boys were arrested. After a long lecture, the man decided to let the boys go. He would forgive them if they cleaned off the paint. Lionel was so relieved that he followed the man out of the building just to say thank you.

What happened to the other nine?

When Jesus healed ten men who were sick with leprosy, only one came back to thank him. The sick men had stopped Jesus and begged him to heal them. Jesus said, "Go show yourselves to the priests." So the ten took off running to find the priests. As they were running they were healed. When the one man realized he was healed, he turned around and ran back to Jesus to thank him. It didn't escape Jesus that the other nine didn't bother to thank him. He told the thankful man to go home because his faith had made him well.

What About You?

• When someone thanks you for something, do you want to do more stuff for that person?
• How often do you thank God for what he does for you?

Talkin' About It

Thank God for everything he has done for you.

Thank God that he gives us the victory through our Lord Jesus Christ.

1 Corinthians 15:57

Read Luke 8:40-56

Cindy heard sobbing coming from her mother's bedroom. She stood quietly outside the door. One part of her wanted to knock and say, "Mom, I'm sorry!" But, the other part wanted to say, "That's what you get!" and stomp out of the house. She didn't do either. She just stood there listening to her mom cry. Pretty soon Cindy heard her mom praying—for her! "Lord, help Cindy know that I love her. I forgive her for the angry words she said to me." On and on Mom prayed, pouring out her love for Cindy and asking God to take care of her.

Parent's often seek God's help for their children.

Jairus' daughter was sick, in fact, she was dying. Jairus believed that Jesus could help her, so he hurried to get him. By the time Jesus got to Jairus' house, the little girl was dead. People were crying and moaning. Jesus said, "Stop crying, she's just asleep." Everyone laughed at him, so he sent everyone except her parents out of the room. Then he said, "Child, get up!" She did! She came back to life. A parent's faith paid off.

What About You?

• Do you think your parents pray for you? About what?
• How often do your parents do things for you?

Talkin' About It

Jesus' miracles are awesome. Thank him for answering this parent's prayer and showing once again what his awesome power is like.

Do Mothers Cry?

Jesus went in, took her hand, and the girl came back to life. •

Matthew 9:25

The Bossy Sister

Read Luke 7:1-10

"Orders, orders, orders. The only words Myra ever says are orders," complained Claudia.

"I wish Mom could be here when we get home from school. I'm sick of Myra bossing us around," agreed Will. "Just 'cause she's the oldest, she thinks she can tell us what to do. I'm sick of her orders!"

A Roman commander knew all about giving orders.

This Roman commander believed that Jesus could heal his sick servant by just saying the words. Jesus didn't even have to come into the guy's house. In fact, the commander was in such awe of Jesus that he felt he wasn't good enough to have Jesus come into his house. He asked Jesus to heal the servant by just saying the words. Jesus did and the servant was healed. Jesus was blown away by the Roman commander's great faith.

What About You?

• How does your faith compare with the Roman commander?
• Why was Jesus amazed at the Roman's faith?

Talkin' About It

Can you imagine having that much faith? Ask God to help your faith in him grow stronger every day.

No one can please God without faith.

Hebrews 11:6

Read Mark 11:22-24

Miracles! Who hasn't wanted a miracle to happen at some time in life? Maybe you wished the school building would burn down, or that you could be just a little sick so you could miss a test. Or maybe you wanted a real miracle, like for someone sick to be healed.

Does God still do miracles today?

Sure he does. Some things that we take for granted every day are miracles—like when the sun comes up, or we have air to breathe. But, we tend to get hung up on the fact of wanting miracles which relate to our personal needs. Such as the healing of a loved one, or special help relating to grades, money, or friends. Sometimes God does answer those prayers and do miracles for us. Hurrah! But, don't ever forget that even a plain, old, normal day is full of God's miracles.

What About You?

• What miracle have you wished for God to do?
• Has he done a miracle for you? What is it?

Talkin' About It

Think about all that God does for you every day. Thank him for daily miracles. Tell him what specific things you want him to do for you.

Fix It; God!

That's why I tell you to have faith that you have already received whatever you pray for, and it will be yours. Mark 11:24

I'm Not Listening!

Read Matthew 13:1-23

Mark sat still and looked straight ahead with no expression. He was supposed to be listening to Dad give "THE LECTURE" which came along every couple of months. It consisted of: "cleanyourroomhelpoutwithchoresbenicetoyourbrothertakeresponsibilityforyourself . . ." Mark had heard it all a hundred times. After each lecture, Mark tried to do what Dad wanted—he really did. But, after a week or so, he'd get too busy or tired of the effort it took, and he'd slip back to his old ways.

Mark is just like a guy Jesus talked about.

This guy heard the Word of God and tried for a while to obey it. But he didn't keep learning about it, so when life got a little tough, he gave it up. Some other guys heard the Word of God too. Satan came and grabbed it away from one man before the guy believed it. Another man let worry drown out the Word. The last man accepted God's Word and let it grow in him. Then he went out and told others about it.

What About You?

• Which of the men in Jesus' story are you like?
• What do you have to do after receiving the Word for it to grow in you?

Talkin' About It

Ask God to help you understand his Word. Ask him to help you want to study it and let it grow in you.

> I will put my teachings inside them, and I will write them on their hearts.
>
> Jeremiah 31:33

Read Matthew 13:24-30, 36-43

Isaiah is a good kid. Not a goody-two-shoes or anything like that, but a good kid. He would never consider doing drugs or getting high on booze. For the most part, Isaiah does his homework and is only mildly rebellious to his parents. So why are we even talking about him? Isaiah has started hanging out with some guys that aren't the cream of the crop. These guys have been known to try some drugs, blow off school, and even push some girls to go farther than they wanted to.

Not the best influence.

Hanging out with those kind of guys is like throwing bad seeds into a field of crops. It happens slowly, but those weeds will come up and choke out the good crop—taking the food and water that the good crop needs. The influence of bad people (Satan's workers) does that in a person's life—chokes out any desire to live for God or tell others about him. Just as weeds are gonna be yanked out and burned, Satan and his followers will be destroyed someday.

What About You?

• Honesty time. Are there some bad influences in your life? Who?
• How do bad influences pull you away from God?

Talkin' About It

Granted, it's not easy, but you gotta make choices. Tell God if you know some of your friends are bad influences. Ask him to help you be strong enough to get away from them.

Bad Seed

Then the people who have God's approval will shine like the sun in their Father's kingdom. Matthew 13:43

It's the Real Thing

Read Mark 4:30-32

The first year that Coca Cola® was sold at soda fountains, sales averaged only nine a day. The popular beverage was born in a pharmacist's backyard in Atlanta, Georgia. Dr. Pemberton took it to a local soda fountain and they sold it for five cents a glass. Now, Coca Cola® can be found in nearly 200 countries and hundreds of millions of servings are sold each day. Something big came from something little.

Jesus said his kingdom is like that.

It began with one guy—Jesus—talking about God's love. A few people believed and joined him. Then a few more. His people will keep sharing the message of God's love with those around them, and one day God's kingdom will be the biggest and most important kingdom ever. Something big came from something little.

What About You?

• Have you joined God's kingdom?
• How are you helping the kingdom grow?

Talkin' About It

Thank God that you're part of his kingdom. It's awesome that it will be the biggest ever some day. Ask how you can help it grow.

Praise the LORD, my soul.

Psalm 104:35

Read Luke 15:4-7

Mom had a long day ahead of her. She needed to get to work early. But she had to drive Peter to school and he wasn't ready yet. When she went to his room to hurry him along, Mom hit the ceiling. Junk from the closet, shelves, and drawers was dumped all over the floor. "What are you doing?" Mom demanded.

"I want my Cubs hat, and I can't find it," Peter explained.

"You've got a hundred hats, grab one and come on!"

"I don't want one of the other ones, I want to find the Cubs hat!" Peter shouted back.

Have you ever lost something special?

You must have felt pretty great when you found it, right? Well listen to this—Jesus looks for people that don't know him, or who have turned away from him. Even though there are many other people who love him, he cares about each person, individually. When a lost person comes back to God, there is a major party in heaven!

What About You?

• Have you ever felt lost in a crowd or like you don't matter to anyone? How does that feel?
• How does it feel to be important enough to cause a party in heaven?

Talkin' About It

Tell God how you feel about being special enough to him to cause a party in heaven. Thank him for caring that much for you.

I Want THAT One

There will be more happiness in heaven over one person who turns to God and changes the way he thinks and acts than over 99 people who already have turned to God and have his approval.

Luke 15:7

Drop It, Already!

Read Matthew 18:21-24

Bailey was totally caught in the grip of anger. Yep, Bailey was totally mad at Samantha because Samantha had laughed at her in front of the whole class. Sam knew it was a dumb, insensitive thing to do, but it just sort of popped out when Bailey got her tongue twisted while giving a book report. Sam had even apologized, but Bailey was not willing to forgive. She was holding on to her anger like a shark holds onto its food.

Sorry Bailey, your anger will get you nowhere.

Jesus made a great point about forgiving others with a story about a man who owed a bunch of money to a king. He couldn't pay the debt, so the kind king canceled the debt.

Then this guy turned around and had another man thrown jail for not paying a small debt. Think about it—God has forgiv en you a lot, and will forgive you even more. Doesn't that make it easier to forgive a frien for whatever wrong is done to you.

What About You?

• Honesty time. Are you holding a grudge against anyone? Who and why?
• Think of times when other people have forgiven you.

Talkin' About It

Thank God for his forgiveness. Thank him that he doesn't get tired of forgiving and just stop. Ask him to help you let go of things and forgive others.

Forgive us as we forgive others.

Matthew 6:12

Read Matthew 20:1-16

"Thirty math problems!" moaned Moses. "It's gonna take me all night to do these."

"I know," agreed A. J. "I don't understand this stuff enough to do even one problem." At lunch they complained more.

When Jeff joined them, A. J. asked what he thought of the monster math assignment. "Oh, I don't have to do all thirty," said Jeff. "I came late today 'cause of Student Council, so Mrs. Smith said I only have to do ten problems."

Does that sound fair?

It's like a man that hires workers for the day. They agree on a wage and the workers get busy. Later in the day he hires more workers; still later he hires more. At the end of the day, he pays all the workers the same amount. The guys who worked all day yell about it. But, the boss gets to decide how to use his money. Think about it—that's like God's forgiveness. Some of us are forgiven a lot, some a little. But the bottom line is that no one deserves his forgiveness, so there's no reason for yelling. God forgives because he loves us not because we worked for it. He forgives anyone, at any time, who comes to him.

What About You?

• Why did the men who worked all day think this arrangment was unfair?
• How do you feel about some being forgiven a lot, and some a little?

Talkin' About It

Thank God that you don't have to earn his forgiveness. Thank him for forgiving over and over.

It is God's kindness that saved you.

Ephesians 2:5

That's Not Fair!

Tell Me a Story

Read Matthew 13:10-17

Remember when you were a kid and you curled up on Mom or Dad's lap and listened to a good book? Those were great learning times. You may have learned the alphabet and how to count by reading those books. There were probably a few books that you wanted to hear over and over and over.

Have you ever wondered why Jesus told stories when he was teaching?

Jesus spent a lot of time explaining things about God and heaven to his followers. But, other people were always hanging around him, maybe to see if he would do things for them. They didn't really care about learning what he wanted to teach them. He used simple stories to help them understand how to live for God. But, even with the simple stories they didn't understand because their hearts weren't really interested in learning.

What About You?

• What have you learned from Jesus' stories?
• Do you really want to learn how to live for God? Even if it means changing things in your life?

Talkin' About It

Many of Jesus' stories are to help you learn how to treat other people. Thank him for his stories. Ask him to help you live for him and treat others with kindness.

Knowledge about the mysteries of the kingdom of heaven has been given to you.

Matthew 13:11

Read Matthew 22:2-14

"Carol will play the part of Aunt Eller," Mrs. Clemons announced. This part in "Oklahoma" was Carol's first big part and she wanted to do a great job. She learned her script right away and practiced the songs diligently. But, when Mrs. Clemons put in a square dance, Carol balked. She was clumsy on her feet, and she didn't want to look silly in front of the whole school. Mrs. Clemons insisted, but Carol wouldn't even try. Mrs. Clemons finally said, "Carol, I'm the director, and you need to do what I say. If you can't do that, you can be replaced in this part."

Scary words—you can be replaced.

Jesus emphasized that point in his story about the wedding banquet. None of the invited guests could come because they were too busy. The king replaced them with people from the street. In the same way, God has invited people to come to heaven. When they refuse to come, they can be replaced. Others who come in but aren't serious about heaven will be thrown out into the darkness. Judgment happens.

What About You?

• Have you accepted the invitation to come into heaven?
• Are you willing to do whatever God asks you to do?

Talkin' About It

Thank God for inviting people to heaven. Thank him that he looks at people's hearts to know if they are serious about obeying him.

The LORD is great. He should be highly praised.

Psalm 48:1

You Can Be Replaced

Be Ready!

Read Matthew 25:1-13

Letoyna had one page of math homework to do. She planned to do it right after her favorite TV show. But then Janet called. When she got off the phone, she sat down to do it, but her new Teen magazine was on the desk so she looked at it for a while. Eleven o'clock came, but her math homework never did get done. Letoyna went to bed thinking, *I'll get the answers from Janet tomorrow at school.*

Boy was Letoyna surprised when Janet said, "No way! I took time to do my homework, you should have, too. I'm not giving you the answers."

Just then Miss Jones said, "Turn in your papers now." Letoyna was cooked!

You should have been ready!

Jesus told a story about some bridesmaids who were ready for their wedding banquet and some who were not ready. When the bridegroom showed up, ready for the banquet, the unprepared ones had to go get ready. They missed the party! Like the bridesmaids who were prepared, you should always be watching for Jesus to come back! There won't be time to accept him when he comes—you gotta be ready and waiting

What About You?

• Are you eager for Jesus to come back? Why or why not?
• Why isn't it wise to put off being ready for Jesus?

Talkin' About It

Don't put off accepting Jesus 'til you're older. If you haven't accepted Jesus as your Savior, talk to him about that now.

So stay awake because you don't know the day or the hour.

Matthew 25:13

Read Matthew 25:14-30

"Can you believe this project?" moaned Paul.

"I think it sounds like fun," said Renee. "We each start out with a make-believe $1,000, and we can invest it, or put it in savings, or whatever we want."

"That part isn't the problem," said Paul. "The bad part is that our grade is determined by how much money we have at the end of the quarter. One bad investment and it's failing time."

Use what you've got!

Jesus told about a man who gave money to three men. The first two men invested their money and had twice as much to give back to the man. The third man buried his money because he was afraid of losing it. The owner of the money was angry that the man hadn't used the money better, so he took it away and gave it to the first man. God has given each of us many abilities. He wants us to use them for him—telling others about him, serving him. If we don't, God may take them away from us.

What About You?

• What abilities and talents has God given you?
• How can you use them for him?

Talkin' About It

Thank God for the abilities he has given you. Ask him to show you ways to use them for him.

Serve eagerly as if you were serving your heavenly master and not merely serving human masters. Ephesians 6:7

Use It or Lose It

Walk the Talk

Read Matthew 21:28-32

"Michael, will you take the trash cans out to the curb?" Mom asked.

"Not right now, I'm busy," Michael responded.

"Scot, will you take the trash cans out to the curb?" Mom asked.

"Sure, Mom, right away," Scot said. But, Scot kept on playing his video game, and never got around to doing the job. However, Michael finished what he was doing, and he took the trash cans out as Mom had asked.

Which boy was truly obedient?

Obeying—do you hear a lot about that word? Jesus said it's good when we know the right things to say about God. But, it's just as important to put those good words into practice—live your faith. Some people who can't find the right words to say about God live for him. That's the way it should be.

What About You?

• When have you said one thing but done something else?
• How do you feel when you do not obey?

Talkin' About It

Ask God to help you obey you parents and obey him. Ask for strength not to just say the right words, but to live them too.

Why do you call me Lord but don't do what I tell you?

Luke 6:46

Read Luke 12:16-21

"Mom, I really want a Chicago Bulls jacket," Ryan begged. "Daniel has one, so I should get one, too."

Mom sighed, "Daniel is 16 and has a job. He earned the $150 to buy the jacket himself." Ryan wasn't giving up yet, "I look like a geek without one. All the cool guys at school have team jackets."

Don't measure your worth by possessions.

There's no future in it. Jesus told about a rich guy that had so many crops he couldn't store them all, so he built bigger barns to store them in. He had all the money he needed, so he decided to party for the rest of his life. This guy put a lot of emphasis on money and fun, and he didn't think about God at all. It's more important to know God than to have lots of money and stuff.

What About You?

• What "thing" do you feel you need to have?
• Is there anything more important to you than God? What?

Talkin' About It

If your priorities are messed up, tell God about it. Ask him to help you keep things in perspective. Ask him to help you remember that it's more important to know him than to have lots of stuff.

Your heart will be where your treasure is.

Matthew 6:21

You Can't Take It with You

You Count

Read Luke 15:8-10

"Great job, Lemar. We're all proud of you for getting a C on this English exam. Your hard work is showing." Dad couldn't say enough good things about Lemar. Meanwhile, William brought home his usual A on every paper and test. William was confused. *Why are Mom and Dad making such a big deal over Lemar's C ?*

A changed life is worth cheering about.

One person who turns his or her life around and starts living for God causes a major party in heaven. Jesus explained this with the story of a woman who lost one of her ten coins. She still had nine coins, but she wanted that one, so she looked everywhere for it. When she found it, she called all her friends to celebrate with her. That party would be nothing compared to the celebration the angels put on in heaven when even one person comes to God.

What About You?

• How does it feel to know angels cheer when one person comes to God?
• Why does God care about just one person?

Talkin' About It

Thank God for caring about each person. Thank him that every person is important to him.

God's angels are happy about one person who turns to God and changes the way he thinks and acts. *Luke 15:10*

Review Scripture from past week

Have you ever seen a mom and dad gently teaching their child to walk? They walk along behind the little one, arms outstretched in case of a fall. They patiently show the little tyke what to do, over and over. And when the baby takes his first step, the mom and dad rejoice and celebrate. They want to teach the baby everything they can.

Jesus wanted to teach people everything he could, too.

Jesus told stories to help people understand how to live for God. Jesus wanted everyone to love God and understand how to obey him. People listened to his stories and learned how to live in a way that pleased God.

What About You?

• What have you learned from Jesus' stories?
• Do you want to learn more about living for Jesus?

Talkin' About It

Ask God to help you understand more about living for him. Thank him for the help that Jesus' stories are.

Love the LORD your God with all your heart, with all your soul, and with all your strength.

Deuteronomy 6:5

One Foot in Front of the Other

Don't Touch Him

Read Luke 10:25-37

The puppet show had just ended, and the kids on the team went out to mingle with the audience. This audience was different from any they had performed for before. It was all terminally ill children. They couldn't applaud or even laugh much. Heidi and Heather went around the room together showing the children a puppet up close, letting kids hold it if they wanted. But, Heidi refused to go to one child over in a corner, "I heard the nurse tell Mrs. Hill that he has AIDS. I'm not getting close to him." Heather couldn't believe it, "You can't catch it just by talking to him." But, Heidi wouldn't budge, "No way, I'm not going."

Ever hear of the Good Samaritan?

Jesus told a story about a guy who was beaten up by robbers and left on the road to die. Two guys passed by who should have helped him, but they didn't. A third guy had good reasons not to help the poor man, but he did. The Good Samaritan went out of his way to help an undesirable man, to show him God's love. It cost him time and money, but he did it.

What About You?

• How do you feel about people who are different from you?
• How can you show love to those who are different?

Talkin' About It

Ask God to make you brave because showing his love to someone different won't be easy. Your friends may make fun of you—but it's still the right thing to do.

Love your neighbor as you love yourself.

Leviticus 19:18

Read Luke 15:11-32

Jenny felt like she was going to explode. Anger boiled inside her until it filled every part of her. She wanted to blast into the lunchroom and rip Tyra's heart out in front of the whole student body. Tyra's decision to share Jenny's secrets with Rick was unforgiveable, especially since a lot of those secrets were about him. *I will never be friends with Tyra again. In fact, I'll never even speak to her again.*

You can lose a lot if you're unwilling to forgive.

Learn about it from one Bible-time Dad whose son ran away from home. The kid asked for his inheritance money before his dad even died. He took the money to another country and blew every cent. One day he was at his job, feeding pigs, and realized they had more to eat than he did. He swallowed his pride and went home to ask his dad for a job. But, his dad was so glad to see him, he forgave the boy and threw a big party! If he hadn't forgiven, he would have lost his son forever.

What About You?

• Forgiveness isn't easy. When have you been too angry to forgive?
• When have you lost a friend because of being unable to forgive?

Talkin' About It

Thank God that he doesn't get so angry with you that he can't forgive. Thank him for his continuous forgiveness.

*F*orgive as the Lord forgave you.

Colossians 3:13

What Have You Got to Lose?

Nagging

Read Luke 11:5-13

"Mom, this is really important to me," said Gail. "Why won't you believe that I want to go to gymnastics camp?"

Mom sighed, "I don't know what's really important to you. You change your mind every other day and go with whatever whim hits you at the moment. I can't afford a $500 whim for gymnastics camp." It took a few days of walking the fine line between repeatedly asking and not being a pain in the neck, but Gail finally convinced Mom she was serious about attending gymnastics camp.

When something is important to you, keep bringing it up.

When you want something from your parents, you keep asking them. You can keep asking God things, too, because he wants to give you good gifts. He wants to know what is important to you. Don't give up if your prayers aren't answered right away. God is very generous, but he wants you to think about what you pray for.

What About You?

• Do you get discouraged if God doesn't answer your prayers right away?
• Have you ever prayed about something repeatedly? How was your prayer answered?

Talkin' About It

Thank God that he wants to answer your prayers. Ask him to help you think about what you pray for. Ask him to help you know what to ask him.

Ask, and you will receive. Search, and you will find. Knock, and the door will be opened for you. Luke 11:9

Read Luke 18:2-8

"Mr. Roseland, my grade on this paper is wrong," Paul scribbled across his paper. He left it on Roseland's desk, but he didn't hear anything about it. The next day he stopped Mr. Roseland in the hallway and asked about it.

The teacher said, "Oh yeah, stop by my room after school."

But, when Paul stopped, by he wasn't there, so Paul left a note about the incorrect grade. He did the same the next day, and the next. Finally, Mr. Roseland stopped him in the hall, "Paul, you are certainly persistent. Let's go change that grade right now."

Persistence paid off.

It can for you, too. God is surely willing to answer your prayers. He loves you more than anyone else will ever love you. Sometimes he seems to hold off on his answers, but it isn't because he doesn't care. He may want you to think about how important the reason for your prayer is. He may hold off to encourage you to spend more time talking to him. Whatever the reason— believe he cares and don't stop praying!

What About You?

• When have you wanted to give up instead of continuing praying for something?
• How long is "a long time" to pray for something?

Talkin' About It

Tell God you get discouraged when you have to wait a long time for his answers. Ask him to encourage you and help you to hang in there.

Never stop praying.

1 Thessalonians 5:17

Justice Served

Hurrah for Me!

Read Luke 18:9-14

Braggart. That's the word most people thought of when they thought of Robert. Robert was good at a lot of things like schoolwork, sports, and chess. The frustrating thing was that he boasted obnoxiously about his abilities. Robert built himself up by pointing out how dumb or un-coordinated other people were. Robert thought he was better than anybody else, and he was very happy to announce that to anyone who would listen.

Don't build yourself up by pushing others down.

A certain Pharisee was pretty proud of himself. When he prayed, he thanked God that he was better than other men, especially the lowly tax collector. He even told God about all the wonderful things he did for God. Meanwhile, the tax collector prayed, asking God to forgive his many sins. He didn't tear anyone else down, he just talked to God about himself. That tax collector was forgiven his sins, but the Pharisee wasn't—he was too hung up on being proud of himself.

What About You?

• What ability or talent do you have that you're proud of?
• Have you ever put someone else down? Why?

Talkin' About It

Ask God to give you a right attitude about yourself and other people. Tell him you are truly sorry for your sins.

Everyone who honors himself will be humbled, but the person who humbles himself will be honored. Luke 18:14

Read Matthew 13:47-50

The whole gang was going to the high school basketball game together. It was the biggest game of the year; a victory meant a trip to the state finals. Trouble was, not every guy in the gang had a ticket. Then one Einstein got the idea of the whole group of 12 or 13 guys walking in together. That way the guys with no tickets could be concealed in the middle and sneak in. What he didn't count on was that the ticket taker had once been a junior higher—he wasn't fooled. "Sorry guys, this game is sold out. Ya gotta have a ticket to get in."

That's how it's gonna be at heaven's gate.

You can't ride into heaven on your parent's coattails. The decision to be a Christian is one you gotta make for yourself. In the same way that a fisherman drags his nets out of the water and throws out all the junk but keeps the good fish, the angels will look at everyone who comes to heaven's gate. The people who have done right and accepted Jesus will be kept. All the rest will be thrown into a burning furnace.

What About You?

• How many different ways can you get into heaven?
• Have you made a decision about heaven?

Talkin' About It

Thank God for making a way to heaven. If you haven't made a decision about Jesus, talk to God about it now.

The Son of Man must be lifted up. Then everyone who believes in him will have eternal life. John 3:14-15

Hey Kid, Ya Gotta Have a Ticket

Computer Games

Review Scripture from past week

You probably work on a computer at school. Do you enjoy playing games on a computer? Why? You have to make choices and think quickly. Computers make learning fun. As you try to win each game, you are learning interesting facts and skills without even realizing it.

Jesus knew something about how people learn.

That's one reason Jesus often told stories when he was teaching. People listened to his story more closely than to a straight lesson. They tried to anticipate what the outcome of the story was. Then, after Jesus had them hooked with the story, he could make a point that taught something about how to live for God. Good lesson to remember as you read Jesus' stories—they aren't just for entertainment. They will teach you how to treat other people, and how to share God's love with others.

What About You?

• What have you learned from Jesus' stories?
• Who do you know that needs to hear about Jesus?

Talkin' About It

Ask God to help you learn from Jesus' stories. Ask him to help you let his love show through you.

Your words are truth.

John 17:17

Read Matthew 4:18-22

There may be times when it sounds wonderful to move away from your family. But, think about it—would you *really* like living away from your family; or not seeing your friends? It's not uncommon for a world-class gymnast to do that. Dominique Dawes is a female world champion gymnast. Dominique left her family when she was very young. She lives with her coach in Maryland and trains for hours every day. Dominique doesn't have time to do much of the "stuff" that most kids do, like hanging out with friends or going to the mall. She is committed to the sport of gymnastics. She left home and family to devote all her energy to her sport.

Sounds like Simon and Andrew.

They were fishermen. That's all the two brothers had ever done. When Jesus came and asked them to follow him, they dropped their nets and went to be "fishers of men." James and John did the same thing. They were fishermen, too. When Jesus called these two brothers, James and John left their father and followed him. All four of these men knew that Jesus, and his work for God, was worth leaving family and home and devoting all their energy to.

What About You?

• How important is Jesus' work to you?
• What does it mean to be "fishers of men"?

Talkin' About It

Ask God to help you understand how important his work is. Ask him to give you courage to share his message of love with others.

Leavin' Everything

Come, follow me! I will teach you how to catch people instead of fish!

Mark 1:17

Leavin' the Trash Behind

Read Matthew 9:9-13

A kid born into poverty, in a family with lots of kids, living in the projects, doesn't have a very promising future. Usually, a kid born into those circumstances continues in that path—poverty and rotten family life. Unless he finds something to lock into, something to which he can devote himself. That's what happened to Kevin Johnson of the Phoenix Suns basketball team. K. J. found out he was good at basketball. He locked into his sport, turned away from the temptations around him, and pulled himself out of the projects.

Levi did a similar kind of turnaround.

Tax collectors were notoriously dishonest. They cheated people and kept the extra money for themselves. They were general creeps, and no one liked them. Church leaders were probably surprised when Jesus asked Matthew, the tax collector, to follow him. Maybe they were even more suprised when Matthew left behind all that easy money and followed Jesus. He was so excited about Jesus that he threw a big dinner and invited lots of other tax collectors to meet Jesus.

What About You?

• What do you need to turn away from so you can follow Jesus?
• Do you know anyone who you think would never follow Jesus?

Talkin' About It

Ask God to help you be as excited about sharing him as Matthew was. Ask for courage to tell people whom you wouldn't normally hang out with.

I've come to call sinners, not people who think they don't have any flaws.

Mark 2:17

Read Matthew 3:1-17

Three straight World Championships! The Chicago Bulls were the best basketball team in the world. A pro basketball team is made up of 15 or so players, and every one of them contributes to the team. Each guy knows he is important, that he has a job to do, but imagine being the 15th guy on a team that stars Michael Jordan! You do your job and do it well, but the player who gets most of the attention and credit is Michael.

He couldn't play the game all by himself!

Every star needs a supporting cast. Even a famous rock singer has backups "o-o-o-oing" behind him. John the Baptist was that kind of guy. He went around telling people to get ready because Jesus was coming. Some people wanted to follow John and believe he had power, but John pointed them to Jesus. John said that he wasn't even good enough to tie Jesus' shoes. When Jesus came to him to be baptized, John said, "No way. You should be baptizing me!" But, John did baptize him and afterward a voice from heaven said, "This is my Son whom I love."

What About You?

• When have you had to be a supporter to someone else? Was it hard?
• John spent his life talking about Jesus. How often do you talk about him?

Talkin' About It

Ask God to help you be willing to take a back seat sometimes. Tell him you want to focus people's attention on him.

Being a Sub

Prepare the way for the Lord! Make his paths straight!

Matthew 3:3

Acting on Impulse

Read Matthew 14:22-33

Todd plays third base for the Pony League Marlins baseball team. Third base is called the "hot seat" because balls come at you hard and fast. Todd is willing to stretch out and sacrifice his body to catch a line drive. For example, at the last game Todd was in position, glove on his left hand as usual. He was bent over and ready for anything. The batter hit the ball, and it flew like a shot, straight over third base. Todd didn't even have time to think, on impulse he stuck out his bare right hand and caught the powerful line drive.

You want to know about impulsive? Read about Peter.

Peter was a passionate kind of guy. Late one night, Peter and the other disciples were in a boat. The lake was rough and the waves were tossing the boat around some. When they saw a man walking on top of the water toward them, they were all terrifie But the man said, "Don't be scared. It's me, Jesus."

Impulsive Peter cried out "If it's really you, let me walk to you on the water."

"Jump in," Jesus called. S Peter did—and he was doing fine until he realized that he was walking on water, then he got scared and sank. Jesus said he should have had more faith.

What About You?

• When have you jumped into something without thinking?
• How can you tell that Peter loved Jesus?

Talkin' About It

Peter's love for God should be catching. Ask God to give you th kind of energy in witnessing for H

May goodwill and peace fill your lives through your knowledge about Jesus, our God and Lord! 2 Peter 1:2

Read Mark 14:3-9

In 1980 the United States Olympic Hockey Team pulled off the impossible. They beat the Soviet team. Throughout the Olympic Games, Americans were glued to their TV sets watching this scrappy team beat incredible odds and make it to the gold medal round. When they won the gold medal, America went wild! After the games were over, President Reagan invited the members of the team to the White House. He honored them for their abilities and their sportsmanship and told them America was proud of them.

Honoring someone shows what you think of him or her.

When Jesus was at Simon's house a woman came in carrying an expensive jar of perfume. She opened the jar and poured the perfume on Jesus' head. Some of the men in the room got angry because she wasted the expensive stuff. It could have been sold, and the money would have helped feed the poor. The woman had her head on straight though. She wanted to honor Jesus. She knew that was more important than helping the poor.

What About You?

• How can you honor Jesus?
• How did the woman show Jesus was first in her heart?

Talkin' About It

Ask God to show you if anything in your heart has crowded in front of him. Ask his help in getting your priorities straight.

Beating the Odds

You will always have the poor with you, but you will not always have me with you.

John 12:8

Tryin' Harder

Read Luke 19:1-10

A guy that is shorter than everybody else has gotta have some limitations, right? He can't expect to achieve a high level of success in a field where tall people excell. Don't tell that to Spud Webb. You might think Spud has no business playing professional basketball where most players are 6'3" or more. Spud is only 5'7", but that didn't stop him from making it in the NBA and even winning the slam-dunk competition in 1986. Maybe he had to try harder than anyone else, but he made it!

Sometimes you gotta be creative!

Like Zacchaeus. Short Zacchaeus wanted to see Jesus. Trouble was, he was in the back of a crowd of tall people. Zacchaeus was a dishonest tax collector who didn't have many friends, no one was going to let him up to the front of the line. So, Zacchaeus got creative—he climbed up a tree so he could see Jesus. Jesus saw him and told him to come down because he wanted to have lunch with Zacchaeus. After talking with Jesus, Zacchaeus decided to stop cheating people and even to pay back all the people he had ripped off.

What About You?

• How do you feel when you have been dishonest with someone?
• When have you made things right with someone you have cheated?

Talkin' About It

Ask God to show you things in your life that you need to change. Ask him to help you make things right with your friends and family.

The Son of Man has come to seek and to save people who are lost.

Luke 19:10

Read 1 Corinthians 12:12-28

Have you ever been part of a team? Baseball? Basketball? Football? Soccer? How about a team that is putting on a play or singing a concert? Another kind of team is one that works on a project for a school class. What happens to a team if some members don't do their part of the work? Can a baseball team play well if only 1 or 2 players are trying, and the others are sitting down? What if only 2 singers sing a concert, and all the others take a nap?

Each part of a team is important.

You are part of God's family if you have accepted Jesus as your Savior. As a member of God's family, you have a job to do for him. That job is important to God's work on earth. If you don't do what you're supposed to do, the rest of the team can't work as smoothly. The followers of Jesus you read about this week each found a way to do what Jesus wanted them to do. Be creative and serve God.

What About You?

• How do you feel about having a job to do for Jesus?
• When have you felt you were definitely doing something for him?

Talkin' About It

Thank God that you can do work for him. Ask him to show you ways to serve him.

Work as a Team

You are Christ's body and each of you is an individual part of it.

1 Corinthians 12:27

Ya Get Back What Ya Give Out

Read Ephesians 4:25-32

*S*tomp! Stomp! Slam!!!
"I hear Hurricane Donni is home," Dad said.
Mom sighed, "She is always so unhappy these days. I don't know what she is so angry about. She doesn't seem to like being with us anymore." That was an understatement. Donni had nothing kind to say to anyone in her family, especially her brothers and sisters. They dreaded having her around these days.

Would you like to be treated the way you treat others?

The best guideline for how to live together is to treat other people the way you would like them to treat you. Everyone has good days and bad days. But, you don't want other people to be angry with you for no reason, to lie to you or cheat you—so don't do those things to them.

What About You?

• How well do you get along with others?
• Is it easier to get along with friends or family members? Why?

Talkin' About It

Ask God for his help in getting along with others. Ask him to make you strong enough and patient enough to treat others the way you would like them to treat you.

Everyone must live in hamony, be sympathetic, love each other, have compassion, and be humble. I Peter 3:8

Read Ephesians 5:1-5

Beth admired everything about Amy Grant. She loved Amy's music, her hair, her choice of clothes. In fact, Beth admired Amy Grant so much that she tried to be just like her. She copied Amy's clothing styles, wore her hair like Amy's, and even tried to talk like Amy. Beth knew all the words to all of Amy Grant's songs.

Imitation is the sincerest form of flattery.

It's OK to have heroes, but the best choice of someone to copy is God. Study God to see what he is like. Does he keep bad thoughts in his mind? Does he say bad words or mean things about others? Be kind and loving in all you do, because this is the way God would act. People who act like God are the ones who will be welcomed into God's kingdom. But, people who enjoy being mean and ugly will have no place in God's kingdom.

What About You?

• Is there someone you try to imitate? Who is it?
• How can you learn how to copy God?

Talkin' About It

Ask God to help you learn more about him so you can copy his behavior. Thank him that you can learn about him from his Word.

Carbon Copy

Imitate God, since you are the children he loves.

Ephesians 5:1

Light Up My Life

Read Ephesians 5:8-14

Jamie read through the list of supplies he was going to need for the coming school year. When he came to *solar calculator,* he stopped. *What is a solar calculator?* he wondered. He asked Dad to explain and found out that a solar calculator has a little panel on it that collects light. Then, that light is turned into power to make the calculator work. Without light, the calculator doesn't calculate.

Kind of like a Christian, huh?

People who know God live differently from those who don't know him. Where does the power come from to do that? God. He gives the power for Christians to be different from those around them. A Christian stands out beause he doesn't try to be like those who don't know God. He is like a light for those around him, showing them what God is like.

What About You?

• How are you different from your friends who don't know God?

• Are you tempted to be like non-Christians? How do you keep from doing that?

Talkin' About It

Tell God you want to be different from those who don't know him. Ask him to give you power to live the way he wants you to live.

Be very careful how you live. Don't live like foolish people but like wise people.

Ephesians 5:15

Read Ephesians 5:15-20

I thought I was just coming to a sleep-over, thought Mary. *How did things get so out of control?* Mary had looked forward to Betty's birthday sleep-over for weeks. Betty's group of friends were popular, and Mary was thrilled to be included in their party. It was late when everyone got settled down in their sleeping bags, then Betty pulled out the magazines full of pictures of naked men. Mary had to make a choice—pretend to be asleep, say "No thanks, I don't want to look," or just join the group.

Which choice shows a love for God?

Everyday is full of choices: be happy, do homework, what to wear, what to do. You don't even realize you're making some choices because they have become habit for you. One wise choice is to spend your time with people who love God. Choose to find out how God wants you to live. Then choose to show God's love to those around you by the way you live.

What About You?

• When was a time you made a good choice?
• When was a time you made a bad choice?

Talkin' About It

Ask God to help you make good choices. Thank him for the help he gives you.

It's Your Choice!

Live in love as Christ also loved us.

Ephesians 5:2

I'm Sick of Obeying!

Read Ephesians 6:1-3

"I'll be glad when I'm grown up and don't have to obey anyone!" Cindy shouted. She thought her parents had too many rules. They told her she was too young to date, couldn't hang out with Elissa cause she was a bad influence, had to keep her room clean, do her homework, not wear certain clothes, and on and on. Life was just one big RULE!

Obedience doesn't end when you grow up!

Guess what? There is always someone to obey. When you're grown up, bosses tell you what to do. The law sets up rules. The biggest obedience is to God. Keeping his rules will give you a long and happy life because he loves you even more than your parents do. Learning to obey starts at home.

What About You?

• What rules do you have trouble obeying?
• How do you show respect to your parents?

Talkin' About it

There are times when obeying is no fun. Ask God to help you with those times. Ask him to help you respect and honor your parents.

Children, always obey your parents. This is pleasing to the Lord.

Colossians 3:20

Read Ephesians 6:10-25

Jessie gasped and closed her eyes as the drug czar shot the policeman right in the heart. "I hate it when the hero dies," Jessie said. Dina agreed as they watched the movie hero fall to the ground. But, suddenly about 50 policemen burst into the room and captured the bad guy. Then the "dead" policeman stood up! He was wearing a bullet-proof vest and though shaken, was not hurt by the gunshot to the chest.

Are you wearing your bullet-proof vest?

Well, the Bible actually calls it the armor of God. You didn't think you had to fight the battle against Satan alone, did you? God has prepared the shield of faith for you to carry. You can wear the vest of truth, the breastplate of righteousness, and the helmet of salvation. You have God's Word which you can use as a sword. You are totally protected when wearing God's armor. Above all else, use your built-in walkie-talkie—prayer. Keep in close touch with God.

What About You?

• How do the different pieces of God's armor protect you?
• How do you get this suit of armor to wear?

Talkin' About It

Thank God for his protection. Ask him to help you learn to wear this protection and to teach you how to use it.

Receive your power from the Lord and from his mighty strength.

Ephesians 6:10

Wear Your Life Protector

Don't Lose Your Temper!

Read Ephesians 4:26

How many times a day do you get mad? Do you usually get angry with friends or family members? When you get mad, does everyone know it because you shout and scream, or do you just clam up and not talk to anyone? When you lose your temper, only bad things will result. Things said in anger really hurt. Even if you apologize and chalk it up to temper, the way you make a friend feel by your harsh words is not easily forgotten.

When you get mad, watch your mouth.

Everyone gets mad because everyone wants things to go his own way. We're all a bit selfish on some points. The bottom line is: don't say things that are going to hurt others and make them feel crummy about themselves. When you are angry, go talk to the person who made you angry and calmly settle the problem.

What About You?

• What makes you angry?
• How do you usually act when you are angry?

Talkin' About It

Ask God to help you keep your temper in control. Ask him to keep you from saying mean things to others.

Don't go to bed angry.

Ephesians 4:26

Read Mark 8:31

Wow. If I had known what this day was gonna be like, I'd have pulled the covers over my head and stayed in bed all day! Kendra thought, staring at the surprise Spanish quiz. Kendra wished she could do what the hero in the popular "Back to the Future" movies did—go back in time to change what would happen in the future. Then she would have studied Spanish last night.

Jesus knew what his future held.

He knew it wasn't going to be pleasant. In fact, he told his disciples three different times that some of the big shots in the nation and the church were going to do terrible things to him. They would end up killing him. Sounds like a good reason to hide, doesn't it? But Jesus didn't. He went through every rotten thing because he loves people and wanted to make a way for us to come to heaven. Besides, he knew he wouldn't stay dead. He told his friends that he would come back to life three days after he died.

What About You?

• How do you feel about Jesus —realizing that he knew what the future held for him, and he went through it willingly?
• Does what happened to Jesus mean anything to you personally?

Talkin' About It

Thank Jesus for what he went through. Thank God for his plan that made a way to heaven for you.

A Crystal Ball

The Son of Man would have to suffer a lot. . . . He would be killed, but on the third day he would come back to life.

Luke 9:22

A Hero's Welcome

Read Matthew 21:1-11

Crowds of people jammed the airport. They were shouting and cheering. When the World Championship baseball team came off the plane, they got a hero's welcome. Tomorrow there would be a parade with the team riding in fancy convertibles, people would line the streets, cheering again. Everyone loves heroes. But, the team knows that if the next year doesn't bring as much success, that same crowd will boo and jeer.

Jesus had a hero's welcome.

When he rode a donkey into Jerusalem, people lined the streets and cheered for him. They called him a king and shouted, "Hooray for God! Hooray for the Son of God!" Some of the fanatics even laid their clothes on the ground for Jesus' donkey to ride over. Jesus was their hero! Jesus knew their cheers didn't mean much. In a few short days, he knew those same people would be shouting for his death.

What About You?

• When you say you love Jesus do you mean it?
• How do you think it felt to hear people cheering for him, when Jesus knew they didn't really mean it?

Talkin' About It

Tell God how you feel about him. Ask him to help you learn to love him more.

Hosanna! Blessed is the one who comes in the name of the Lord!

John 12:13

Read Matthew 26:14-16

Life is good, thought Cheryl. She had lots of friends and a special best friend. But, one afternoon Cheryl heard two kids talking in the bathroom. They were laughing about a juicy bit of gossip they had heard—about her! That was bad enough, but even worse the creeps got their info from Cheryl's best friend!

Have you ever been let down by someone you thought you could trust? Feels pretty crummy doesn't it? When a "friend" stabs you in the back, it hurts more than if a stranger does because a friend should always be on your side and support you.

Is your best friend named Judas?

Some of the church leaders were jealous of Jesus because he was too popular with the people, and he had too much power. They began looking for ways to get rid of him. These creeps found a weak link in the chain of Jesus' friends—Judas. For a lousy 30 pieces of silver, Judas turned Jesus over to them. Judas arranged to take soldiers with him to a garden. When they saw which man he kissed on the cheek, they would know that was Jesus.

What About You?

• Why were the church leaders out to get Jesus?
• How do you betray Jesus in your life?

Talkin' About It

Tell God you're sorry for ways you betray him. Ask him to help you be true to him. Thank him for what Jesus went through for you.

They offered him 30 silver coins. From then on, he looked for a chance to betray Jesus.

Matthew 26:15-16

Who Can You Trust?

Saying Goodbye

Read Matthew 26:17-30

Becca swallowed hard. Every time she thought about this being the last day of camp, her eyes filled with tears. It was gonna be hard to say goodbye to her new friends. They were all from other states, so who knew when they'd see each other again? They exchanged addresses and phone numbers and promised to write every week. As they huddled together, the girls giggled over the silly things that had happened during the week. Then it was time to go. Becca hugged each friend and told her how special she was.

Saying goodbye is never easy.

Jesus gathered his disciples around him for one last meal together. They celebrated the Passover Feast in Jerusalem. But the disciples didn't know it was their last supper with Jesus until he told them that one of them was going to turn him in to his enemies. Each of his friends wondered how anyone could do that. Each of them wondered, *Could it be me?*

What About You?

• How do you think the disciples felt about someone betraying Jesus?
• How do you think the disciples felt about Jesus saying he was going to die?

Talkin' About It

Thank God for Jesus' death and the pathway it opened for you to be able to go to heaven.

This is my blood, the blood of the promise. It is poured out for many people.

Mark 14:24

Read Luke 23:2-49

The movie hero lay on the floor, gasping for breath as the flood waters rose around him. Ginny sat on the edge of her chair, every muscle tight with anticipation. *Would he make it? Would the rescuers come in time?* Suddenly the screen went blank, then "To Be Continued" flashed across the screen. Ginny screamed, "I want to know the outcome RIGHT NOW!"

Jesus' death ended with "To Be Continued."

The same people who cheered when Jesus came into Jerusalem a few days before now shouted, "Crucify Him!" When they had the chance to request a prisoner's release, they chose for a murderer to be freed. Jesus was taken away by soldiers to be beaten and nailed to a cross. But, even as he was dying on the cross, he forgave the sins of a robber being crucified next to him. Jesus died on the cross out of love for mankind. But, the story didn't end with Jesus' death—it was to be continued.

What About You?

• Why did the crowd that cheered Jesus before, now want him to die?
• Have you accepted Jesus as your Savior?

Talkin' About It

Thank God that his plan didn't end with Jesus' death. Thank him that this was one time it was good to have the story continued.

*G*od loved the world this way: He gave his only Son so that everyone who believes in him will not die but will have eternal life.
John 3:16

To Be Continued . . .

A Man's Gotta Do What a Man's Gotta Do

Read Luke 23:50-56

Jered's palms were sweaty, his head hurt. He argued back and forth with himself. But his argument always came back to "What's the right thing to do?" Sometimes you gotta do what you gotta do. Jered knew that a bunch of guys had cheated on the math test. They got the answers from the math teacher's student assistant. He knew everyone would hate him, but he said no to cheating with them, and he turned them in to the teacher.

You gotta be able to live with yourself.

Jesus was dead. When he died, the sky went black and the heavy curtain in the temple ripped. That made some people believe that he was the Son of God. Joseph of Arimathea did a brave thing after Jesus' death. Joseph was a member of the group of Jews that condemned Jesus to death, but he didn't agree with them. He asked Pilate to give him Jesus' body, then he buried Jesus in a brand new tomb which he owned. Joseph could have gotten into big-time trouble for this. Council members weren't supposed to believe in Jesus. Joseph took the chance.

What About You?

• How could you show courage in your faith?
• Does it matter a lot what other people think of you?

Talkin' About It

Thank God for examples of courage such as Joseph of Arimathea. Ask him to help your courage for him to increase.

After he took [the body] down from the cross, he wrapped it in linen. Then he laid the body in a tomb cut in rock, a tomb in which no one had ever been buried. Luke 23:53

Review Scripture from past week

The story of Jesus' last few days on earth is more than a history lesson. These things really happened. Some kids blow off what Jesus did. They say, "Oh that's nice," or "Some people really need that," or even "So what?"

Here's what—he died because he loves YOU.

God's plan came together. He and Jesus knew exactly what they were doing. It all began with Adam and Eve's sin. The first time God was disobeyed, the door to heaven slammed shut. But, God knew the best thing for mankind was to be in heaven with him. So, he came up with this plan of love that would open the door of heaven to people again. Jesus came to earth knowing what he would have to go through. It wasn't pretty and it wasn't make-believe. But, he did it because he loves you.

What About You?

• Have you faced the fact that this plan is for you? Have you accepted Jesus as your Savior?
• There's no other way to heaven. Is there someone you need to tell about Jesus?

Talkin' About It

Thank God for his plan of love. Thank him that the door to heaven was reopened by Jesus' death and resurrection.

God sent his Son into the world, not to condemn the world, but to save the world.

John 3:17

Face Reality

VICTORY

Read Matthew 28:1-8

Forty-five seconds left. It seemed to Laurin that the clock was crawling. Her team had only a one point lead, and the other girls had the ball. The crowd was roaring and the cheerleaders were screaming, "V-I-C-T-O-R-Y. Victory, victory, that's our cry!" Laurin watched as the other team threw the ball down the court and worked it toward the basket. But, just then the buzzer sounded and Laurin's team won!

Victory is the point of the game, right?

The bad guys thought they had won when they killed Jesus. But remember, the story was to be continued. In the second half Jesus won! He rose from the dead just like he said he would. Jesus' victory was over the grave and over sin. He is alive and back in heaven, helping God take care of us. When you believe in what Jesus did, you have victory over death, too because of the promise of eternal life.

What About You?

• Would God's plan have been complete without this second half?
• How do you think Jesus' friends felt when they heard he was missing from the tomb?

Talkin' About It

Yippee! Celebrate this victory with God. Thank him that Jesus is alive!

He's not here. He has been brought back to life as he said.

Matthew 28:6

Read John 20:11-18

March 18, 1995 a two-word fax: "I'm back" sent chills rippling through the sport world. Michael Jordan, undoubtably the best basketball player ever to play the game, was coming out of retirement. His return was greeted with amazement, disbelief, cheers, and relief. For Chicago Bulls fans it felt right to have M. J. back in the red and black uniform.

Jesus' comeback was even more incredible.

The women who discovered that Jesus' body was missing from the tomb ran back to town; all except one. Mary stayed behind, overcome with grief. When she turned around and saw a man she thought was the gardener, she asked him where he had put Jesus' body. When he spoke her name, Mary realized the man was Jesus. He was back! Jesus would be with his people forever now.

What About You?

• How do you think Mary felt when she realized Jesus was standing there?
• Why did Jesus have to come back to life for the plan to be complete?

Talkin' About It

Thank God for Jesus' complete victory. Thank him that Jesus is with you always.

I will still be with you for a little while. Then I'll go to the one who sent me.

John 7:33

I'm Back

Look Beyond Yourself

Read Luke 24:13-35

Karl must have eaten dinner, but he didn't remember a single bite. When the family sat down to the table, his parents announced that they were separating and would probably get a divorce. Karl felt like he'd been kicked in the stomach. Nothing about this seemed right or normal.

That must be how the two guys on the road to Emmaus felt.

They were walking to Emmaus. As they walked, they talked about what had happened in Jerusalem—Jesus' death and the rumors that he was alive again. A stranger came up and walked along with them. He asked what they were talking about. They thought he must be the only guy in the country that didn't know what had happened. When they got to Emmaus the men invited the stranger in to eat. When he gave thanks for the food, they suddenly knew: HE WAS JESUS! They had been so caught up in their grief that they didn't recognize him. As soon as they did, he disappeared.

What About You?

• When have you been caught up in your own problems?
• How do you think the two men felt when they recognized Jesus?

Talkin' About It

Thank God for the miracle of Jesus' appearances after his resurrection. Thank him for the encouragement and excitement of realizing that Jesus was and is alive.

The Lord has really come back to life.

Luke 24:34

Read John 20:24-29

People from Missouri are known for needing to have things proven to them. In fact, Missouri's nickname is the "Show-me State." That means that you can't just tell a Missourian that something has happened and expect him to believe—you gotta show proof.

Wonder if Thomas was from Missouri?

Jesus had appeared to the disciples a couple of times since he came back to life, but Thomas was not with them when Jesus came. They told Thomas all about it, but Thomas wouldn't believe because he hadn't seen Jesus himself. So, one day when all the disciples, including Thomas, were together, Jesus came. He let Thomas touch the wounds in his hands and side. That's what it took. After that Thomas believed Jesus was alive. Jesus was glad Thomas believed, but he was even happier about the people who believed without needing to see him.

What About You?

• Who was Jesus talking about who believed without seeing?
• Do you believe that Jesus is alive?

Talkin' About It

Thank God for his patience with those who do not believe right away. Thank him for taking the time to show Thomas the truth.

Blessed are those who haven't seen me but believe.

John 20:29

Keep On Keeping On

Read John 21:4-14

Devona couldn't seem to get her life on track. She was pretty screwed up. When she admitted to the counselor that her dad had abused her, she thought it would help. But, it didn't. It was hard for her to get excited about anything, including schoolwork or friends. She just didn't see the point.

You gotta keep on plugging away.

Peter and his friends were trying to get their lives back to normal after Jesus' death. They were fishermen before Jesus called them to follow him, so they went back to being fishermen. One morning they brought their boat in after fishing all night without catching anything. A man was standing on shore who told them to drop their fishnet on the other side of the boat. They were be and didn't have the energy to argue. So, they dropped the ne and it came up so full of fish that it nearly tore when they tried to pull it up. The man on shore was Jesus! He helped them get the fish in and then cooked breakfast for his friends.

What About You?

• Do you think Peter and his friends were still discouraged after Jesus helped them? Why?
• Was it easier for them to get life back to normal after that? Why?

Talkin' About It

Thank God for Jesus' appearances to his followers. Thank him for the ways he encourage you today.

They knew he was the Lord.

John 21:12

Read Acts 1:1-11

A distinguished looking man in a dark suit opened the airport locker and took out a briefcase. It had a tapeplayer inside, which he clicked on. The voice on the tape said, "Your mission, should you be willing to accept is . . ." Once the mission was given the voice said the tape would self-destruct.

Jesus left a mission for his followers.

After Jesus' resurrection he spent some time on earth, showing his followers that he was really alive again. When it was time for Jesus to go back to heaven, he told his followers that the Holy Spirit would be coming to give them God's power to help them live for him. He told them that he had a mission for his followers. That mission was for them to go all over the world and tell people about him. Right after Jesus told his followers this, he began to rise up into heaven. He disappeared into heaven as they watched!

What About You?

• Do you feel like you have a mission from Jesus?
• Was the mission Jesus gave his disciples *only* for them? Why or why not?

Talkin' About It

Thank God for the mission his people have in the world. Ask him to help you discover how to serve him.

Your Job, Should You Be Willing . . .

You will be my witnesses to testify about me in Jerusalem, throughout Judea and Samaria, and to the ends of the earth.

Acts 1:8

You Win!

Read 1 Corinthians 15:3-4

When a school sports team is having a winning season, the student body gets more and more excited. Larger crowds come out to the games and the cheering is louder than ever. Posters plastered all over the school encourage good games and victory. If the team should win it all and be state champions, each student in the school claims the joy of being Number One.

Jesus' victory makes you Number One, too.

Jesus won over death. He put Satan in his place and showed that no one is more powerful than God. Jesus hung around on earth in his resurrected body until his followers believe that he was truly alive. Then, h gave them a job to do and he took off for heaven. Each member of God's family can claim Jesus' victory, too because each of them will win over death someday. The door to heaven i open to each of them. Jesus dic it all out of love. Not love for a faceless world of humans—love for you personally.

What About You?

• What are you going to do with his love?
• Have you decided to follow Jesus?

Talkin' About It

Thank God for the incredible plan that allows you to look fo ward to heaven. Thank him for Jesus' victory.

Christ died to take away our sins as the Scriptures predicted. He was placed in a tomb. He was brought back to life on the third day as the Scriptures predicted.
1 Corinthians 15:3-4

Read Acts 9:36-42

"Laura, will you help me fold these clothes?" Mom asked. "I've got to be at a meeting in twenty minutes, and I'm running out of time."

Laura rolled her eyes and gave a huge sigh. She obviously didn't want to give any help to Mom.

Her attitude didn't go unnoticed as Mom said, "Never mind. I'd rather be late for the meeting than put up with your attitude."

Great way to win friends and influence people.

Laura should hear about Dorcas. Dorcas had friends coming out the wahzoo because she was a kind person who enjoyed doing nice things for other people. Dorcas' thing was sewing, so she made robes and clothes for people all the time. When Dorcas died unexpectedly, her friends were really sad. They sent for Peter and asked if he could do anything. He sure could, well actually God could. God helped Peter raise Dorcas back to life. Her friends were so happy to have her back. Many of them put their faith in God because of what happened!

What About You?

• How willing are you to help when your parents ask?
• What things can you do to show God's love to others?

Talkin' About It

Thank God for people who serve others, such as Dorcas. Ask him to show you ways to help others and to give you the right attitude about doing it.

If this is the way God loved us, we must also love each other.

1 John 4:11

Doing Nice Stuff for Others

Doin' Little Things

Read Matthew 25:31-40

Mom and her stupid contest, thought Jerry.

Mom's contest was to get Jerry and his brother John to keep their rooms clean. So, for one week, Mom checked their rooms everyday. At the end of the week, the one who had kept his room the cleanest was to be served breakfast in bed for one week by the loser. Guess who lost? You got it, Jerry. So, he's serving John breakfast in bed. *I hate being a stinkin' waiter,* Jerry fumed

Hey, Jer, serving others is a way of serving God.

Do you have trouble thinking what a kid could do to serve God? Jesus said that anytime you give a drink to the thirsty, or food to the hungry, kindness to newcomers, or clothes to the homeless, you are serving God. Being nice to strangers, visiting elderly people, even doing errands for them is serving God. Doing these kinds of things for others is the same as doing them for Jesus.

What About You?

• What things have you done to serve others?
• Do you enjoy doing things for others? How's your attitude?

Talkin' About It

Honesty time. Are you too selfish to want to help others? Ask God to help you work on your attitude.

The King will answer them, "I can guarantee this truth: Whatever you did for one of my brothers or sisters, no matter how unimportant they seemed, you did it for me."
Matthew 25:40

Read Mark 12:41-44

Way back in 1908 a marathon runner from Italy was leading the Olympic marathon race. But, he had just about given his all. The young man ran into the Stadium to circle the track on the last leg of his run, but he was so tired that he began running the wrong way. The officials showed him he was going the wrong way, but the poor guy was so exhausted that he fell down, got up, fell down, got up, fell down, got up, and fell down again. He had given it everything he had, and he couldn't make it across the finish line. The officials helped him finish the race, but that disqualified him, and he lost the Olympic gold medal.

Sometimes giving your all is good.

Jesus noticed a woman who gave her all. All her money that is. Jesus and some of his friends were in the temple, watching rich people give lots of money in the offering box. Right after that, this woman came and dropped in 2 measley coins. Jesus turned to his disciples and pointed out that she really gave more than the rich man; he could afford what he gave, but she gave all the money she had.

What About You?

• Do you give any of your money to God's work?
• How much of your time and energy do you give to God's work?

Talkin' About It

Thank God for the chance to give money to his church or missionary work. Ask him to help you remember to give.

All of them have given what they could spare. But she, in her poverty, has given everything she had to live on.

Mark 12:44

Giving your All

Be a Little Flexible

Read Acts 8:26-39

Dan hopped out of bed. He had no plans for the day, and he was looking forward to bumming around. So, when his dad came in and suggested that Dan help him clean the garage and wash the windows, Dan was ticked. "Come on, Dad, I just want a day off," he complained. Dan knew this was the best weekend to help Dad, But he sure wasn't excited about changing his plans.

Good thing Philip wasn't that inflexible.

It wasn't like Philip wasn't interested in serving God. He already was serving God by going around teaching about him. So, when an angel told him to change his plans and go to a certain place, Philip could have said, "Nope, I'm busy serving God here." Good thing he didn't. Philip went where the angel told him to go, and he got to explain the Scriptures to a man who was reading them but couldn't understand them. He even got to baptize the man. Philip must have been happy that he changed his plans.

What About You?

• How flexible are you when your plans are changed?
• Have you ever felt like God changed your plans? When?

Talkin' About It

Ask God to help you be more flexible and by doing so to have chances to serve him.

Philip told the official the Good News about Jesus.

Acts 8:35

Read Acts 6:8-15; 7:54-60

Manny is a Christian and he goes to church every week. He reads his Bible and prays every night. He gives offerings in church every week. But, you know what? None of Manny's friends at school know that Manny is a Christian. There's a very good reason for that—listen to what Manny says: "I'm afraid that the guys at school will tease me, or think I'm a sissy, or just in general make my life miserable if they find out I'm a Christian. So, I keep it quiet."

Manny needs some of Stephen's bravery.

Stephen loved God very much. He was always talking about God and teaching people about him. But, the guys that didn't love God tried to shut Stephen up. They threw him in jail, and they told lies about him. But, that didn't stop Stephen. Finally, they decided to kill him. But, Stephen wasn't afraid. While they were throwing stones at him, his face looked like an angel's, and he asked God to forgive the people who were killing him. Stephen's courage helped him serve God right up until the minute he died.

What About You?

• Do your friends know that you believe in God?
• How could you have courage for God?

Talkin' About It

Ask God to help you be brave in little ways and then to let that courage grow, so you can be brave in big things.

Brave Enough to Serve

So Stephen said, "Look, I see heaven opened and the Son of Man in the position of authority that God has given him!"
Acts 7:56

Gettin' a Second Chance

Read Acts 15:36-41;
Colossians 4:10-11

Kyle blew it. He had totally broken Mom and Dad's rules about what time to be home and where it was or wasn't OK for him to hang out. They would probably never trust him again. The hard part was that Kyle was really sorry for his disobedience. He had learned a lesson from it. But, Mom and Dad were very disappointed in him. He'd probably not get to go out with his friends again 'til he was 18 years old.

Second chances happen once in a while.

John Mark got one. He had gone on a working trip with Paul and Barnabas. They traveled to different cities and started churches. But, for some reason, in the middle of the trip, John Mark went home. This didn't set well with Paul. So, when Barnabas wanted to bring John Mark on another trip some time later, Paul said, "No way." H felt so strongly about it that he and Barnabas split up and went on their own trips. But, a while later, Paul did give John Mark a second chance, and he became good friend of Paul and an important part of Paul's ministry.

What About You?

• When have you gotten a second chance after you've blown i
• How good are you about givir others a second chance?

Talkin' About It

Everyone needs a second chance sometime. Thank God for all the chances he gives you to do better. Tell him you want to be tha fair with your friends and family.

Whenever you pray, forgive anything you have against anyone. Then your Father in heaven will forgive your failures.

Mark 11:25

Read Galatians 6:2

You've read six stories this week of six different ways people served God. Did you read them and think, *Oh yeah, that's cool. These make great stories, but they don't have much to do with me. I'm just a kid.*

Serving God isn't something you get licensed for at 21 years of age.

Anyone can serve. Serving God really begins with an attitude of the heart. Telling God that you are available and asking him to show you ways to serve him is a good place to begin. Serving God can be something as simple as being kind to someone new or someone other kids blow off. It can be donating your time to work in a food pantry or nursing home. You might be able to serve by working in the nursery at church or playing with a little kid who doesn't have a dad at home. The ball is in your court. Ask God to make you aware of opportunities around you.

What About You?

• Are there things you do to serve God already? What are they?
• What are some other ways you could serve him?

Talkin' About It

Tell God you love him and want to serve him. Ask him to make you aware of ways to do so. Ask him to give you courage and strength to serve him.

Serve your

Help carry each other's burdens. In this way you will follow Christ's teachings.

Galatians 6:2

Fill 'Er Up

Read Acts 2:1-4

Monica and her mom held their breath as the car rolled up to the gas pump. It died just as it got close enough for the hose to reach the car's gas tank. *Whew, at least we didn't have to walk. Now we can put in more gas and head out shopping,* Monica thought.

No gas means no power.

When Jesus left earth to go back to heaven, he arranged to leave fuel or power for his church. All his followers were together in a room when there was suddenly the sound of a strong wind blowing, then what looked like tiny flames appeared above each person. That was Jesus' gift of power—the Holy Spirit. The Holy Spirit would stay with each person and be their power to live for God.

What About You?

• Does the Holy Spirit still stay with Jesus' followers?
• How is the Holy Spirit fuel for the believer?

Talkin' About It

Thank God for the Holy Spirit that stays with you always and helps you live for God.

Each of you must be baptized in the name of Jesus Christ so that your sins will be forgiven. Then you will receive the Holy Spirit as a gift. Acts 2:38

Read Acts 3:1-10

It was an incredible sight. The stars twinkled in the dark, Norwegian night. At the top of an enormous ski slope, a lone skier stood poised, ready to zoom down, holding the flame that would light the Olympic torch. The flame had traveled across many countries, passed from runner to runner. Now the young Norwegian came down the ski slope with the flame held high. At the bottom, he passed the torch on to another person who ran up the steps and dipped the torch into the huge basin to light the Olympic flame.

The torch was passed from runner to runner.

One man couldn't complete the entire job himself. When Jesus left earth, he wanted his work to continue. So, he passed the torch on to his followers. The Holy Spirit came to be the power for the work to continue. Jesus' followers, like Peter and John, carried on Jesus' work of telling people about God, healing people, and even raising dead people back to life. Peter and John wanted everyone to know and praise God.

What About You?

• How seriously did Jesus' followers take his work?
• How do you feel about the "torch" being passed to you?

Talkin' About It

Being part of God's church means doing his work. Ask him to show you what to do. Ask him to give you courage and strength to do it.

All the believers were filled with the Holy Spirit.

Acts 2:4

Passing the Torch

Trouble Won't Stop Us

Read Acts 5:17-42

Trisha was a member of the church puppet team. The team performed musical programs with puppets, drama, and mime. But, now what? Everything they had was stolen; puppets, props, costumes. Should they give up? Did God want them to stop doing their programs? *No,* thought Trisha, *God wouldn't let it stop this way. We've got to keep going. Trouble won't stop us!*

That's about the same thing the members of the first church said.

The leaders of the old, established church didn't like the energy and excitement of these upstart Christians. The old guys didn't believe in Jesus and what he had done. So, they tried to shut the Christians up. They threw some of them in jail, but an angel set them free. Then they threatened to kill them, but one wise old guy stopped them. They ended up beating them, then letting them go. But, none of that trouble stopped the Christians. They had a message to tell—and they kept right on telling it.

What About You?

• What would you do if someone threatened to beat you for talking about Jesus?
• Where would the church be today if those Christians had stopped talking about God?

Talkin' About It

Ask God to help you hang on during hard times. Ask him to keep you from getting discouraged.

Scripture also says that by the authority of Jesus people must be told to turn to God and change the way they think and act so that their sins will be forgiven. This must be told to people from all nations.

Luke 24:47

Read Acts 2:42-47; 4:32-37

"We've been asked to help a refugee family get settled here in the U.S." Pastor Ron announced. "The family consists of a mom and dad, a teenaged son, and a preteen daughter. They escaped with the clothes on their backs and nothing more. So, they need clothes, coats, just anything that you need to live. If you've got anything you can donate, bring it to my house and we'll deliver everything together."

The early church knew how to share.

The members of the early church were as close as a family. When one of the Christians needed something, someone came to his aid, even if he had to sell his possessions in order to help. They made sure that no one in the church was needy. The apostles preached about Jesus and everyone was happy being together.

What About You?

• How have other Christians shared with you?
• How does your church help needy people?

Talkin' About It

Ask God to show you how you can help others.

What's Mine Is Yours

The whole group of believers lived in harmony. No one called any of his possessions his own. Instead, they shared everything.
Acts 4:32

That's Impossible!

Read Acts 5:12-16

Jon slumped in a chair with the remote control in hand and hopped from one TV channel to the next. As he zipped through, he noticed a program that looked like a church service. Next time through, he stopped there because he saw the TV minister blowing on a woman. The woman fell to the floor, then stood up shouting, "I'm healed! I'm healed!" *From being blown on? That's impossible*, thought Jon.

Does God give people the power to do miracles today?

In the days of the early church, God gave some of his followers the power to do miracles. They healed sick people and raised some dead people back to life. People heard about this and brought sick friends and relatives to be healed. Some confused people thought that Peter's shadow falling on the sick person had the power to heal. Truth is, God helped his followers heal the sick and raise the dead so that people would believe in God's power and become part of his family.

What About You?

• When have you prayed for a miracle?
• How would you react if you saw someone do a miracle?

Talkin' About It

Thank God for miracles. They still happen today, but usually not by the hand of a human. Ask God to help his people keep doing his work so that more and more people will believe in him.

> *More men and women than ever began to believe in the Lord.*
>
> *Acts 5:14*

Read Acts 13:1-5

Jon continued channel-surfing through all 116 TV channels available to him through the miracle of cable television. He got a kick out of the channels that ran nothing but info-mercials. One guy had invented a new product that supposedly made fat melt from the body. But, instead of putting it in a store, the guy bought time on cable TV and hired a skinny celebrity to say how fantastic his product was. The guy must have felt this was the quickest way to get the news of his product out to the most people.

When you believe in something, you want to tell everyone about it.

The members of the early church totally believed in God's love. They told everyone around them about Jesus, and they did miracles when God gave them the power. When God told them to send Paul and Barnabas out to other countries to tell them about Jesus, the church members were happy to do so. They prayed for these first two missionaries and sent them to talk about God to people who had never heard.

What About You?

• Does your church support missionaries? Do you know who they are and what countries they are in?
• Does being a missionary mean you must go to a foreign country?

Talkin' About It

Pray for the missionaries you know. Ask God to remind you of them daily so you pray for them.

Wherever you go, make disciples of all nations: Baptize them in the name of the Father, and of the Son, and of the Holy Spirit.
Matthew 28:19

Come, See, Go, Tell

What's Your Church Like?

Read Psalm 133

When you need something, who is there to meet your need? Who takes care of you when you are sick? Who gets clothes for you? Who encourages you and teaches you? The answer to each of these questions is probably someone in your family. Even though your family may bug you to the point of craziness, deep down inside you know they love you, and you love them, too.

Your church is a family, too.

God's instructions to the first church were to treat each other like family. That first church is the example for our churches today. Church members should help each other any way they can, whether it's providing food for the sick, helping the elderly with yardwork, or working together to spread the message of God's love. God wants his family members to live together peacefully, care for each other, and do his work.

What About You?

• How do people in your church care for one another?
• How are you involved in your church's work?

Talkin' About It

Thank God for your church and the way the people care for you and your family.

See how good and pleasant it is when brothers and sisters live together in harmony!

Psalm 133:1

Read 1 Corinthians 13:1-4

Mallory used to love it when the class read a book aloud. But, since Gloria-that-doesn't-speak-English had come to school, it wasn't much fun anymore. The rest of the class practically fell asleep while Gloria stumbled over word after word.

Why doesn't she learn English? thought Mallory. *This is so-o-o-o-o boring!*

Some of the kids called Gloria names because she couldn't speak English. Mallory had never actually done that, but she had laughed at their "Gloria jokes."

Mallory is a Christian.

And, she thinks she is a pretty good one. So, what difference could that make to Gloria? Some people may never go to church or read the Bible. Their only idea of what God's love is like comes from watching you. Do you show God's love by being kind and patient with others?

What About You?

• Is impatience a sin?
• Do you try to show love, even if it means being kind and patient when you don't feel like it?

Talkin' About It

Tell God what kinds of things make you impatient. Ask him to help you show his love to others by being kinder and more patient to others. Thank God that he is always patient with you.

If we love each other, God lives in us, and his love is perfected in us.

1 John 4:12

Show Some Kindness

Read 1 Corinthians 13:5

Mallory watched Gloria pick up a lunch tray and go to a corner table by herself. "Come on, Mal," her friends called. Mallory hesitated for just a second. *What if Gloria does eat by herself? It really isn't my problem. The only thing important about Gloria is that she helps the grade curve in English!*

Hang on a second, Mallory.

Put yourself in Gloria's place: new language, new school, new neighborhood, even a new country. If Gloria ever needed a friend, it's now.

It's never easy to go against what our friends are doing, but there comes a time when we all need to stop thinking about ourselves and treat others the way that shows God's love. You know the old Golden Rule—do unto others the way you would have them do unto you.

What About You?

• What do you think Mallory should do now?
• Have you ever been on the receiving end of selfish actions? How did you feel?

Talkin' About It

Being the first one in the crowd to be nice to someone new is not easy. Ask God to help you be strong enough to treat others the way you would want to be treated.

People should be concerned about others and not just about themselves.

1 Corinthians 10:24

Do Unto Others

Read I Corinthians 13:5

"Hey guys, let's ask Gloria to sit with us for lunch today," Mallory suggested quietly. Her friends exploded in laughter. "Come on, she's all by herself." When they saw that she was serious, Mallory's friends stopped laughing.

Jenna, their unofficial leader spoke up, "If you want to eat with that geek, go ahead. We're not!" Then the whole group left, giggling as they walked away.

Now what?

Mallory could be mad at them for treating her like this. She could be mad at Gloria, who has no idea what is going on. Of course, neither would help anything. Mallory has taken the first step toward showing God's love to Gloria. Getting angry at her friends would be a step backward. Getting angry and holding grudges only hurts you. Mal knows this is her chance to show God's love, not keep score.

What About You?

• Do you think you are a patient person? Can you think of an example?
• How do you feel when someone is angry with you?

Talkin' About It

It's not easy to keep your temper when you've been treated wrongly. When that happens to you, tell God about it and ask for his help to keep showing love.

*A*bove all, love each other warmly, because love covers many sins.

I Peter 4:8

Grudges Don't Help Anyone

Whatever Happened to Fairness?

Read I Corinthians 13:6

Mallory was still smarting a bit from her friends' treatment as she changed into her gym clothes. When she went around the corner to the gym, she saw something that gave her chills. All her friends were huddled together near Gloria. They were saying mean things about Gloria and laughing like crazy. Poor Gloria might not know what they were saying, but she could tell it wasn't nice!

This wasn't fair.

Gloria hadn't done anything to deserve this. Mallory knew her friends were acting like this just because of her suggestion to have Gloria eat lunch with them. She quietly walked over to Gloria and stood beside her.

Showing love means taking a stand. God's kind of love wants everyone to be treated fairly. Mallory knew Gloria didn't deserve ridicule for just being new to school or born in a different country.

What About You?

• When have you seen someone picked on for no reason?
• Does it bother you when people are treated unfairly? How about when you are?

Talkin' About It

Most people have a sense of fairness and want everyone to be treated right. If you have trouble with this, talk to God about it. Especially tell him if there is one person that you kind of like to see get in trouble. Work on your attitude toward that person.

> *Love means that we live by doing what he commands. We were commanded to live in love.* 2 John 6

Read 1 Corinthians 13:7

Mallory took a deep breath and looked at her friends. "Come on, guys, this isn't fair. You're really mad at me, not Gloria." she said quietly. Her friends stopped laughing and looked straight at her. Mallory took another deep breath and turned to Gloria, "Come on, let's go to class."

Wow, that was brave!

Mallory showed God's love all around—by protecting Gloria from the girls' mean comments, and by not attacking her friends for their behavior. She showed what a loyal friend she is. Each of her friends is probably thinking about that right now. Everyone wants a friend who will stand up for them when others are saying mean or untrue things.

What About You?

• When have you been a loyal friend—or needed a loyal friend?
• How do you feel about a friend who has stood up for you?

Talkin' About It

Mallory showed a lot of strength today. Do you think you could be as strong? Ask God to help you be the kind of friend that you would want for yourself.

Shield with Love

What matters is a faith that expresses itself through love.

Galatians 5:6

Staying Put

Read 1 Corinthians 13:8

The game of the day in gym class was volleyball. That was Jenna's specialty. She slammed and spiked her team to victory. When class was over, Mallory said, "Great game, Jenna. You're really good!"

Jenna looked at her suspiciously. But, when she saw that Mallory was sincere, she softened up. "Thanks. I really like volleyball. I hope I make the team next year."

"Well, if you play like today, no problem," Mallory answered.

"You're walking home with us today, right?" Jenna said casually.

Mallory looked toward Gloria. "Well, I . . ."

"OK, OK, Gloria can come, too," Jenna spouted in exasperation. Everyone laughed. "Look, I'm—we're sorry, right guys?" Jenna said softly. "If you want us to get to know Gloria, we'll try. You're to good a friend to lose."

Love won!

True love that comes from the heart never fails. It jus goes on and on and on.

What About You?

• How do you think Gloria fee about Mallory and her friends?
• Who do you love?

Talkin' About It

Thank God for his love that never changes. Thank him for the people in your life who lov you.

I may speak in the languages of humans and of angels. But if I don't have love, . . . I am nothing. 1 Corinthians 13:1-2

Read 1 Corinthians 13:1-8

What if you play basketball better than anyone ever has? What if you have the most beautiful singing voice that has ever been heard? What if you have the most complex scientific mind since Einstein? If you have all these abilities and gifts, but don't really love others, you don't really have anything.

The Bible says the most important gift is love.

You know how great it feels to know someone loves you and is loyal to you. It isn't always easy to love others—when you're tired or you've had a rotten day or someone is being especially creepy. But, that may be when showing love is the most important. Paul explains in 1 Corinthians 13 how important it is to love people around us—even when they aren't easy to love.

What About You?

• Think of someone you know who is easy to love. Why is that person easy to love?
• Think of someone you know who is hard to love. Why is that person hard to love?

Talkin' About It

Some people are not easy to love, but that doesn't let you off the hook. Ask God to help you be more loving and patient to those around you. Thank him for his help.

No Excuses

Love never stops being patient, never stops believing, never stops hoping, never gives up.

1 Corinthians 13:7

I Want to be in the Theatre

Read Luke 9:23

"To be or not to be, that is the question. Whether 'tis nobler…" Sandee strutted around the room as she quoted the famous lines. When she finished, her fellow English students exploded in applause.

After class, Melanie caught up with Sandee in the hall. "You're really good," she said.

"Thanks," said Sandee. "I want to devote my life to the arts. My goal is to win at least three academy awards."

It's good to have goals in life.

But, when you give your life to the Lord and you decide to live for him, you have to check those goals against what he wants for you. Jesus said that anyone who wants to follow him has to put aside his own desires and plans. Jesus might have something different for you to do. That may be hard to accept, but it is important to remember that God only wants the best for his followers.

What About You?

• What goals and dreams do you have for your life?
• Are your dreams from God? Have you talked with him about them?

Talkin' About It

Thank God that he wants only the best for you. Trust him. If he changes your plans, believe that what new plans he gives you will be wonderful!

Those who serve me must follow me.

John 12:26

Read John 8:31-32;
2 John 9

"I made the team!" Tom shouted as he ran through the house. The school football team was GOOD, and it wasn't easy to make—but Tom did it! He was a little surprised at practice the next day when the coach handed each player a book the size of a Chicago phone directory. "These are your plays, men," he said. "Knowing these plays and excecuting them is what makes this a great football team. Learn every one."

If you don't know the plays, you won't win games.

Seems like there is always something to be learning, doesn't it? While football plays and school lessons are impor-tant, there isn't anything more important than life. Is there a playbook for life—something that tells you guidelines and good plays versus bad plays? Sure there is. It's the Bible. Learn it, and you will know what God is like and how he wants you to live.

What About You?

• How often do you read the Bible?
• What is your favorite Bible verse?

Talkin' About It

Do you understand you can't know God without reading the Bible? Ask God to give you a hunger for his Word. Ask him to help you understand it.

I have kept my feet from walking on any evil path in order to obey your word.

Psalm 119:101

Playbook or Phonebook?

Can We Talk?

Read Matthew 7:7; John 14:13-14, 15:7

Mom picked up the phone to make a call. Just before she started dialing she heard Maria's voice on the line. Mom hung up and checked every few minutes for an hour to see if Maria was off the line yet. Finally, Mom broke in and asked to use the phone.

When Maria came downstairs later, Mom asked, "What do you find to talk about for all that time?"

Maria's response was immediate, "I was talking to my best friend. We talk about everything."

That's the kind of friendship God wants with you.

Do you talk to God about everything and anything? He wants to know how you feel about things, what's important you, even what guy or girl you like. Tell him what is important you. The great thing about this friend is that, as you get to kno him better and talk to him mor you can ask him things. And, when you pray in Jesus' name, God will do those things for yo

What About You?

• The keys are knowing God b ter and praying in Jesus' name. Why are these important?
• Do these verses mean you ca ask God to make you rich or famous and he will? Why or why not?

Talkin' About It

Imagine—God wants to be you friend. Is that awesome or wha Talk to him. Tell him the things that are in your heart, both go and bad. Get to know him and let him get to know you.

If you ask me to do something, I will do it.

John 14:14

Read John 13:34-35; 1 John 4:11-21

"Mr. Crow is going to give us our lab partners today," said Jim.

"I know. I wonder who's gonna get stuck with Len? I just hope it's not me!" wished Lantei.

"I know. He's trouble for any partner he gets."

When Mr. Crow handed out the partners, Lantei was the lucky guy who got Len for a partner. Lantei blew a gasket, stomping around the room, he wrote off the idea of getting a decent grade on this project.

Not exactly a show of love!

Being kind to other people, especially unlovely people, is a great way to show God's love to anyone who is watching.

You can "talk love" as much as you want. You know what I mean—all the right words that sound so Christian. But, if you can't put some of that talk into action, it's not much good. Some people may never listen to a sermon, but they may learn about God by watching you.

What About You?

• When have you had the chance to show love to someone? Did you?
• How does it look to others if Christians are fighting and arguing?

Talkin' About It

Ask God to help you show love to others. Tell him if there is someone you find especially hard to love. He will help you.

Actions Speak Louder Than Words

We must love each other because love comes from God.

1 John 4:7

Doing Your Job Well

Read John 15:5,8,16

William got a job delivering newspapers. He was up and working every morning by 4:30. He folded and wrapped the papers, then delivered them for the next two hours. It was quite a schedule. After a few weeks, William was worn out. He started getting sloppy, some of the papers he delivered weren't wrapped well or weren't put in plastic. William wasn't doing the job he was supposed to do.

Christians should be busy doing God's work.

That work is to tell others about how much God loves them. You can even show people God's love by being kind and considerate. That may be the first contact some people have with God. If you love God, you will be busy doing God's work. He will help you, and what you do for him shows God you love him.

What About You?

• How can you show God's love to a specific person?
• What are you already doing for God?

Talkin' About It

Tell God you want to be productive for him. Ask him to show you things you can do for him.

You give glory to my Father when you produce a lot of fruit and therefore show that you are my disciples. John 15:8

Read 1 Corinthians 12:12-31

"Five guys go out on the floor," Coach Jordan said. "Some of you may have good nights and some may have less than average. That's OK. We aren't looking for any superstars to be born here. You guys are a team and you'll do fine as long as you play like a team. Every one of you is necessary for the team to work."

Mark was glad to hear that. In his heart, he wanted to be the superstar of the team, but it was good to hear that he had an important role, even as a sub.

Every person on a team is important.

In the same way, every part of a body is important. What good is a foot all by itself? Or the head or the hand? For the body to work well, every part must do it's job. Every part of God's family has a job to do, also. When each part does it's job, then more and more people hear about God's love. No one job is more important—ministers are important, so are singers and typists. Do the job God gives you.

What About You?

• What job can you do for God right now?
• What job have you wished God would give you?

Talkin' About It

Thank God that anything you can do for him is important. Tell him what job you would like to do for him. Ask him for opportunities to serve him.

So God put each and every part of the body together as he wanted it.

1 Corinthians 12:18

A Hand Without an Arm

What Can I Do?

Review Scripture from past week

OK, let's be honest. Are you thinking: What can I do for God? I'm only a kid. I don't have a career that is a ministry. I can't do much work in the church. So, what am I supposed to do for God?

Actually, you have some great opportunities to show God's love.

You can share God's love through friendships and by giving good advice to those who ask. You can let kids at school, your friends, and your family know you are a Christian. Be ready to make any changes God asks of you. Living for Christ is a daily process. Just be open to him and he will use you.

What About You?

• Do your friends know you are a Christian?
• How can you share Christ with your schoolmates?

Talkin' About It

Ask God to help you be consistent in how you live for him. Ask him to lead you where he wants you to be.

A person may plan his own journey, but the LORD directs his steps.

Proverbs 16:9

Read Genesis 18:1-15

In a busy household, phone messages can easily get lost. Lew's mom came up with a plan to be sure messages were delivered. She put a huge bulletin board in the kitchen beside the phone. It was divided into columns, one for each family member. Mom put a notepad and pencil beside the bulletin board so when anyone took a message for another family member, all he or she had to do was write it down and stick it in the appropriate column.

God had an even more unique way to deliver messages.

He sent angels to deliver them. When he wanted Abraham and Sarah to know that they were going to have a baby, God sent three angels to tell them. Abraham and Sarah had waited a long long time for this news and Abraham might have started having some doubts. When he heard the news from the three men standing in front of him, he couldn't blow it off as a dream or think he misunderstood some sign. The angels ate with him, and when they told him the news, they came right to the point.

What About You?

• How do you get messages from God?
• Do you ever get confused as to whether a message is from God, or something you made up in your mind?

Talkin' About It

Thank God that he makes sure his messages are delivered to his people. Thank him for his special angel helpers.

Message Board

You are my rock and my fortress. For the sake of your name, lead me and guide me.

Psalm 31:3

Page 289

Get Outta Here!

Read Genesis 19:1-3, 15-25

Lori looked at the door in horror! *I could just die,* she thought. Her dad had come to get her from the party because he didn't think she should be there. Secretly, Lori was glad to be rescued, but it was totally embarrassing to have her friends see her daddy come get her.

But the bottom line was—Lori's dad rescued her because he loved her and cared what happened to her. She had gotten sucked into a situation she didn't want to be in. Dad helped.

God sent angels to get Lot out of a bad situation.

Lot and his family were living in a rotten city where no one cared a bit about God. In fact, God was so fed up with the people there that he decided to destroy the whole city. But, God knew that deep in his heart, Lot wasn't like the creeps in Sodom. God wanted to save Lot and his family. God sent two angels to tell Lot to get out of the city. When Lot didn't start moving immediately, the angels literally dragged him and his family out of town. Just in time, too—fire fell down from heaven and burned up the whole city!

What About You?

• When have you been rescued from a bad situation?
• How does this story make you feel about God's protection?

Talkin' About It

Thank God for knowing what's going on with you all the time. Thank him for helping you and protecting you.

But whoever listens to me will live without worry and will be free from the dread of disaster. Proverbs 1:33

Read Numbers 22:1-35

*C*an't we go any faster? thought Zoe. Mom was driving over the speed limit, but Zoe wanted to go even faster. She wanted to be early for the "loading of the vans" for the youth group outing. Position is everything, and she wanted to be sure she got one of the back seats. When their car came around a bend in the road and they saw a roadblock set up ahead, Zoe nearly lost her cool. Mom inched the car along until a policeman came over. "We're detouring all traffic, ma'am. There's a water main break in the next block, and the street is washed out."

Some roadblocks are for protection.

Kind of like what Balaam and his donkey kept coming up against. Balaam was about to disobey God and hurt God's people, so God sent an angel to stop him. Trouble was, Balaam couldn't see the angel standing in the middle of the road, only his donkey could see it. Every time the donkey came face to face with the angel, the donkey ran off the road, then Balaam beat it. Finally, God let Balaam see the angel, too. God was trying to protect Balaam by sending the angel to stop him.

What About You?

• Has God ever put a roadblock in your life?
• Can you fool God into thinking you're obeying when you're really not?

Talkin' About It

Thank God for watching out for you. Ask him to help you pay attention when he tries to protect you.

*T*he LORD is a stronghold for the oppressed, a stronghold in times of trouble.

Psalm 9:9

Don't Run the Roadblock

Baby Announcement

Read Judges 13:2-5, 20

Marcie didn't get excited about many things—especially where her family was concerned. But, this news definitely had her excited. Marcie's oldest sister was going to have a baby! *This baby is going to have anything he or she ever wants, including a great babysitter,* Marcie promised herself. Her sister, Linda, and her husband had waited a long time for this baby. When the doctor told her she was pregnant, Linda had kissed him!

Would you kiss an angel?

How about if the angel had great news for you? God once sent an angel to visit Manoah's wife. She didn't have any children, but she wanted a baby very much. The angel told her that she would soon have a son. Her boy would serve God all his life, so the angel had special instructions for him.

What About You?

• How would you feel about great news which you have waited a long time to hear?
• Would you want proof that the person telling you the news is really an angel?

Talkin' About It

Babies are happy news. Thank God for sharing special news.

So the woman had a son and named him Samson. The boy grew up, and the LORD blessed him. Judges 13:24

Read I Kings 19:3-9

Maddy felt crummy. She was having one of those days when absolutely everything went wrong. At lunch time, she went outside and sat under a tree, determined not to talk to anyone. 'Course that wouldn't be a problem since all her friends were mad at her anyway, and she didn't even know why! The more Maddy thought, the worse she felt. Pretty soon, she closed her eyes and leaned her head back against the tree. A bit later the smell of red licorice brought her back to her senses. When she opened her eyes, her best friend Lynn was holding out a handful of red licorice to her.

Friends know what will make you feel better.

Elijah was bummed out because he had a king and queen mad at him, and he felt like the only person left who loved God. Elijah ran away into the desert, sat down, and prayed that he could die. God knew he just needed encouragment, so God sent an angel to bring food and water to Elijah—two times! Then Elijah felt better and continued on his way.

What About You?

• How do your friends make you feel better?
• How do you feel about God knowing what will make you feel better?

Talkin' About It.

Thank God that he cares when you are sad and discouraged. Thank him for helping you feel better.

If any of you are having trouble, pray.

James 5:13

Red Licorice

A Saving Alibi

Read Daniel 6

Mr. Morris walked up to the lunch table and said, "You boys have been accused of trashing the locker room during third period. A witness saw you all go into the room together." Shawn was not one of the guys who did the damage, but since he was sitting with them now, he looked guilty.

Mr. Morris was about to hand out punishment, when Coach Edmunds came up. "I don't know about these other guys, but Shawn was with me third period, helping put the basketballs away."

Do right and you stand a better chance of being saved.

Daniel comes to mind. He was in big-time trouble and he hadn't done a thing wrong.

The problem was that some other guys were jealous of him so they tricked the king into making a law that got Daniel in trouble. Now the king had to throw him into a den of lions because that was to be the punishment. The king and God knew that Daniel had not done anything wrong. God sent an angel to keep the lions' mouths shut, so Daniel spent a night with hungry lions and came out absolutely fine!

What About You?

• When have you been accused of something you didn't do?
• When have you been protected from punishment?

Talkin' About It

Ask God to help you do right and avoid even looking like you have done something wrong. Thank him for his protection.

God is our refuge and strength, an ever-present help in times of trouble.

Psalm 46:1

Review Scripture from past week

Does it ever seem to you that someone is always telling you what to do? After all, you have parents, teachers, older siblings, counselors, policemen, and on and on who have rules for you to obey. As hard as it may be to swallow, remember:

The rules are usually for your own good.

All the people handing out rules want you to make it to adulthood. God has rules for you to follow, too, 'cause no one cares more about you than he does. He wants you to live safely, to learn more about him, and to love him. His angels are around you all the time, protecting you, guiding you, and perhaps even giving you instructions. You can be thankful that God takes care of you every day.

What About You?

• When have you been aware of God's care and protection?
• Do you think you've ever seen an angel? What do angels look like?

Talkin' About It

Thank God for watching over you and caring for you. Thank him for angel protection and guidance.

In the fear of the LORD there is strong confidence, and his children will have a place of refuge. Proverbs 14:26

Rules and More Rules

Passing the Test

Read Daniel 3:1-30

Sara was in the middle of the biggest science test of the whole year—it counted for a major percentage of the final grade. The problem was whether to put down the answers Mr. Larry wanted, which said evolution was true, or the answers she believed in her heart were right, which were that God created the universe and everything in it. She had tried to explain her beliefs to Mr. Larry when the class covered the evolution material, and he got angry that she even brought it up. Sara was afraid what would happen if she put her creation answers on the test.

Should she take a stand?

Shadrach, Meshach, and Abednego refused to bow down and worship a statue of the king. They believed in God and would worship only him. vain king threw them into a bu ing hot furnace and sat down t watch them burn up. But, God knew the boys hadn't done any thing wrong, so he sent an ang to protect them. The king could believe it when he saw four gu walking around in the furnace, hurt at all. He brought the boys out, and they didn't even smell like smoke!

What About You?

• Have you ever gotten into tro ble because you refused to do something wrong?
• In your heart, do you believe God will protect you when you haven't done anything wrong?

Talkin' About It

Thank God for his protection. A him to give you courage when you need to make a stand for h

Praise God . . . He sent his angel and saved his servants, who trusted him.

Daniel 3:28

Read Luke 1:26-38

Liza was only two years old and many of the words she said didn't come out clearly. Her older sister's friends loved to talk with her just to hear how she would pronounce words. Their favorite Liza-ism was, "Great news!" which came out "Gweat news!" sort of like Elmer Fudd would say it. She always began with "Gweat news" when she had something to tell you, such as "Gweat news, the dog threw up!" or "Gweat news, Mommy took me to McDonalds." The kids gave Liza bits of information just to hear her shout the "Gweat news" proclamation.

Mary received some truly "Gweat news!"

Imagine how young Mary felt when God sent an angel to tell her, "Great news, Mary. You're going to have a baby, and he will be the Son of God." God's Son, Jesus, was coming to earth as part of the plan to save people from sin. Mary had always lived to please God, and he chose her to be the mother of his Son. He knew she would take good care of little Jesus.

What About You?

• When have you received some "great news"?
• Why was Jesus coming to earth?

Talkin' About It

Thank God for the "great news" he gave Mary. Great news that changed your life and gives hope for the future.

You will . . . give birth to a son, and name him Jesus.

Luke 1:31

Great News

News Break

Read Luke 2:8-14

Donnell settled down with a big bowl of ice cream to watch his favorite TV show. Tonight's episode was supposed to be especially good, and he couldn't wait to see how it came out. Just at the climax of the story, the network news team cut in with an emergency news break about some war heating up a zillion miles away. Donnell was ticked when his program came back on in time to show the credits—now he would never know how the story ended.

How come news breaks are always bad news?

A bunch of sleepy shepherds sitting out in their field one night, before TV was even invented, actually had a good news break. Really—they were just sitting there minding their own business when an angel suddenly appeared in the sky with a news break. The angel announced that a baby had been born that night in Bethlehem who would be their Savior. Before the shepherds could catch their breath, the sky was filled with angels who praised God together!

What About You?

• How do you think the shepherds felt about this good news break?
• Why did the group of angels praise God?

Talkin' About It

Thank God for the good news break of Jesus' birth.

Glory to God in the highest heaven, and on earth peace to those who have his good will! Luke 2:14

Read Matthew 1:20; 2:13, 19-20

At 2:00 A.M. Carolyn suddenly appeared at her mother's bedside with all the sheets and blankets from her bed in her arms. Mom groggily sat up and asked, "What are you doing?"

Carolyn looked frustrated that Mom would even ask such a silly question. "I brought you my laundry like you told me to do," she said, not very kindly.

Then Mom realized that Carolyn had dreamed a conversation, and she gently guided her back to bed.

Not all dream talk is make-believe.

Three different times Joseph got instructions from God while he was sleeping. But, God didn't just put thoughts into Joseph's mind, each time he sent an angel to give Joseph a message. One time the angel told Joseph that baby Jesus was coming. Another time he told Joseph how to protect the baby from bad guys who wanted to hurt him. Joseph knew his dreams were messages from God, not just dreams.

What About You?

• Can you remember an unusual dream you have had?
• Why did Jesus need to be protected?

Talkin' About It

Thank God that he knows everything that is going to happen. Thank him for protecting Jesus.

Dream Talk

I know whom I trust. I'm convinced that he is able to protect what he had entrusted to me until that day. 2 Timothy 1:12

We Can't Be Stopped

Read Acts 5:17-20

Only a few seconds were left in the football game. The University of California had the ball, but they were trailing by one point. The players knew that they had time for one play, but when that play ended, the game would be over, and they would lose. When the ball was snapped, the players ran down the field tossing the ball sideways or backwards to each other in passes called laterals. They ran all the way down the field like this and scored the winning touchdown!

Peter and John couldn't be stopped either.

They were thrown in jail by church leaders who thought they were too popular with the people. Everyone knew that Peter and John taught about God and that he had given them power to heal people. But, they hadn't done anything to deserve being in jail. So, God sent an angel to open the jail doors and set Peter and John free. The angel told them to get back to preaching about God's love.

What About You?

• Do you let obstacles stop you from doing what you know you should do?
• When have you felt strongly enough about something to be persistent until you got it?

Talkin' About It

Thank God for protection. Thank him that he knows everything that is going on.

Every day in the temple courtyard and from house to house, they refused to stop teaching and telling the Good News that Jesus is the Messiah. Acts 5:42

Read Acts 12:1-11

People all across America were glued to their TV sets watching the rescuers try to free little Jessica who had fallen into a well. The two-year-old had been trapped in the ground for several days, crying and calling for her mommy. All the time her rescuers tried to figure some way to safely rescue the little girl, people all across the country were praying for her safety. When they lifted Jessica out of the well, people everywhere cheered.

God answers prayer!

Peter's friends were earnestly praying for his safety. He had been thrown in prison again because he kept talking about God. Because the police were so afraid he might escape, he was heavily guarded and chained to two different guards. But, God answers prayer—he sent an angel to free Peter and walk him right out of the prison, past all those guards! When Peter was safely out, the angel disappeared, and Peter hurried to find his friends.

What About You?

• When have you earnestly prayed for someone's safety?
• How does this story show you that God answers prayer?

Talkin' About It

Thank God for helping both Jessica and Peter. Thank him for watching over you.

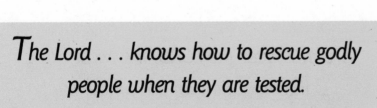

The Lord . . . knows how to rescue godly people when they are tested.

2 Peter 2:9

News Bulletins

Review Scripture from past week

What are the different ways you get information? International and national news usually comes through radio and TV or now, the Internet. You can get more detailed information from newspapers and magazines. At home, you may get information by notes from Mom or Dad. At school, there are loudspeaker announcements or maybe a daily news sheet.

We are bombarded with information.

God has news for us, too. His information comes through his Word, the Bible. In many of the stories you read this week, God's information was passed on to his people by angels. He must have wanted the people to know that the information was important and they shouldn't ignore it. Isn't it great that God knows just the right way to give you information so you will listen to it?

What About You?

• When has God spoken to you?
• What is the best way for him to get your attention?

Talkin' About It

Thank God for speaking to each of his people in the right way to make those people listen. Ask him to help you listen better.

> We must fear the LORD, the Most High. He is the great king of the whole earth.
>
> Psalm 47:2

Read Matthew 6:5-8

Robbie brought the ball down the floor and his teammates spread out around the court. "Over here, Robbie!" yelled Kris as he broke free of the defense. Robbie ignored him and kept dribbling around in circles. Finally, Robbie made a break for the basket and tried to force an underhand lay-up, rolling the ball off his fingers. It didn't go in. Robbie was a hot dog. He wanted to be the "star" so everyone would think his abilities were awesome! His hot doggin' didn't have the best results for the team. They missed good chances to score because Robbie wouldn't pass the ball.

Ever heard of a prayer hot dog?

Jesus said not to be a prayer hot dog—the kind of person who prays out in public just for show. The point of prayer is not to have other people say how great you are; hot dogs who want that should not expect their prayers to be answered. Jesus said to pray in private—God will still hear you.

What About You?

• How do you feel about praying in public?
• Can you pray about more personal things when you pray privately?

Talkin' About It

Talk to God like you would to a friend. Tell him what you worry about and what you need his help with.

When you pray, go to your room and close the door. Pray privately to your Father who is with you. Your Father sees what you do in private. He will reward you. *Matthew 6:6*

Using a Model

Read Matthew 6:9-13

"Math is like the dumbest thing in the world. I can't do this!" Janell complained—loudly.

Dad sat down and looked at the problems with Janell. "Well, these are tough problems," he conceded. "But, all you have to do is look at the model or sample problems here. They show you how to do the problems you have."

It really helps to have a model to follow.

Jesus knew that, so when he taught his followers how to pray, he gave them a sample prayer to go by. With that sample, he showed what to include in a prayer: praise to God, thanks for his help, requests to be more like him, and requests for forgiveness. This prayer isn't for show, it's to be prayed from the heart—to be more like God.

What About You?

• Can you say the Lord's Prayer?
• What would you like to praise God for?

Talkin' About It

Thank God for the Lord's Prayer sample. Use it as a pattern while you pray.

Ask and you will receive so that you will be completely happy.

John 16:24

Read Ephesians 1:3-15;
Hebrews 13:15

Joiya sat down at the piano and groaned. She was sick of playing this thing. Since Joiya was seven, she had practiced piano about three hours a day. As you might guess, she played superbly now. But, after six years of playing piano, she was getting pretty sick of it. Sometimes it felt like work instead of pleasure. But, it seemed like everytime Joiya was ready to give up her music, someone would come up out of the blue and tell her how much they enjoyed her music and how talented she was. She needed to hear that again right now.

Compliments can be very encouraging.

God likes to hear compliments, too. When you pray, praise him for all the wonderful things he has done. He likes to hear what things you really appreciate. Praise him that he knew all about you even before you were born. Praise him for his awesome plan that makes a way for you to go to heaven. Praise him for the Holy Spirit who always stays with you.

What About You?

• What would you most like to praise God for?
• What part of God's character amazes you most?

Talkin' About It

Praise God for all he has done for you. Thank him for your favorite parts of his creation.

Point Out the Good

We should always bring God a sacrifice of praise, that is, words that acknowledge him.

Hebrews 13:15

Say Thanks Once in a While

Read Mark 6:41; Romans 7:25; Ephesians 5:4; Philippians 1:3

"Mom, I need my blue sweater washed tonight!" called James. Mom got up from her easy chair and washed the sweater. The next morning James put it on and left without a word.

Only a couple of days later, James needed his black jeans washed. Mom ignored his request, so the next morning when he got dressed, the jeans were still in the laundry. James was plenty mad and let Mom know it.

She responded with, "I'm happy to do things for you, James, but I would appreciate a simple thank you once in a while."

Do you remember to say thank you?

It's no fun when people make constant demands of you, and never even think to show their appreciation. Do your parents ever have reason to feel that pain? Wonder how God feels about that? How much of your prayer time is spent asking him to do things for you in comparison to thanking him for what he's already done? Jesus thanked God nearly everytime he prayed. Quite an example for us!

What About You?

• What has God given you? Make a list.
• How often do you say thank you to him?

Talkin' About It

Thank God for five things he has given you. Thank him for answered prayer.

Everything you say or do should be done in the name of the Lord Jesus, giving thanks to God the Father through him.

Hebrews 3:17

Read Luke 15:11-21; 1 John 1:9

They say confession is good for the soul, and I feel totally crummy, so maybe I'd better confess, thought Ray. It was strange—he took money out of Mom's wallet and got away with it—Mom thought she had spent it and forgotten about it. But, Ray couldn't sleep, couldn't eat, couldn't live with himself.

Guilt can wear you down.

You can fool people sometimes—get away with things. But, you can't fool God, ever. He may not come down heavy on you, he may just quietly wait for you to confess. When you confess your sins to God, he forgives and forgets. Don't waste energy trying to hide things from other people or from God, confess and you'll feel better.

What About You?

• Do you need to confess anything to another person? What?
• Do you need to confess anything to God? What?

Talkin' About it

Tell God you're sorry for the wrong things you do. Thank him for his forgiveness.

Confess, You'll Feel Better

Wash me, and I will be whiter than snow.

Psalm 51:7

If You Want It, Ask for It

Read Matthew 7:7-8;
Philippians 4:6; James 1:5-8

"I need three notebooks for school," Margaret announced.

"What kind?" Mom asked.

"I don't know," said Margaret.

Mom ran to the store after dinner and bought three notebooks. When she gave them to her, Margaret said, "Oh, I forgot. They have to be spiral bound."

So, Mom went back to the store. She came back with three spiral bound notebooks.

But Margaret said, "Oh, I forgot, they have to be different colors. And, oh yeah, one has to be 100 pages and one has to be 75, and one has to be 3-subject."

Why don't you ask for what you really want?

That includes when you pray. Does it seem pushy to tell God exactly what you would like him to do? You shouldn't feel that way—the Bible says to ask God for what you want. In fact it says that some people don't have what they want because they don't ask him. When you are close to God, you can ask for exactly what you want, 'cause you'll be asking for what he wants to give you.

What About You?

• When have you asked God for something specific?
• When you pray, do you believe God will answer?

Talkin' About It

Honesty time. Tell God exactly what you need. Believe that he loves you and will answer your prayer.

Never worry about anything. But in every situation let God know what you need in prayers and requests while giving thanks.

Philippians 4:6

Read James 4:2

How do you usually pray? "Now I lay me down to sleep," or "God is great, God is good, let us thank him for this food." Those are fine starters. But, as you know God longer, you should be able to talk to him like you do a friend. You should be able to tell him the things you need, the things that worry you, what you would like him to do for others.

Believe that God will answer you.

A big part of prayer is having faith, believing that your prayers go farther than the ceiling of your room. You don't have to kneel down and do a big fancy prayer. God is with you all the time, so you can talk to him in your thoughts. But, don't expect God to just know what you want him to do. Take time to talk to him and be still sometimes and listen to him talk to you.

What About You?

• Have you ever spouted the words of a memorized prayer without thinking about them?
• Which of the lessons this past week do you need to pay attention to in your prayer life?

Talkin' About it

Tell God you're sorry that you don't pray more often or don't think about the words you say to him. Thank him for listening to you.

> *You don't have the things you want, because you don't pray for them.*
>
> James 4:2

Just Like Talking to a Friend

Changing Teams

Read Acts 9

Lou Brock was one of the greatest baseball players of all time. He played outfield for the Chicago Cubs. The St. Louis Cardinals were the arch rivals of the Cubs. When those two teams played, trash talk flew and tempers flared. Each team wanted to win so much the players could taste it. Then one crummy day, Lou Brock was traded from the Chicago Cubs to . . . you guessed it, the St. Louis Cardinals. Now Brock had to play for and support the team he had hated before.

Changing teams isn't easy.

The Apostle Paul went through a similar experience. He hated Christians so much that he made it his life work to make them miserable—even to the point of putting Christians in jail whenever he could. Then Jesus called Paul to follow him. Suddenly, Paul was on the other team. He had to convince the Christians that they could trust him, and he had to deal with his former friends who still hated Christians. Paul handled all of it and spent the rest of his life teaching about God's love.

What About You?

• Do you think Paul ever wanted to go back to his old team?
• Have you ever had a similar experience of changing teams?

Talkin' About It

Thank God for the example of Paul, who worked through the hard times and kept telling people about God.

The prize that shows I have God's approval is now waiting for me. The Lord, who is a fair judge, will give me that prize on that day.

2 Timothy 4:8

Read Acts 4:36-37; 11:22-26

Any football fan can tell you who Walter Payton was: famous running back for the Chicago Bears. Payton was nicknamed "Sweetness" because of his smooth running style. He racked up more yards and points than almost any other player. Another name that is not so well known is that of Matt Suey. The less glamorous job of blocking for Payton fell to Suey. He often cleared the way so Payton could make his fantastic runs.

Every team needs a workhorse.

Someone who is dependable and steady. That was Barnabas. He often traveled and taught in the shadow of the great Apostle Paul. Barnabas was dependable and an encourager, he even sold some land he owned and gave the money to the poor. He wanted to help everyone, and he wanted all people to know about Jesus' love.

What About You?

• How do you feel about working behind someone else? Would you rather be the "star"?
• Why are people like Barnabas important?

Talkin' About It

Thank God for dependable, steady people like Barnabas. Thank him for encouragers. Ask him to help you find ways you can serve him

Barnabas was a dependable man, and he was full of the Holy Spirit and faith.

Acts 11:24

The Best Team

Read Acts 18:24-28;
Romans 16:3-5

Mo was captain, so he got to choose which players he wanted on his baseball team. Fran chose for the other side. They took turns choosing, each one going for the best players. Everyone knew that Tom would be the last one chosen. He couldn't catch, hit, or run. He had nothing to offer either team. Plus, all he did was complain and criticize the other players. Neither side wanted him for their team.

Teammates have to work together.

Take Priscilla and Aquila. They were married to each other, and they worked together to tell people about God. When they heard Apollos preach,

they realized he didn't know th whole truth about God. So, they told him the rest of the story. Priscilla and Aquila were great team who worked togeth er well to share God's love.

What About You?

• When have you worked with a partner?
• How could you work with a partner to share God's love?

Talkin' About It

Thank God for examples of people who shared his love.

May God, who gives you this endurance and encouragement, allow you to live in harmony with each other by following the example of Christ Jesus. Then, having the same goal, you will praise the God and Father of our Lord Jesus Christ. Romans 15:5-6

Read I Corinthians 4:17; I
Timothy 4:11-12;
2 Timothy 1:5

Andrea Jaeger was only 14 years old when she won her first professional tennis tournament. She was only 18 when she played at Wimbledon, the most important tennis tournament in the world. Many people saw Andrea coming up, improving her game, and threatening the old established tennis stars. But they thought, *she's just a kid, she can't be a serious tennis player.*

Kids can accomplish things, too.

Timothy sure proved that. He was a young man, but he had been taught about God from the time he was a child. Paul kind of took Timothy under his wing and took him on some of his missionary trips. Paul even sent Timothy out to do check-up work on some churches Paul had started. Even though Timothy was young, he could still be an example of God's love by the way he lived.

What About You?

• What can you do to serve God as a young person?
• How did Timothy serve God?

Talkin' About It

Thank God that he uses people of all ages. Thank him for wanting you to do his work.

Don't let anyone look down on you for being young. Instead, make your speech, behavior, love, faith, and purity an example for other believers. I Timothy 4:12

Too young!

Read Acts 2:14-41

Babe Ruth was one of the most famous baseball players of all time. His record number of home runs stood for years. The Babe was not known as a shy guy, he was loud and proud. He partied a lot, which eventually brought his career to an end. One of Babe's last home runs is famous. He stepped up for his turn at bat and suddenly pointed his finger to center field as if to say, that's where the ball's going. That's exactly where he hit it over the wall. Not a shy guy at all.

Peter wasn't a shy guy either.

Want an example? One time when Peter was teaching about Jesus' love, some guys started making fun of Christians. Peter would have none of that. He explained Old Testament Scriptures to them and that Christians acted differently from other people because they had the Holy Spirit helping them live right. Peter told them if they turned away from their sin, they could have the Holy Spirit, too.

What About You?

• Are you usually shy and quiet or proud and loud?
• Peter could say what he did because he knew the Scripture. How well do you know the Bible?

Talkin' About It

Ask God to make you brave about sharing his Word. Ask him to give you courage to stand up for him and other Christians when you need it.

Whoever calls on the name of the Lord will be saved.

Acts 2:21

Not a Shy Guy

Read Acts 16:16-34

Have you ever run a marathon race? Imagine the strength, endurance, and mental toughness it takes to run 26.3 miles. Imagine the excitement of being the first woman to finish the race. Rosie Ruiz won the 1980 Boston Marathon. But, since none of the officials or other runners had ever heard of Ruiz, they checked up on her and discovered she hadn't run the entire marathon—she took a subway for part of the race route. That was dumb!

She didn't learn that from Silas.

He always tried to do what was right. Like the time he and Paul were in prison again. This time they had healed a demon-possessed slave girl; her owners got mad and had Paul and Silas tossed in prison.

During the night, there was an earthquake and the prison doors fell off. All the prisoners could have escaped, but they didn't. When the jailer saw that they had stayed, he knew there was something special about Paul and Silas. He asked them how he could be saved. Paul and Silas introduced the jailer and his whole family to God.

What About You?

• When have you tried to do right when everyone else seemed to be doing wrong?
• Do you think it's obvious to your friends that you are a Christian?

Talkin' About It

Ask God to give you strength to stand for right. Ask him for chances to share your faith because of doing right.

Believe in the Lord Jesus, and you and your family will be saved.

Acts 16:31

Doing What's Right

Don't You Want to Tell Someone?

Review Scripture from past week

This week you've read about six people who shared their faith in God with those around them. Six different styles. Not everyone is a Paul or a Peter. The way you live your life and share your faith depends on what kind of person you are.

You gotta be yourself.

Are you an outgoing, talkative, preacher-type person? Are you a quiet, behind-the-scenes worker? Maybe you're at your best one-on-one, just being a friend to someone. Whatever your style, God can use it. Be willing to let him.

What About You?

• Which of the people you read about this week do you most identify with?
• How courageous are you about sharing your faith?

Talkin' About It

Tell God you would like to share your faith with your friends. Ask him to show you how you can best do that.

I will give you thanks, O LORD, with all my heart. I will tell about all the miracles you have done. Psalm 9:1

Read Luke 11:28; Romans 10:17; 1 Peter 2:2-3

"I need to call Marta and find out what our Spanish homework is," said Kara.

"Why don't you know what it is?" Dad asked.

"I don't know. I guess I wasn't paying attention."

Dad shook his head, as only a Dad can do. "How do you expect to learn the material if you aren't paying attention in class? You need to hear Spanish spoken in order to learn it."

Kara moaned, "I know, but I don't understand what he's saying, so it's boring!"

Hearing it spoken makes the Word easier to learn.

When the Scripture passage is read in your church worship service, do you listen or tune it out? Hearing God's Word read aloud is a great way to begin learning it. You know how you listen to a favorite song over and over and soon you know the words? Same process—the more you hear the Bible read, the more you'll learn it.

What About You?

• How much time do spend each day reading the Bible?
• Do you enjoy hearing the Bible read aloud?

Talkin' About It

Ask God to help you understand the Bible. Ask him to give you a hunger for it.

Pay Attention in Class

Blessed are those who hear and obey God's Word.

Luke 11:28

Is Your Homework Done?

Read Acts 17:11;
Revelation 1:3

"I'm going out to play basketball," yelled Kara.

"Wait a minute," Mom stopped her. "Is your homework done yet?"

"All I have is Spanish," Kara answered.

"Well, that's homework, isn't it?" Mom countered.

"Mo-o-o-m, I don't understand it," Kara wailed.

You're not gonna learn it by ignoring it!

How did you learn the alphabet? How did you learn to count? Anything that you have learned in your life you spent time on. As you got older, the lessons got harder, so you had to spend more tim on them. You have to do that with the Bible, too. If you read a verse that doesn't make any sense, look up other verses on the same subject—read the whole chapter so you understand the background. The Bib can change your life. Be willing to spend time on it.

What About You?

• What do you do when you read a verse you don't understand?
• What are some things you can do to make the Bible more understandable?

Talkin' About It

Thank God for his Word. Ask him to help you understand it and apply it to your life.

Also take salvation as your helmet and the word of God as the sword that the Spirit supplies. Ephesians 6:17

Read Psalm 119:9, 11

"How am I supposed to remember all this junk?" moaned Kara. "Who cares what the Spanish word for bathroom is?"

"The Spanish people probably do," laughed Dad. Kara glared at him. "Honey, the only way you can learn Spanish is to memorize it. Just go over and over and over it, until it's stuck in your brain. Then you don't have to think about what a Spanish word is, you just know it."

Know God's Word so well that you don't have to think about what it says.

The Bible is God's Word to you, and it can help you with any problem you have. But, you don't always have a Bible with you when you need it, so what do you do? Memorize it. Learn verses of the Bible that have special meaning to you or help you be strong about living for God. When you memorize them, they are hidden in your heart, and you can remember them any time you want.

What About You?

• How often do you memorize Bible verses?
• How does remembering a Bible verse help you?

Talkin' About It

Thank God for his Word that can be such a help and encouragement to you. Ask him for help to learn Bible verses.

Exam Time

*T*ake to heart these words that I give you today.

Deuteronomy 6:6

Thinking in Spanish

Read Psalm 1:2-3;
Philippians 4:8-9

"When is the big Spanish test?" asked Dad.

"Manana," answered Kara.

"You know," said Dad, "I've been noticing lately that when I ask you a question, you answer in Spanish, without needing to stop and think. That's good because it shows you are understanding the language better."

Can you make decisions to honor God, without even thinking about it?

If you know anything about computers, you know their success is based on what is put in the program. You put junk in, you get junk out. Same thing with our minds: put trash in, trash comes out. God says to think about the Bible all the time, that way it's teachings become part of your thoughts and the way you live.

What About You?

• Compare how much time you spend thinking about the Bible and how much time you spend watching TV?

• Do you think about lessons the Bible naturally, or do you have to make yourself think about them?

Talkin' About It

Ask God to help you forget the trash and put good stuff from the Bible in your head.

Blessed are those whose thoughts are pure.

Matthew 5:8

Read James 1:22; 2:14-20

Kara was so nervous she thought she was going to throw up. Today's Spanish test counted for about 1/4 of the total grade. She had been doing so poorly in this subject that she really needed a good grade on this test. When Mrs. Lupus handed out the papers, Kara took a deep breath and jumped in. This would show if she had really learned the material or not.

Put it into practice.

Reading, studying, and memorizing God's Word are good starting points. But, it doesn't mean a thing if it doesn't get into your life. You can read and memorize all you want, but if it doesn't change the way you live, you fail the big test. You can memorize a zillion verses, but if you are disrespectful to your parents and fight like crazy with your brother and sister, you haven't learned a thing. Think about it.

What About You?

• How have your put God's Word to practice in your life?
• Does this mean that you never, ever do anything wrong?

Talkin' about It

Realize this is a process. Ask God to help you put the Word into practice once a day as a starting point.

I will show you my faith by the things I do.

James 2:18

The Big Test

You Be the Teacher

Read Matthew 28:19-20

"I passed! I passed! And guess what?" Kara was so excited she could hardly contain herself. "Mrs. Lupus said I have improved so much that she wants me to help tutor some fifth graders who are just beginning to learn Spanish! Can you believe it?" Dad and Mom and Kara celebrated her hard work with dinner at her favorite restaurant.

Share what you have learned!

That's the next step in learning God's Word. When you read it, study it, memorize it, and let it make a difference in your life. Get excited about it! You won't hesitate to tell others because it's the best news in the whole world, and you want to share it with everyone

What About You?

• Have you ever told anyone else about God's love?
• Who do you know who needs to hear about God's love

Talkin' About It

Ask God for courage to talk with your friends about God. Ask him for the right words to say and a sensitive heart to know when the right time is.

Go everywhere in the world, and tell everyone the Good News.

Mark 16:15

Read Psalm 119:98

A secret weapon—have you ever wished for one? Like when someone is giving you a hard time or a teacher seems to be constantly on your case, or your parents are acting like cell guards. Haven't you wished for some super-human defense?

Guess what? You have one!

There are lessons in the Bible to get you through any tough circumstance. Remembering Bible verses and the lessons they teach can give you strength when you need it, help you see a situation from a different viewpoint, or help you be more patient. Learn it and hide it in your heart— there's your secret weapon.

What About You?

• What subject do you need to know verses about?
• How does knowing Bible verses become a secret weapon?

Talkin' About It

Ask God to help you memorize verses and be able to recall them when needed.

Secret Weapon

Your commandments make me wiser than my enemies, because your commandments are always with me. Psalm 119:98

A Special Gift

Read Matthew 7:16-20;
Acts 1:4-5; Galatians 5:16

The best part of having a sister that's six years older than you is that you can ask her advice on clothes and hair and stuff like that. Jamilla and Jessie had gotten past the fighting stage and become good friends in the last year. Now Jessie was leaving for college, and Jamilla would miss her—a lot. The day Jessie left, Jamilla went back to her room and found a box on her bed with a note on top. Inside the box was a big picture of a grinning Jessie and Jamilla taken at the beach last summer. The note said, "Love you J'illa. Write me every day, and don't forget me!"

A special gift to help you remember.

When Jesus left earth to go back to heaven, he left a special gift, too. He gave the Holy Spirit. The Holy Spirit stays with you always when you ask Jesus into your heart. He helps you grow and become more like Jesus. God doesn't judge a person by the work he does, but Jesus did say that your life would show it if the Holy Spirit lives in you.

What About You?

• What does the Holy Spirit do for you?
• How do you know if the Holy Spirit is living in you?

Talkin' About It

Thank God for the Holy Spirit and for his constant help and reminders of what Jesus has done for you.

I pray that your love will keep on growing because of your knowledge and insight.

Philippians 1:9

Read Galatians 5:22

Loving and joyful are not two titles you would ever hang on old Mrs. Prunepit. Her name was really Pruitt, but everyone called her Prunepit because she griped about everything, from kids cutting across her lawn to laughter coming from neighbors' windows. The only thing about Prunepit that you could count on was that every Sunday morning at 9:30 she would stride out the door and down the block to the big, old church on the corner. She sure wasn't a good advertisement for the church.

Your actions show what is in your heart.

You can say all the right "Christian words" about being saved and the Holy Spirit and all that, but if your life doesn't show it, no one is going to believe it. When the Holy Spirit lives inside you, it shows by the way you treat people. Do your actions show love for God and those around you? Is the joy of the Holy Spirit bubbling out of you? Joy doesn't mean laughing every minute. It is a deeper feeling of happiness that comes from understanding all that God has done for you.

What About You?

• Are you usually a "Prunepit" or a joyful person?
• How do you usually treat your family?

Talkin' About It

Ask God to help you show love and joy by the way you treat others.

I have told you this so that you will be as joyful as I am, and your joy will be complete. John 15:11

Are You a Prunepit?

Peace or Pieces?

Read Galatians 5:22

"You little creep, get out of my room!" Elissa chased her little brother Eric all the way down to the family room, screaming the whole way. The sad thing was that Eric hadn't done anything except stick his head in Elissa's room to ask her a question. Before he could get two words out, she went to pieces.

No one in Elissa's family would ever say she was easy to get along with.

Two more evidences of the Holy Spirit living inside you are patience and peacefulness. Patience is tough, especially where family members are concerned. But, the Holy Spirit can help you learn to live peacefully with those around you. Others will notice if you are a peaceful person. Patience means you don't push others to keep your idea of when and how things should be done. It also means you don't try to hurry God along.

What About You?

• How are you at keeping the peace?
• Do you consider yourself patient? Why or why not?

Talkin' About It

These two may be the toughest things to live out. Ask God to help you show peace and patience when you need it most.

So let's pursue those things which bring peace and which are good for each other.

Romans 14:19

Read Galatians 5:22

Everyone made fun of Patty. There was no real reason to, except she didn't have clothes as nice as the other kids, and her family wasn't as sophisticated as other suburbanites. Patty was very smart, in fact, she was usually at the head of the class. But, Patty didn't have any friends, and she was the butt of many cruel jokes. Maria actually felt sorry for Patty, but what could she do?

Be kind, Maria.

If Maria is showing the fruit of the Holy Spirit, she would be kind. A kind person wants to be nice to others in any way she can—even if others are mean. Kindness is not just what you show your friends, it is for anyone you meet, especially those who are different from you. Showing this kindness sets you apart from other people because they are only kind to their friends.

What About You?

• Who could you show this kindness to?
• How does it make you feel when someone is kind to you?

Talkin' About It

Thank God for someone who has been kind to you. Ask him to help you show kindness to someone to whom others are mean.

Christian Snobbery?

Be kind to each other, sympathetic, forgiving each other as God has forgiven you through Christ. Ephesians 4:32

U - Turn

Read Galatians 5:22

Danielle was leading the pack in the mile run. Her school was doing great, and if she finished first, they would win the whole track meet. The finish line was in sight when Danielle suddenly did a strange thing. She turned around and ran straight back through the group of other runners . . . away from the finish line.

Why run against the crowd?

Sometimes you have to. It's easy to go along with the crowd—do what everyone else is doing. But, what if your friends don't care diddly about God, and you do? If the Holy Spirit is living in you, it shows by your faithfulness to God— that means being true blue to

him. That might mean you have to run against the crowd. But, the Holy Spirit will help you live for God through any hard situation. He will give you the strength you need.

What About You?

• Do you need to turn away from what your friends do and take a stand for God?
• Does it frighten you to go against the crowd?

Talkin' About It

Thank God for his help and strength. Ask him to help you live for him.

The LORD protects faithful people.

Psalm 31:23

Read Galatians 5:23

Kiri threw open her locker door so hard that it rattled four lockers down. She threw her books in and slammed the door shut. The crowd of kids in the hall parted like the Red Sea so Kiri could pass through. Her temper's reputation was well-known.

Self-control is a fruit of the Spirit.

Self-control means controlling your temper and having patience. A self-controlled person doesn't overdo on good things either; like eating too much or watching tons of TV or playing video games for hours. Having self-control means your life is balanced between fun and work and friends and church.

What About You?

• What do you need more self-control in?
• How does self-control show that you live for God?

Talkin' About It

Ask God to help you have self-control in your life. Ask him to help you live for him so your friends will know you are a Christian.

Be firm in the faith.

1 Peter 5:9

Self-controlled or Sin-controlled?

Copycat

Review Galatians 5:22-23

Micah found out that in middle school, it's important to look like everyone else—wear the same type clothes, same hair styles, walk the same way, talk the same way. In fact, Micah is afraid to look or act differently from his friends. He doesn't want to feel weird and stick out like a sore thumb.

So, how do you live for God then?

Nobody said it would be easy, but you don't have to do it alone. The Holy Spirit is God's gift to you, and he is always with you. He will remind you of what to do and how to live. You only have to listen to him. Living for God is not something you can fake, because there is certain evidenc that the Spirit helps show in your life. If it is missing, it's obvious you're not letting the Holy Spirit do his work in you.

What About You?

• Do you think you should show the fruit of the Spirit immediately?
• Which part of the fruit do you need the most help with?

Talkin' About It

Thank God for his patience wit you. Ask him to help the fruit of the Spirit grow in you.

But the spiritual nature produces love, joy, peace, patience, kindness, goodness, faithfulness, gentleness, and self-control. There are no rules against things like that.

Galatians 5:22-23

Read Acts 9:19-31

In 1984, a tiny gymnast with a great big smile won the heart of America. Mary Lou Retton got perfect scores in the floor exercise and the vaulting events of the Olympics. The sixteen-year-old won the gold medal in the All-Around. The amazing thing was that this tiny bundle of energy had never before competed in a major gymnastic meet.

Nothing like starting at the top!

That's definitely what Paul did when he began his preaching career. After his dramatic conversion on the road to Damascus, Paul was blind for a while. When God gave him back his sight, Paul did a career turn around. His goal in life had been to persecute Christians, now he wanted to teach everyone that Jesus is the Son of God. He preached with so much power that God's enemies began planning how to kill him.

What About You?

• Do you know someone who is so bad you think he or she could never become a Christian?
• When have you wondered how the changes in your life would work out for good?

Talkin' About It

Ask God to give you courage and energy, like Paul's, to share his love with others.

We know that all things work together for the good of those who love God—those whom he has called according to his plan.
Romans 8:28

Blasting into the Limelight

We're Just People

Read Acts 14:8-18

When Michael Jordan came out of retirement to play basketball again in 1995, the news media treated him like a hero. The Chicago Bulls practice center was surrounded, night and day, by the newsmen. At his first game, M. J.'s every move was scrutinized to see if he still had the magic. After that first game, Michael hinted that he'd like the reporters to back off. "I'm just a man," he said. They had been treating him like a national hero.

Save your worship for the God who deserves it.

Paul and Barnabas were in Lystra and they saw a man who was crippled. The man was listening to Paul speak about God. Paul saw that he believed, so he healed the man. When the people around them saw this, they started shouting that Paul and Barnabas were gods! They wanted to worship Paul and Barnabas. Paul put a stop to that right away. He told them to worship the one true God.

What About You?

• Who is your "hero"? Why?
• Does your hero ever get in the way of your worship to God?

Talkin' About It

Ask God to help you keep him in first place. Ask him to help you choose good heroes to admire.

Never make your own carved idols or statues that represent any creature in the sky, on the earth, or in the water.

Exodus 20:4

Read Acts 16:13-15

Ever wonder how much good stuff you miss because you don't pay attention? Sunshine found out the hard way. Mom was still talking, but she had already given Sunshine a list of chores to do on this beautiful spring day. The one Sunshine hated the most was taking everything out of the cupboards and washing the shelves. Anyway, Sunshine wasn't listening to Mom. Her mind was on what she would rather be doing. After Mom left, Sunshine unhappily emptied the cupboards. When Mom came back later, she was surprised that Sunshine was cleaning the cupboards, "I said you didn't have to do that, weren't you listening? I had decided to do it myself and throw some things out."

Now Sunshine

wished she had listened.

She should have been like Lydia, a saleswoman who was doing pretty well for herself. Lydia heard Paul teaching about God's love and Jesus' death and resurrection. She could have closed her mind and not paid any attention to Paul, but she didn't. Lydia listened to him and was saved. Paul baptized her and her family and she invited Paul and his friends to stay in her home.

What About You?

• When have you not paid attention and been sorry later?
• What did Lydia do as soon as she believed?

Talkin' about It

Ask God to help you pay attention to his Word. Ask him to help you act on it, not just listen.

She was listening because the Lord made her willing to pay attention to what Paul said.

Acts 16:14

What Are You Missing?

God or gods?

Read Acts 17:16-34

"World history class is so cool!" Angela announced to her friends. "We've been talking about all different kinds of religions and how people worship and what they believe."

Raven was in the same class, but she had a different opinion. "I think it's sad. People have always wanted to worship a god, but they miss knowing the real God and end up with all these weird religions and gods that can't help them at all."

Paul saw the same thing in Athens.

When Paul went into that famous Greek city, he saw statues and altars everywhere, but not to the true God. He even saw an altar to *An Unknown God*. That did it, Paul had to tell them about the real God. So, he preached about creation and how humans and fake gods couldn't do any of the stuff that God could do. He told them about judgment too, and that they should turn away from their idols and love God.

What About You?

• Do you know anyone who is caught up with false gods?
• Would you be brave enough to do like Paul and tell about the true God?

Talkin' About It

Everyone seems to want to worship someone. Thank God that you know him and can worship the true God.

Never worship [other gods] or serve them, because I, the LORD your God, am a God who does not tolerate rivals.
Exodus 20:5

Read Acts 20:7-12

"Our church services are about an hour too long," grumbled Keith.

"They only last an hour," said Mom.

"My point exactly," Keith grumbled again. "Church is so boring I can't stay awake. Some Sunday I'm gonna fall asleep and slide right off the pew."

Listen to what happened to Eutychus!

Paul had so much to say about God that when he started preaching, he couldn't stop. One night he had been preaching for a long time. A young man named Eutychus was sitting in a window listening. It was getting late, and Eutychus got so tired that he fell out of the window. People ran to check on him and discovered that he was dead. But, Paul ran out crying, "He's alive!" He fell down on top of Eutychus and brought him back to life. Then Paul went back inside and preached all night!

What About You?

• What excites you so much that you can't stop talking about it?
• Do you pay attention in church, sleep, or goof off with your friends?

Talkin' About It

Thank God for people who are so excited about him that they can't stop talking about him. Ask him to help you pay attention in church so you can learn more about him.

Can't Stop Talking

I'm not ashamed of the Good News. It is God's power to save everyone who believes, Jews first and Greeks as well.
Romans 1:16

I Did My Best

Read 2 Timothy 3:10–4:8

Lia had trained for this race for a solid year. It was the race of her life. The mile run in the state track meet had been her goal since she started running about three years ago. She had the race planned out in her mind, her body was in top shape, and she was ready. It was a close finish, but Lia came in second. At first, she was disappointed, then she realized it was OK because she had done her best.

Paul was able to say he had done his best, too.

Paul's last letter was written to young Timothy. Paul had been teaching Timothy how to carry on the work of sharing God's love. He wanted

Timothy to know that it wouldn't always be easy, but it was important to keep sharing the Good News. Paul was able to say that he had done his best and he wanted Timothy to be able to say the same thing.

What About You?

• Can you say you've done your best at sharing God's love with others?
• What could you do better?

Talkin' About It

Ask God to help you take his work seriously. Ask him to help you realize there are people around you who need to hear about him.

Be ready to spread the word whether or not the time is right. Point out errors, warn people, and encourage them. Be very patient when you teach. *2 Timothy 4:2*

Read 2 Timothy 4:7

Some kids idolize musicians. Some pattern themselves after athletes. But, think about it, musicians and athletes are human. True, some of them are Christian, but they are still human. They can easily slide off the pedestal that admiring fans place them on.

Who makes a good role model?

The best is obviously Jesus. He was perfect and is our example for how to live. But, in the struggle to be Christian in a non-Christian world, you can learn some tips from Bible characters like Paul. His human emotions fought against his desire to be like Jesus, just as yours may do sometimes. Paul hung in there, and when his life was over, he could say he had fought a good fight and run a good race.

What About You?

• When does your desire to be like Jesus have to fight against human emotions?
• What have you learned from Paul?

Talkin' About It

Thank God for hanging in there with you. Ask him to help you stick with your desire to live for him. Ask him to keep you from getting discouraged.

A Good Role Model

I have kept the faith.

2 Timothy 4:7

Noah Stands Out

Read Genesis 6–8

Kia thought she was gonna explode. She felt pressed on from every side—like being at the bottom of a pile of people. *Peer pressure. Man, it's a killer because I want to have friends, and I want them to like me. That means I sometimes have to do things I don't really want to do. Otherwise my friends might dump me.* How can she escape this pattern?

Take a lesson from Noah.

Literally everyone in Noah's day had turned away from God—except Noah. People must have made fun of old religious Noah, but he didn't let that sway him. When God told him to build a big boat 'cause a humongous flood was coming, people must have really thought Noah had flipped. No matter, Noah did what God told him was right—and he survived the flood! Then God hung a rainbow in the sky to show his promise to never flood the entire earth again.

What About You?

• How do you deal with peer pressure?
• When was a time you stood up to your friends?

Talkin' About It

Thank God for Noah's example. Ask him to help you know what's right and stand up for it.

I will put my rainbow in the clouds to be a sign of my promise to the earth.

Genesis 9:13

Read 2 Kings 11:21–12:16

Excitement filled the air as the athletes and their parents took their seats. The Sports Award Banquet was the culmination of a season of hard work. The most prestigious award, honorary team captain, went to the athlete who had shown good sportsmanship and desire for expertise in play. Everyone expected the award to go to Todd, after all, he was graduating. So, imagine everyone's surprise when the award went to Ryan, the youngest guy on the team.

Little guys can be leaders, too.

Joash became king when he was seven. (Remember when you were seven?) Joash loved God and felt that God's temple needed to be fixed up. So, he came up with a plan to put an offering box in the temple. The money that people gave went to temple repairs. Finally, the temple was fixed up. Not bad for a kid, huh?

What About You?

• Do you consider yourself a leader with good ideas?
• What are some things you would like to do for God?

Talkin' About It

Thank God for putting the story of Joash in the Bible. It's nice to know that kids can do things for God, too.

It is God who produces in you the desires and actions that please him.

Philippians 2:13

Team Leader

New Mom

Read Numbers 27:18-23;
Joshua 6

"She'll never take my Mom's place," vowed Jillian. It had been six years since Jillian's mom died, but it still hurt a lot. Now Dad was going to marry Lily, and Jillian was fighting it with every ounce of strength she had. She didn't need or want a new mom, and she didn't want Lily trying to take Mom's place.

Joshua must have met with that kind of opposition.

Moses led the Israelites for as long as anyone could remember. But, he was getting old and God told him to start training Joshua to be a leader. God promised to speak directly to Joshua and to lead him just as he had Moses. God was true to his word. He helped Joshua capture the city of Jericho in a miraculous way. Joshua wasn't trying to take Moses' place, he was just trying to lead the people as God had told him.

What About You?

• Have you ever resisted a new leader, teacher, coach? When?
• Why was Joshua a successful leader?

Talkin' About It

Thank God for helping Joshua. Thank him for helping you when you obey him.

The LORD said to Moses' assistant Joshua . . . Be strong and courageous.

Joshua 1:1, 6

Read Esther 2; 4–5

It was dangerous, but the success of the mission depended on it. A broken valve on the outside of the spaceship was going to sabotage the whole project. One brave astronaut put on his spacesuit and, tied to the spaceship, went outside the ship to try to fix the problem. He could have died out there. The possibilities of problems were endless.

Maybe Esther was his example of courage.

Esther risked her life to save the Jewish people. Haman hated the Jews and had come up with a plan to wipe them out. What he didn't know was that Queen Esther was Jewish. So, brave Esther went out on a limb to protect her people and reveal Haman's plan. His goose was cooked.

What About You?

• What do you feel strongly enough about to risk your life for?
• Who could you pray for that works in a dangerous place?

Talkin' About It

Ask God to help you be as brave as Esther. Thank him for her example.

Esther sent this reply back to Mordecai, "Assemble all the Jews in Susa. Fast for me . . . I will go to the king . . . If I die, I die."

Esther 4:15, 16

A Dangerous Job

Forgive and Forget

Read 1 Samuel 19:1; 26:9-12

The big event of the 1984 Olympics was going to be the 3,000 meter race in which two of the best female runners in the world would go head to head. Mary Decker for the U.S. and Zola Budd running for Great Britain. Halfway through the race the unbelievable happened, the two runners tangled legs and Decker fell to the ground in excruciating pain. Budd was so upset that she finished the race in tears . . . and lost.

This is when to forgive and forget.

David was just a young boy when he was chosen to be the next king of Israel. A few years later, David killed a nine-foot giant that had scared the whole Israelite army. King Saul was jealous of David's popularity, and he tried to kill him several times. Later, when David had a chance to kill Saul, he didn't. He knew it was best to forgive and forget.

What About You?

• Are you carrying around a grudge toward someone who has hurt you?
• Have you ever been forgiven for a wrong you have done?

Talkin' About It

Thank God for the forgiveness he has given you. Ask him to help you follow David's example and forgive and forget.

The LORD should be praised. I called on him, and I was saved from my enemies.

2 Samuel 22:4

Read Exodus 3

Coach Grayson was demonstrating the difficult skill of serving overhand volleyball. Kelly was only half-heartedly paying attention. Volleyball wasn't her thing and her overhand serves always went right into the net. Through the fogginess in her mind, she heard Coach call someone up to demonstrate the serve. The class waited, but no one came. Kelly snapped to attention when Coach said, "Kelly I called you to come up and demonstrate. Get up here."

Did you want me to volunteer?

Moses couldn't believe it when he was called into duty. God wanted him to lead the Israelites out of slavery in Egypt. But, Moses could think of all sorts of reasons why he shouldn't be the one to do it. God convinced him, though. God worked through Moses to do many wonderful things in his lifetime.

What About You?

• When have you been asked to volunteer for something you didn't want to do?
• Would God ask you to do something and not help you with it?

Talkin' About It

Thank God that he never gives you a job to do without giving you his help and strength to do it.

The LORD is my rock and my fortress and my Savior.

2 Samuel 22:2

Surely You Don't Mean Me

The Hall of Fame

Read Hebrews 11

If you are a sports fan or movie and TV fan, you know that just about every industry has it's grand achievement awards like Grammies for music or Oscars for movies. Being awarded one of these is super cool. The greatest honor is being inducted into the hall of fame for your field. Only the best are in the baseball or football hall of fame.

Did you know there is a spiritual hall of fame?

Hebrews 11 tells about some of God's servants who did their best to serve him. Some of them he used to do fantastic things for his name, some were simple people who showed great faith. Whichever one speaks to you, that person life can show you how God ha helped his people throughout the centuries. This can help yo believe he is still helping his people today.

What About You?

• Which Old Testament charac ter do you find most fascinat ing?
• How does that person's expe rience help you?

Talkin' About It

Thank God for all the examples of service to him that are given in the Bible. Ask him to teach you through those examples.

Faith assures us of things we expect and convinces us of the existence of things we cannot see. Hebrews 11:1

Getting Things Ready

Read Luke 3:1-23

"This is so totally cool. I can't believe Hillary Clinton, the First Lady of the United States, is coming to our school," Tia was excited. Everyone was. A couple of weeks before Mrs. Clinton's visit, Tia and her friends noticed lots of strange men in suits walking through the school. Later, they found out the men were from the Secret Service. It was their job to make sure the school was safe for Mrs. Clinton and that everything was ready for her arrival. They wanted everything to go smoothly when she came.

Someone has to lay the groundwork.

That's exactly what John the Baptist did. He got everyone ready for Jesus' arrival. John taught who Jesus was and that he could save people from sin. Then, when Jesus arrived, the people were ready to hear what he had to say. John never tried to be any more than that. He wore camel hair clothes and ate locusts. He said he wasn't even worthy to tie Jesus' sandals. When Jesus was ready to begin his ministry, he asked John to baptize him.

What About You?

• How would you feel about doing the groundwork for someone else?
• Have you ever felt honored to be able to do something for God?

Talkin' About It

Not everyone can be the star. The "helper jobs" are very important. Ask God to use you in any way he chooses. Ask him to help you do your best.

Prepare the way for the Lord! Make his paths straight!

Luke 3:4

Page 345

No Stereotypes

Read Acts 10

Roger wore his hair long, and it was usually greasy. His clothes were ratty too: dirty torn jeans, T-shirts with gang symbols painted on them, denim jacket with a gang symbol painted on the back of it. Roger wasn't easy to get along with, either. He had a negative outlook on life that made him hard to be around. Not the kind of guy you would want to walk up to and say "Jesus loves you!"

Hang on—listen to Peter's experience.

Peter spent his life telling people about Jesus' love, and he wasn't shy about it, either. Peter was very strict about keeping laws that showed he served God. So, when he had a dream telling him it was OK to eat food that had been sacrificed to idols, he went bonkers! But, what God was showing Peter was that when God makes something clean, Peter shouldn't call it unclean. That means don't pre-judge people and decide they don't get to hear about God's love. Let them hear and decide for themselves if they want to accept it.

What About You?

• Is there someone you have decided wouldn't be interested in hearing about God?
• Are there certain people God wants saved and some who he would rather not have in his family?

Talkin' About It

Thank God that he doesn't play favorites—he wants everyone to hear about his love and have the chance to know him.

God doesn't play favorites. Rather, whoever respects God and does what is right is acceptable to him in any nation.

Acts 10:34-35

Read Acts 2:1-14

Pole-vaulting looks like so much fun—flying up into the air and over the bar. But, it's a lot harder than it looks as Joe found out. In the Junior High School City Track Meet, Joe was the only pole-vaulter from his small school. He was allowed three tries to clear the bar at 16.6 feet. On the first try, he wasn't even close, on the second one he hit the bar, on the third one . . . he made it!

Perseverance pays off!

Paul was a great example of hanging in there. Paul's purpose in life was to share the love of Jesus with everyone he met. He wanted everyone to have a chance to hear. One time a man warned Paul about making a trip to Jerusalem. The man said Paul would be tied up there and given a hard time because of his preaching. Paul didn't care! He said he was ready to be tied up, or even to die for the sake of the Lord.

What About You?

• What's the hardest thing you have ever had to do?
• Do you consider yourself to be a person who hangs in there or quits easily?

Talkin' About It

Granted, not everyone hangs in like Paul did. But, thank God for Paul's example. It's a goal to shoot for.

Don't let anyone move you off the foundation of your faith. Always excel in the work you do for the Lord.
1 Corinthians 15:58

Hangin' In There

Choosing Your Team

Read Luke 6:12-16

How would you like to be the guy who put together a championship team? Whether your team is a basketball team, hockey team, or a forensics team that competes in public speaking, putting together a championship team is very exciting. Usually, a winning team is assembled a member at a time and the coach or manager who is choosing the team members looks at each person's abilities and skills.

Jesus put together a winning team.

When Jesus chose the twelve men who would be his closest friends and followers, it wasn't a hit-or-miss process. Jesus chose twelve men to be as close as family to him. He spent hours teaching these men how to carry on his work. The twelve were called apostles and Jesus gave them the job of traveling around, teaching people about him. He even gave them special abilities to use. Jesus knew these men would be devoted to carrying on his work.

What About You?

• Who are your closest friends?
• Would Jesus choose you as one who would be serious about carrying on his work?

Talkin' about It

Ask God to help you be seriou about sharing Jesus' love with others. Thank him for the person who told you about him.

I don't call you servants anymore, because a servant doesn't know what his master is doing. But I have called you friends because I have made known to you everything that I have heard from my Father.
John 15:15

Read Matthew 17:1; John 13:23; 19:26; Revelation 1:9

Beth and Amanda have been best friends since the day they met. The girls are insepa-rable. Beth knows she can tell Amanda anything, and she will understand. When Amanda heard a hurtful rumor flying around school about Beth, she didn't believe it. Not only did she not believe it, she told people it was a stinking lie! Beth knows that whatever happens, she can count on Amanda to be there for her, and Amanda knows the same thing about Beth.

Best friends are awesome!

One of Jesus' disciples became his best friend. John was called the beloved disciple. He trav-eled with Jesus and witnessed many of Jesus' miracles. John was standing at the foot of the cross when Jesus was cru-cified. Jesus even asked John to take care of his mother. John was glad to do that. Jesus understands how important best friends are.

What About You?

• Who is your best friend?
• Do you consider Jesus a friend?

Talkin' About It

Thank God for your best friend. Thank him that he understands how important best friends are.

Be devoted to each other like a loving family. Excel in showing respect for each other.

Romans 12:10

Best Friend

A Great Teacher

Read 1 Timothy 4:11;
2 Timothy 3:10-17

When Casey was called on to read aloud in class, he always said "No way!" Most of the teachers and students thought he was just uncoop-erative. But, Mrs. Lewis was smarter than most. She figured that Casey acted the way he did because he couldn't read. So, Mrs. Lewis pulled Casey aside and confirmed her beliefs. She arranged to meet him before and after school every day and patiently taught Casey how to read.

A great teacher can make a great student!

Paul called Timothy his son. He spent a lot of time with young Timothy, teaching him about God and how to work in churches. When he felt he was ready, Paul even sent Timothy out alone to check on churches they had started. Paul wrote Timothy two letters, which are in our Bible now—1 and 2 Timothy. He wanted to tell Timothy that life would be tough, but not to give up. He told Timothy never to be ashamed of the Good News he was sharing!

What About You?

• How would you feel if some-one told you life was going to be tough?
• Where would Timothy get the strength to get through the hard times?

Talkin' About It

Thank God for teachers you've had. Ask him to help you keep learning about him so that someday you can be a good teacher.

My child, find your source of strength in the kindness of Christ Jesus.

2 Timothy 2:1

Read 2 Timothy 1:6-14

The examples of God's servants in the New Testament are awesome. What do you need? The courage of Paul, the bravery of Peter, the tenderness of John? Remember, you don't have to try to be something you aren't. God can use you no matter what personality you have. You just need to be willing for him to use you.

Take a stand for Jesus.

It won't always be easy, but taking a stand for Jesus in your family, neighborhood, and school is the right thing to do. God wants you to be proud of him and eager to share his love with the people around you. You don't have to do it by yourself. His strength is available to help you be brave and strong. Ask him to show you times when you can take a stand for him. Be willing to start small. When you have success in little things, you may be willing to try bigger things.

What About You?

• Which New Testament person do you most admire?
• What can you do for God?

Talkin' About It

Thank God that there are ways for everyone to serve God. Thank him that you are important to him.

Stand Firm

Never be ashamed to tell others about our Lord.

2 Timothy 1:8

Do You Hear Something?

Read 1 Samuel 3

"Paul Randall Thomas," Paul heard his name ring out loud and clear. *Oh man, what have I done now?* he thought. When Mom didn't call again, Paul decided to ignore her. A few seconds later he heard, "Paul Randall Thomas!" Again he sat quietly without responding. Then a third time, much louder, Mom called, "PAUL RANDALL THOMAS!" Paul slowly put down the book he was reading and went to find out what he was in trouble for now.

Samuel once heard someone call his name, but it wasn't his mom!

Samuel worked in the temple for the priest, Eli, because Samuel's mother had promised God that her child would serve him. One night Samuel was sleeping when he heard someone call his name. He ran to see what Eli wanted. But, it wasn't Eli who called him. Samuel heard his name three times, and he hurried to answer each time. Finally, Eli realized it must be God calling Samuel. So Samuel answered God the next time and God gave him a special message.

What About You?

• Do you answer right away when your parents call? Why or why not?
• Would you be brave enough to answer God if he called you?

Talkin' About It

Ask God to help you answer when he calls. Ask him to help you be willing to do whatever he wants you to do.

God didn't give us a cowardly spirit but a spirit of power, love, and good judgment.

2 Timothy 1:7

Read 2 Kings 5:1-15

Have you ever felt like this: The adults in your house are going nuts looking for something or trying to solve some "mystery" and you know the answer. For instance, Mom and Dad are tearing the family room apart looking for the remote control, and you know exactly where it is, but they are so caught up in the hunt that they don't listen to you trying to tell them.

How do you get grown-ups to listen to a kid?

Naaman was an officer in the army. That's a very powerful position, but he wasn't feeling so powerful. He had leprosy, a nasty skin disease that was so contagious that people who had it were not permitted to live near healthy people. Naaman's wife had a young slave girl who felt bad for him. She knew that he could be healed by God's prophet, Elisha. She talked Naaman into going to Elisha, and sure enough Naaman was healed.

What About You?

• When have you been able to help someone?
• When have you been pushed aside because you are a kid?

Talkin' About It

Thank God that he uses kids as well as adults. Ask him for chances to serve him.

Listen to Me!

Even a child makes himself known by his actions, whether his deeds are pure or right.

Proverbs 20:11

Page 353

A Kid Leads the Way

Read 2 Kings 22:1–23:3

Jade's family life was certainly not what it should be. Her dad was hardly ever home, and when he was home, he was usually beating up on someone. Jade couldn't say she loved her dad. Her mom struggled to keep the family going with what little money she could scrape together and hide from her husband. If he found it, he'd spend it on booze. Jade wished with all her might that she could get her mom to leave—just take the kids and leave. She was afraid that one of these times Dad would beat Mom bad enough to really hurt her.

What can a kid possibly accomplish?

Quite a bit if you're an eight-year-old king named Josiah. The adults of the kingdom surely knew they should be serving God. They probably knew they were not doing such a good job of that. But it took young boy's shock to knock some sense into the people. Josiah cleaned all the idols out of the temple and punished anyone who still wanted to worship idols. A kid with power brought people back to God. Jade needs some of Josiah's strength.

What About You?

- Have you ever tried to give advice to adults?
- Could you handle the responsibility of being king?

Talkin' About It

Ask God to help you be a gentle leader. Ask him to help you lead by the way you live for him.

Even when I am afraid, I still trust you.

Psalm 56:3

Read Luke 18:15-17

Jennifer plopped down in the family room and started shaking the few Christmas packages under the tree. It was only a matter of time before her four-year-old sister Taylor came in.

"Santa's comin' Santa's comin'!" Taylor sing-songed.

"Oh grow up," Jennifer moaned. "What are you so happy about?"

Taylor looked surprised, "'Cause Santa's comin'."

Jennifer rolled her eyes, "Yeah, right. Don't you know Dad's been out of work for six months?" Taylor didn't even pretend to see what the connection was between Dad's unemployment and Santa coming.

A child's trust is so pure.

Jesus said the faith that little children have is the best. Children don't ask for anything in return, they just believe what they are told. He said that adults need that kind of pure, simple faith to get into heaven. Jesus loved children. When his disciples stopped parents from bringing children to him to be blessed, he said, "Don't stop the children from coming to me."

What About You?

• Do you consider yourself trusting or cynical?
• How do you feel about the promises in the Bible?

Talkin' About It

Thank God that he cares about children. Ask him to give you a simple pure faith.

ChildLike Trust

Jesus said, "Whoever doesn't receive the kingdom of God as a little child receives it will never enter it." Luke 18:17

The Boy Who Shared

Read John 6:1-15

"Is that your kid?" the opposing coach asked Jason's mom as he pointed toward Jason.

"Yes, that's my son," she responded. She wondered why the coach of the team that Jason's team had just creamed was interested in her son.

"I just wanted to tell you that he is the most unselfish basketball player I have ever seen. There were plenty of times when he had good shots, but he chose to pass off and give someone else a chance to score. That's amazing in a boy his age."

It's noticeable when you share.

You've heard the story of the little boy who came to hear Jesus teach. He had five loaves of bread and two fish with him for his lunch. But, for some reason, the other 5,000 people who came to hear Jesus speak didn't bring anything to eat. The little boy was willing to share his lunch with Jesus, who took it and blessed it and used it to feed more than 5,000 people.

What About You?

• If Jesus took your lunch and fed 5,000 people with it, how would you feel?
• Would you give Jesus anything he needed from you?

Talkin' About It

Thank Jesus for using the little boy's lunch. It's cool that a kid was involved in such a great miracle.

If we love each other, God lives in us, and his love has reached its goal in us.

1 John 4:12

Read Acts 23:12-22

Little brothers are a total pain. Joy knew because she had the world's biggest pain as a brother. Michael's favorite thing was to hide outside her bedroom door and eavesdrop on her conversations. When he heard the phone ring, he made a beeline to the door and listened to her side of the conversation, then made up the other side. Michael was quite willing to share his half-made-up stories with Mom when he got mad at Joy.

Eavesdropping actually helped Paul one time.

The great apostle Paul was in prison again. Church leaders who were jealous of his popularity kept putting Paul in prison. But, this time they were very serious. Some of the church leaders promised each other they wouldn't eat or drink until Paul was dead. But, they didn't know that Paul's nephew was eavesdropping on them. He warned Paul and the authorities. Paul was sneaked out of the prison in the middle of the night. The little boy saved Paul's life!

What About You?

• Have you ever eavesdropped on someone? When?
• If you heard some important news, would you be brave enough to do what Paul's nephew did?

Talkin' about It

Ask God to use you to do something important for him. Ask him to help you be brave enough to serve him.

Encourage each other and strengthen one another as you are doing.

1 Thessalonians 5:11

Eavesdropping

Serving God

Review Scripture from past week

Does it encourage you or discourage you to hear how kids have been used to serve God? When you read of all the things kids in the Bible did, do you feel like you should be doing more? Like perhaps you missed your chance?

Every day is a chance to serve God.

Every day you are given chances to stand up for your faith in God. You may be around kids at school who don't know God, but they can see what he is like by watching how you live. At home, too, you have chances to live for God and show his love to your family members.

What About You?

• Can you name something you have done for God?
• How often do you feel you show God's love to your family and friends?

Talkin' About It

Tell God you want to serve him. Thank him for chances you have had in the past to serve him. Ask him to make you aware of new chances to share his love.

Always be ready to defend your confidence in God when anyone asks you to explain it.

1 Peter 3:15

Read 1 John 3:18; 4:7-8

Paul caught the ball and started down the court. Just as he cut to the basket, Todd stepped in front of him and threw his elbow up. It caught Paul in the side of the head, and he sprawled on the floor. Paul jumped up with his fists clenched, ready to give Todd some of his own medicine. Tension filled the air as the teammates stood face to face. Fortunately, the coach broke it up and got the guys busy running drills.

Some people are not easy to get along with or work with, let alone love.

The easiest thing would be to punch out their lights. But, God doesn't want us to handle things that way. The Bible says the best thing to do is love others. How do you do that when the other guy is a first-class creep? Ask God to help you. He's got love to spare, and he would be happy to share some with you.

What About You?

• Who in your world right now is tough to love?
• Can you think of a time when you may have been hard to love yourself?

Talkin' About It

Love is not always easy, and some people are hardly ever easy to love. Ask God to show you how to love them.

God is love.

1 John 4:16

Getting Along with Everyone

Great Job!

Read Romans 12:18; 14:19;
15:2; Ephesians 4:12

Frank took the tape off his throbbing ankle. *I'm getting worse instead of better,* he thought. *I can make jump shots right and left—unless Coach is watching. I'm probably gonna end up on the bench. Man, if Tim gets to start Friday and I'm benched, he'll never let me forget it!*

Frank walked past Coach's office on the way to the showers.

"Hey Frye," Coach called. "Yes, Sir," Frank said with dread in his heart. He fully expected Coach to tell him he was benched. "Good hustle out there today, son. I like the way you give it your all. You'll be starting on Friday."

Well, that perked Frank up!

A few words of encouragement can pick up a sagging spirit. When someone is feeling bad about himself, a pat on the back and an encouraging word can really make a difference.

What About You?

• What area do you usually get down on yourself about?
• When has someone really encouraged you?

Talkin' About It

Ask God to remind you how good it feels to hear nice things about yourself. Ask him to help you remember to say kind and encouraging things to others.

Turn your burdens over to the LORD, and he will take care of you.

Psalm 55:22

Read Ecclesiastes 4:9-10;
1 Corinthians 9:19-23

Victor ran down the court. There were only a few seconds left in the game, and they were down by one. Victor stopped running and whipped the ball across his body to where Eddie was supposed to be standing under the basket. But, Eddie wasn't there, and the ball bounced out of bounds. In a few seconds, the buzzer sounded and the game was over. The team sadly gathered around their coach. "You know what happened out there tonight?" Coach asked. "You didn't play like a team."

A team works together and helps each other out.

Teammates try to think as one and anticipate each other. The Bible tells us to help each other out; be there to strengthen your friends in the hard times and the good times.

What About You?

• When have you been a member of a team?
• When has a friend helped and strengthened you?

Talkin' About It

Thank God for a time when a friend has helped you. Ask him to help you be sensitive to your friends' needs.

Working Together

> *Two people are better than one because together they have a good reward for their hard work. If one falls, the other can help his friend get up.*
> *Ecclesiastes 4:9-10*

Like You Never Blew It!

Read Matthew 18:21-22;
Ephesians 4:32

The guys trooped into the locker room. Everyone was quiet—until Eddie came in. Then Todd started in on him. "Way to go. You blew the game! All you had to do was run the play right and we would have had a chance for one more shot. We probably would have won!" Many of the guys joined with Todd in picking on Eddie.

Everyone makes mistakes.

You do and so do your friends. We all need forgiveness at some time. The Bible says to forgive people when they blow it. In fact, there is no limit to how many times you should forgive others.

You'll feel better when you forgive others—and so will the people you forgive.

What About You?

• Have you ever been forgiven for something? How did it feel?
• When have you forgiven someone?

Talkin' About It

Is there someone you really need to forgive today? Tell God about it. He'll help you forgive. That's a great way to show God's love.

If you forgive the failures of others, your heavenly Father will also forgive you.

Matthew 6:14

Read Acts 2:42; Hebrews 10:25

The guys all hung their heads and thought about what their coach had just said. His statement that no one person was responsible for their loss gave them something to think about. It would be a lot easier to blame Eddie, than for each guy to accept responsibility for the loss. Frank sort of felt like forgetting the whole team. They played so bad they were an embarrassment to the school. Maybe they should scrap the whole basketball program.

That wouldn't prove anything.

The best way to overcome a tough time is to hang in there and keep on with what you're doing. The Bible encourages Christians to keep meeting together, even if people give them a hard time. When a group sticks together through tough times, it comes out even stronger! You learn a lot about each other when you are under stress!

What About You?

• Have you ever been part of a group that went through a hard time?
• How did your group handle it? Did you come out stronger because of the tough time?

Talkin' About It

It can take a lot of strength to hang in there when the going gets tough. Ask God to help you. Ask him to help you encourage someone else to hang in there, too. Thank him for sticking with you.

Comfort each other!

1 Thessalonians 4:18

Don't Give Up

Page 363

Be A Team

Read Jeremiah 32:39; John 17:21; Acts 2:42

The team was all suited up and ready for the last game. *If we win tonight,* thought Jay, *we make the play-offs.* He could tell that the guys were all pretty tight. But, Jay couldn't believe what happened when the game started. Todd started playing like he was possessed. He wouldn't pass the ball, he jumped into the middle of every struggle. Coach called time out and he didn't look happy!

"This is a team," he said. "We're not looking for any stars. If you can't pass the ball around and play like a team, you're on the bench!" he said to Todd.

A team has no chance if the members don't work together.

A house divided against itself cannot stand. That's the way i is with Jesus' followers, too. W all have the same goal. We want everyone to come to know Jesus. When we fight ar complain among ourselves, pe ple pay attention to that instea of to Jesus. So, let's work like a team—and we'll accomplish a l more!

What About You?

• Have you ever been on a team where someone wanted be the star? How did the rest the team feel?
• Are you pretty good at work ing with others?

Talkin' About It

Ask God to help you keep you focus. Remember what you have in common with other Christians—the love of Jesus!

I am in them, and you are in me, so that they are completely united. In this way the world knows that you have sent me and that you have loved them in the same way you have loved me.
John 17:23

Review Scripture from past week

What kind of body would you have if your legs wanted to go to the mall, your arms wanted to go to a movie, your eyes wanted to read a book, your hands . . . get the picture? A body is one thing with many parts. The reason the body works is because all the parts work together. They don't each try to get their own way. No one wants to be around a person who always wants his own way. The key to getting along with others is known as the Golden Rule.

Do to others as you would have them do unto you.

If you treat other people the way you would like to be treated, most of the time, you're going to come out just fine. You'll have friends, you'll be a good example of a person who follows Jesus, and you'll be pretty happy!

What About You?

• Bottom line—how do you want people to treat you?
• Do you try to treat others the way you'd like to be treated?

Talkin' About It

It is a lot easier to think about yourself instead of how others feel or what is best for the team. That's something to talk to God about. Ask for his help to put Jesus first, others second, and yourself last.

One Body

We love because God loved us first.

1 John 4:19

Read James 1:2-15

Imagine how Roy Riegels felt when he scooped up a fumble by the Georgia Tech football team. Riegels, on the University of California team, ran the ball all the way down the field and across the goal line. He scored!—for the wrong team! He had run the wrong way.

Everyone is gonna have problems.

James said it—problems are coming. But, James said to be happy when you have troubles because those troubles will help your faith in God grow stronger. You can always ask God to help you when you have tough choices to make. The main thing to remember is that when you are tempted to do wrong—always say no!

What About You?

• What problems do you have?
• How do you handle temptation?

Talkin' About It

Being happy for troubles sound a little tough. Ask God to help you see how you grow through troubles.

Be very happy when you are tested in different ways.

James 1:2

Tough Day

Read James 1:16-27

Diane studied clarinet for 10 years. She practiced every day and progressed through the lesson books quickly. So, Diane knew everything there was to know about clarinet. She can tell you how to play any chord, how to take the instrument apart and what it's made of. However, Diane never plays the clarinet in public. She never uses the knowledge she has.

Knowing should lead to doing.

James said that when you know what the Bible says, it should show in your life. If you say you know what the Bible says, but you treat people like you never heard of the Bible, then what good is your knowledge? If you aren't doing what the Bible says, you're kidding yourself.

What About You?

• Is it hard to do what you know is right?
• Have you accepted the gift of salvation?

Talkin' About It

Thank God for the Bible and it's help in knowing how to live. Ask him to help you put it into practice.

If you obey my commandments, you will live in my love.

John 15:10

Get in the Game

Breathe or Die

Read James 2:1-26

Ellen is a nice person. She treats her friends with respect and kindness. No one can find a mean thing to say about Ellen because she treats other people the way she would like to be treated. Ellen has her special friends, but she doesn't save her kindness just for them. Ellen has learned that kindness shared will come back to her.

Faith shows by what you do.

In the same way that a body has to breathe or die, faith has to do something or it is dead. You don't get into heaven by just doing things, but you will do things when your faith is alive and growing.

What About You?

• What do you think people say about the way you treat others?
• How do you show love to other people?

Talkin' About It

Ask God to help you live your faith, to make it alive and growing.

Love your neighbor as you love yourself.

James 2:8

Read James 3:1-18

"Your hair looks like you combed it with a blender," Laura said. She had a habit of bombarding people with words. That's probably why she didn't have many friends. Everyone was afraid of Laura because she often hurt people by what she said.

Friends are made or lost by words.

Think about how a huge ocean cruiser is guided through the water by a small rudder. That small rudder has a lot of control and power to guide a huge ocean liner. Think about how a tiny spark can set an entire forest on fire. Now compare that to the words you say. A word that seems tiny to you can do incredible damage to the person you say it to.

What About You?

• When have you been hurt by someone's unkind words?
• Do you think before you speak?

Talkin' About It

Ask God's help in this difficult area. Ask him to help you think before you speak.

However, the wisdom that comes from above is first of all pure. Then it is peaceful, gentle, obedient, filled with mercy and good deeds, impartial, and sincere.

James 3:17

Watch What You Say

Quit Thinking about Yourself

Read James 4:1-17

Ruthie won the leading part in the school play. Rhoda wanted the part and she wasn't handling her disappointment well. *Ruthie's a little slut,* thought Rhoda. *She practically threw herself at Mr. Hoffman to get that part.* Nasty rumors flew all around the school about Ruthie. Guess where they started?

Demonstrating your faith means getting yourself out of the way.

A person who is demonstrating faith in God is not selfish or self-promoting. This person is happy for other people to succeed. If you need help with this, ask God. You can ask God for help with just about anything and if you are asking with the right motives, he will help you. Let God guide you.

What About You?

• Do you enjoy being around selfish people? Why?
• When have you been selfish?

Talkin' About It

Ask God to help you show love to others. Ask him to control your life.

Place yourselves under God's authority.

James 4:7

Read James 5:13-20

Jenny's whole family was praying for Lionel to get well. Lionel was very sick and had two young children at home. Jenny joined her family in praying for Lionel, but she didn't really believe their prayers were going to make any difference.

James says to pray in faith—believe God will answer you.

That kind of prayer can make the sickest person well. Part of being a good person who wants to serve God is praying for yourself and other people. Don't think you can't pray powerful prayers. Anyone who knows God can.

What About You?

• When have you seriously prayed for something?
• Did you believe that God would answer?

Talkin' About It

Thank God for the privilege of prayer. Thank him that you can talk to him about anything, any time you want.

Pray with Power

Prayers offered by those who have God's approval are effective.

James 5:16

Show your Faith

Review the Book of James

How many people know where you stand about God? Do your friends know you go to church? Do they think you go because your folks make you? What does your faith mean to you? Is it important enough to share it with others?

Faith shows itself in actions.

James wrote a whole book on how to get along with other people. Ways to show people that your faith is a serious part of your life. Faith can be quiet and steady, but it should also make actions bubble out of you—actions of kindness and unselfishness. Actions that will show others what God is like.

What About You?

• What lessons from James do you need to put to work in your life?
• How can you successfully incorporate these points into your life?

Talkin' About It

You can't have this kind of faith without God, ask him to help you.

Do any of you have wisdom and insight? Show this by living the right way with the humility that comes from wisdom.

James 3:13

Read Luke 17:29-36

"Put your books away and take out a sheet of paper," Mrs. Bette said. *Oh no, a pop quiz!* thought Ellie. *The one day I didn't read the homework material, she has a pop quiz. I wish I had time to just glance at the material.* It's too late.

Important business doesn't wait.

Making sure that your friends and family know Jesus is serious business. Why? Because the only way to heaven is through faith in Jesus Christ. He is coming back someday to take his people to heaven for eternity. There will be no warning when he comes, he'll just be here. So, there will be no time to accept him then, it will be too late. It's important to share your faith now.

What About you?

• Are you ready to go with Jesus to heaven?
• Who would you like to tell about Jesus?

Talkin' About It

Tell God the name of someone you want to share his love with.

Then you will also be given the wealth of entering into the eternal kingdom of our Lord and Savior Jesus Christ.

2 Peter 1:11

He's Coming Back!

Here Comes the Judge

Read 1 Corinthians 3:12-15; 4:5

Mrs. Bette graded the pop quizzes and handed them back at the end of class. Bad news, Ellie got a *D* which is about what she expected. 'Course that low grade brought some punishing words from Mrs. Bette as it certainly would from Dad and Mom.

There is a big judgment coming.

The day is coming when all people will be judged for how they lived. If they lived wisely, showing and sharing God's love to others, then they need not worry. But, if they lived selfishly and ignoring God, they should fear judgment. On judgment day God will show that he knows everything about all people, even their thoughts.

What About You?

• What things do you think you're hiding from God?
• How do you feel about judgment day?

Talkin' About It

Confess any secrets you have in your heart. Thank God for loving you.

Your heavenly master will reward all of us for whatever good we do.

Ephesians 6:8

Read Romans 8:38-39;
Colossians 1:5; 1 John 2:28

"There are only 5.6 seconds left in the basketball game, we are down by one point," Coach reviewed. "Bring the ball in, get it to T. J. You set up, T. J. and take a good shot." That's what happened and, impossible as it seemed, the shot went in. They won!

Never give up!

When you asked Jesus to be your Savior, you arranged to win the game. Someday Jesus is coming back to take his people to heaven. You have the wonderful privilege of being one of those people because you are part of his family. So, no matter how tough life gets, never give up. You have the promise of being in heaven someday!

What About You?

• Do you believe that Jesus is coming back for you someday?
• Are you excited to go to heaven?

Talkin' About It

Thank God for the promise that Jesus is coming back. Thank him that you can go to heaven someday.

Now, dear children, live in Christ. Then when he appears we will have confidence, and when he comes we won't turn from him in shame. 1 John 2:28

Signs of the Times

Read Matthew 24:3-14

Tom stepped up to the plate and took a couple of practice swings. Then, as he settled in the batter's box and got ready to hit, he looked over at his coach. The coach slapped his leg, touched his nose, and adjusted his hat. Tom knew those signs meant swing hard, straight away.

Signs tell us what is coming.

There are signs to tell us when Jesus is coming back. There will be wars around the world and rumors of wars. There won't be many people who want to hear about Jesus. It won't be a happy time for believers. When you notice signs like this, hang in there because Jesus will be coming soon.

What About You?

• How do you feel about Jesus coming back for you?
• Have you noticed any signs that point to Jesus' return?

Talkin' About It

Ask Jesus to help you hang in there when things get tough in the world. Thank him for his strength. Thank him for the promise of his return.

Then the sign of the Son of Man will apear in the sky. All the people on earth will cry in agony when they see the Son of Man coming on the clouds in the sky with power and great glory. Matthew 24:30

Read Matthew 6:19-24

Rodney practices basketball every spare minute. He's got the greatest hook shot you ever saw. Trouble is, Rodney's grades stink, he doesn't talk to his parents, he doesn't spend time with friends, and he doesn't go to church. Rodney's great at basketball, but his priorities are a bit messed up.

What's the most important thing in your life?

Are you spending your energy and time to earn money or be more popular with your friends? Stop and think about it—is being popular or rich really the most important thing? There is certainly nothing wrong with those things, but they should never be more important than God and his work. Find happiness in God, not in things.

What About You?

• What is important to you?
• Where does God fit in your list of priorities?

Talkin' About It

Ask God to help you keep your priorities straight, with him in first place.

What's the Most Important?

You cannot serve God and wealth.

Matthew 6:24

Praise Forever!

Read Revelation 7:12; 19

Two special sections in the Chicago Tribune—in one week—to honor one person!!! Yep. Michael Jordan came back to basketball and heard more praise about himself than even he imagined possible. When you've worked really hard at something, it's nice to have your effort recognized.

Praise makes you feel really good.

Someday we're all gonna be together in heaven, and we'll spend all our time and energy praising God. Does that sound like something you want to do for all eternity? Stop and think about all God has done. Think how awesome it will be when you actually see him. We'll have all of eternity to tell him how wonderful he is, but that won't seem long enough because God is so awesome and has done so much for us.

What About You?

• What would you like to praise God for right now?
• What else?

Talkin' About It

Praise God for all he has done for you and for all mankind.

The kingdom of the world has become the kingdom of our Lord and of his Messiah, and he will rule as king forever and ever.
Revelation 11:15

Read Jude 25

How good are you at waiting? When you're waiting for a special day, or someone special to come over, do you get impatient? How do you feel about Jesus coming back? It's a little scary, 'cause we don't know a lot about how it's going to happen. But, we do know that heaven is an awesome place where there is no sadness and no evil. Cool place to be!

When Jesus comes, it will be too late for them to make a decision.

What About You?

• Have you grasped how serious this is? There is one way to heaven. When Jesus comes it's too late to decide. Who do you need to tell?
• Are you eager for his coming?

Do you wonder when Jesus is coming back for his people?

Are you ready? Have you realized that believing in him is the only doorway to heaven? Are you eager to share that with your friends and family?

Talkin' About It

Thank God for his awesome plan. Thank him that you're in the family.

When Is He Coming?

Honor, majesty, power, and authority before time began, now, and for eternity belong to the only God, our Savior, through Jesus Christ our Lord. Amen Jude 25

Topical Index